Overcoming
Unintentional Racism
in Counseling
and Therapy

SECOND EDITION

MULTICULTURAL ASPECTS OF COUNSELING AND PSYCHOTHERAPY SERIES

SERIES EDITOR

Paul B. Pedersen, Ph.D.,
Professor Emeritus, Syracuse University
Visiting Professor, Department of Psychology, University of Hawaii

EDITORIAL BOARD

VOLUMES IN THIS SERIES

Overcoming Unintentional Racism in Counseling and Therapy

A Practitioner's Guide to Intentional Intervention

SECOND EDITION

Charles R. Ridley
Indiana University

Multicultural Aspects of Counseling and Psychotherapy Series 5

SAGE Publications
Thousand Oaks ▪ London ▪ New Delhi

For information:

Sage Publications, Inc.
2455 Teller Road
Thousand Oaks, California 91320
E-mail: order@sagepub.com

Sage Publications Ltd.
1 Oliver's Yard
55 City Road
London EC1Y 1SP
United Kingdom

Sage Publications India Pvt. Ltd.
B-42, Panchsheel Enclave
Post Box 4109
New Delhi 110 017 India

Printed in the United States of America

Library of Congress Cataloging-in-Publication Data

Ridley, Charles R.
Overcoming unintentional racism in counseling and therapy: a practitioner's guide to intentional intervention / Charles R. Ridley.— 2nd ed.
    p. cm.
—(Multicultural aspects of counseling and psychotherapy; v. 5)
Includes bibliographical references and index.
ISBN 0-7619-1981-3 (hardcover) — ISBN 0-7619-1982-1 (pbk.)
    1. Counseling. 2. Racism. 3. Ethnocentrism. I. Title. II. Series.
BF637.C6R53 2005
361'.06'089—dc22   2004024598

This book is printed on acid-free paper.

05   06   07   08   09   10   9   8   7   6   5   4   3   2   1

Acquiring Editor:	Arthur T. Pomponio
Editorial Assistant:	Veronica Novak
Production Editor:	Beth A. Bernstein
Typesetter:	C&M Digitals (P) Ltd.
Proofreader:	Kris Bergstad
Indexer:	Karen McKenzie
Cover Designer:	Janet Foulger

Contents

Series Editor's Foreword

Anyone in the United States who believes that he or she is immune to cultural attitudes about race underestimates the power of modern advertising. Indeed, we all have opinions and attitudes about racial issues, and many of us have good intentions in this area. This second edition of *Overcoming Unintentional Racism in Counseling and Therapy: A Practitioner's Guide to Intentional Intervention* speaks to mental health professionals who strive to offer high-quality mental health services to all clients and to avoid overemphasizing or underemphasizing racial issues. In this revision of the successful first edition, Charles Ridley builds on the premise of unintentional racism to "depoliticize" mental health issues regarding race and return the focus to accurate and successful mental health functioning.

Part I of this book examines assumptions about race and racism in a systematic analysis of propositions and then applies these propositions to four models of mental health, with special attention to judgmental and inferential errors. Part II is action oriented, aimed at helping counselors make changes in their attitudes and opinions so that they can make more accurate and appropriate decisions regarding minority clients. Part III guides counselors toward overcoming both intentional and unintentional institutional racism in the mental health system. Specific change strategies are presented and discussed.

Ridley challenges the predominant notion about overcoming racism: that "when people discover the motivational sources of their behavior, they can better understand themselves and make constructive changes in their personalities." This idea has been a classic assumption of most psychological theories. In applying this premise to racism, practitioners' focus is "usually on the biases, prejudices, and bigotry of racists," working from inside out, and exploring individuals' hidden, unconscious, or unintentionally racist attitudes. Rather than focusing exclusively on the causes of racism, however, Ridley also examines racism's effects, both intentional and unintentional. Racism is always harmful, but it is not always intentional.

Ridley shows how counselors can change some of their specific behaviors to produce desired effects and consequences. In shifting the focus from causal to consequential explanations of racism, he does not minimize personal motivation, however. He provides specific strategies and guidelines that counselors can apply to reduce their racism. In an age when racist attitudes are probably more powerful than ever, this book is an important contribution to the mental health literature.

All of the volumes in the **Multicultural Aspects of Counseling and Psychotherapy** series strive to combine a broad definition of culture with an expanded and inclusive understanding of counseling to provide practical guidance for multicultural counselors. This series has been more successful than we originally dared to hope it would be. By identifying specific gaps in the counseling and psychotherapy literature, the books in this series have made significant contributions to the profession of counseling with regard to multicultural issues. This book, which guides counselors in making culture central to the counseling process, is an excellent example.

— Paul Pedersen
Professor Emeritus
Syracuse University,
Visiting Professor,
University of Hawaii,
Department of Psychology

Preface

Theorists have explained human behavior using two major traditions in the social sciences: One emphasizes the causes of behavior, and the other emphasizes the effects of behavior. Psychological theories focusing on the causes of human behavior are prominent in research and scholarship. Many of these theories are based on a common principle: that behavior is motivated by conscious or unconscious mental processes. These theories assert that when people discover the motivational sources of their behavior, they can better understand themselves and make constructive changes in their personalities. Classical psychoanalysis, with its emphasis on unconscious mental processes and early childhood experiences, elegantly represents this class of theories.

The theories used to explain racism and other forms of oppression typically emphasize the causes of behavior. Research on racism focuses almost exclusively on the biases, prejudices, and bigotry of racists; thus proposals for change generally involve working from the inside out. That is, these proposals encourage individuals first to explore their own hidden bigotry. They assume that once individuals unmask their own motives and begin to accept their bigotry, they will change and treat people of other races in a fair and equitable manner.

In this book, I set forth a different approach, examining racism in mental health counselors and institutions in light of its effects. Racism has many faces. Some racism is intentional, but racism also may be unintentional. Whether intentional or unintentional, racism always is harmful. Counselors with laudable intentions often are the ones most responsible for insidious acts of racism. In the chapters that follow, I pinpoint specific racist behaviors of counselors and institutions and describe how these behaviors adversely affect their minority clients. In this way, I challenge counselors to examine the relationship between their behavior toward minority clients and the consequences of that behavior. For most counselors, this approach will require a paradigm shift in their thinking, from causal to consequential explanations of racism.

This approach does not minimize the relevance of personal motivation. Certainly counselors must come to terms with the causes of their behavior. When they see their bigotry, they should try to stop it. But becoming self-aware and changing on the inside are only partial solutions to overcoming racism. To serve their minority clients better, counselors also must identify their specific racist behaviors, recognize the harmful consequences of these behaviors, and then deliberately change how they behave. Unfortunately, this behavioral part of the solution to counselor racism is usually overlooked. In reading this book, many well-meaning counselors are likely to discover that, despite their efforts to treat all clients equitably, they are unintentional racists.

This volume is intended for all helping professionals, including mental health counselors, psychologists, social workers, psychiatrists, marriage and family therapists, student personnel professionals, nurses, and ministers. The book is analytic in its treatment of the topic, but it goes beyond problem analysis to offer solutions—concrete strategies that professionals can use to overcome unintentional racism in counseling and therapy.

This book is organized into three major parts. Part I, "Examining the Counselor's Unintentional Racism," contains six chapters covering the nature, scope, history, and dynamics of racism in mental health service delivery. These chapters focus in particular on counselor unawareness of the problem. Part II, "Overcoming the Counselor's Unintentional Racism," comprises five chapters, each providing a specific strategy and a variety of practical recommendations. Part III, "Examining and Overcoming the Unintentional Racism of the Mental Health System," is new to this edition. The three chapters in Part III move beyond the behaviors of individual practitioners to the policies and procedures of institutions. The most important lesson in these chapters is that all mental health professionals are stakeholders in mental health service delivery and therefore participate—usually unknowingly—in institutional practices that yield consequences that are antithetical to their intentions.

I hope readers will benefit from this volume by learning to become more competent service providers. More important, I hope ethnic minority consumers of mental health services will benefit by becoming the recipients of improved service delivery.

— Charles R. Ridley
Bloomington, Indiana

Acknowledgments

Many individuals have contributed in various ways to the writing of this book, and I am indebted to each of them. Thomas and Annabell Ridley, my parents, taught me spiritual values and the self-discipline needed to complete this type of undertaking. Faith Phipps, my cousin, awakened in me a passion for writing. Dr. Paul Pedersen had the wisdom to suggest I write a book on this topic. More than anyone else, he has championed my development of these ideas, and I am one of his many protégés whom he has described as becoming "leading insiders." Dr. John Taborn was my intellectual mentor. He laid the foundation for my understanding of racism. Dr. Joseph Ponterotto provided an evenhanded critique and helped shepherd the initial writing process.

The staff at Sage Publications deserves special thanks. Marquita Flemming, aided by Dale Grenfell and Diana Axelsen, provided invaluable support on the first edition. Arthur Pomponio managed the delicate balance of patience, encouragement, and prodding on the second edition. Beth A. Bernstein, Veronica Novak, and Judy Selhorst are top-notch, and they made the project flow as efficiently as possible. The Sage staff believed in this project and made business a pleasure.

I also would like to acknowledge several individuals at Indiana University. Benita Brown typed numerous drafts of the original manuscript. Her work was nothing short of excellent. Rochelle Picou, my administrative assistant, made the completion of the revision possible. She personifies competence and human dignity. Shannon Kelly demonstrated brilliance as an editorial assistant. Her editorial skill is persnickety, and she helped make the text engaging.

I am especially grateful to the team of reviewers: Professors Gerald Corey, Michael D'Andrea, Halford H. Fairchild, Allen E. Ivey, Donald Pope-Davis, Tina Q. Richardson, and Jerome Taylor. Their comments were constructively critical and insightful, and they helped sharpen the presentation. Most important, their enthusiastic endorsement of the project was pretty amazing.

Last but not least, Iris, Charles, and Charliss Ridley were incredible sojourners during this lengthy pilgrimage. They are God centered and lovers of life. I am most blessed for having them in my life.

Part I

Examining the
Counselor's Unintentional Racism

1

Minority Clients as Victims

Picture yourself as the victim of a driver who runs a red light. As a safety-conscious pedestrian, you wait on the sidewalk at the corner until the light turns green. Even though you have the right of way, you look both ways before you enter the intersection, and then you proceed. When you get halfway across the street, however, tragedy strikes. A speeding car knocks you off your feet, leaving you badly bruised and disheveled, with a few broken bones.

Numerous explanations could account for the driver's behavior. He may have been a young man rushing his pregnant wife to the hospital, and he may have been distracted by her labor pains. The driver may have been intoxicated. The driver may have been negligent about auto maintenance, and his car's brakes finally gave out. The driver may have been distracted by a pretty young lady walking down the street or temporarily blinded by the glare of the sun. The driver may have been a suspected burglar who was being pursued by police.

Add an interesting twist to the story. This is not the first time you or members of your family have been victimized while crossing the street. On many occasions, you and your family have encountered cars running red lights. Incidentally, such bad fortune has never struck your neighbor, Mr. Jones, even though he regularly walks the same streets as you and members of your family.

Understanding the Victim

Mental health professionals can gain useful insights that are applicable to counseling by envisioning themselves in the preceding story; these insights include a better understanding of what it means to be a victim and the importance of being sensitive to the victim's plight.[1] This story also sets the stage for the topic of this book—overcoming unintentional racism in counseling and therapy. Following are five brief discussions about victims that counselors should ponder.

Anyone Can Be a Victim

Few people go through life untouched by victimization. Victims of crimes, of physical or sexual abuse, of mental cruelty, of natural disasters, of wars, of jealous lovers, of deception and manipulation, of oppression, of their own careless actions—these and a host of other groups of victims bear the marks of trauma and injury.

Every victim has a unique story. The pedestrian crossing the street did not suspect impending danger. Although anyone in the wrong place at the wrong time can get hit by a car, no two victims have identical experiences. One of the great human tragedies is that some people are victimized many times over. Many people experience the reality of being victims, and we should not close our eyes to the fact that anyone can be a victim.

The Victim May Not Be at Fault

Most often, victims incur damage from forces outside of their control, and frequently those forces take the form of human victimizers. Ironically, individuals sometimes are victims of their own abuse, such as those who set themselves up for failure, choose self-defeating lifestyles, or attempt suicide. Most of these self-abusive people are acting out the unresolved pain of being victimized by others in the past.

Many victims are not responsible for their own victimization, and they should not be blamed for it. A pedestrian may be hit by a car despite making an honest attempt to avoid it. In our society, however, some victims experience double jeopardy—after they are victimized, they are blamed for what has happened to them. Society's fundamental denial of responsibility further cripples such victims, who often internalize feelings of irresponsibility and self-blame. However, victims do not deserve to be blamed for their victimization any more than they deserved to be victimized in the first place.

Intentions Are Not an Accurate
Gauge for Measuring Victimization

People are victimized for many reasons. Sometimes victimization results from malicious intent: a clear and unequivocal decision on someone's part to harm the victim. Sometimes victimization is unintentional; that is, it is an outcome that does not result from malicious intent. Many attempts to prove victimization are really attempts to prove malicious intent. Victimization, however, may reflect something beyond intentionality. It always involves action—the negative behavior of one person toward another. To the injured pedestrian, it does not matter whether the driver of the car was a criminal, a drunkard, or a girl watcher. The only thing that really counts is the harm caused by the driver's actions.

We Need to Understand Victims From Their Perspective

It is easy to think we understand victims' experiences when we really do not. People interacting with victims often discount the emotional toll of victimization. Feelings of shame, self-blame, humiliation, and rage are common in victims, as are a sense of intrusion, violation, and vulnerability, and even a desire for revenge. These feelings may linger long after the actual victimization. Many individuals continue to play the victim role for some time because their feelings about their victimization remain unresolved. As McCann, Sakheim, and Abrahamson (1988) explain, although victims' scars are often invisible, they leave profound, persisting effects. To intervene with victims in a meaningful way, counselors must realize that victims often are in tremendous emotional pain and that many victims have a tendency to avoid their pain. Counselors also should understand that each victim views his or her experience of victimization from a unique perspective.

Understanding victims is a challenge, especially for those who have never been victimized. The tragedy of not being understood as a victim is second only to the tragedy of actually being one. To understand victims fully, counselors require empathy, patience, and the willingness to set aside their own preconceived ideas. Counselors who do not exhibit these qualities likely will misunderstand the unique experiences and perspectives of the victims they seek to help. Tragically, they may victimize their clients further through their lack of understanding.

When Victimization Is Selective and Repeated, It Is Not Just Victimization

When people victimize each other, it is appalling, and it is a blight on society. Although society has increased its efforts to prevent victimization, many forms of victimization remain social enigmas and continue to proliferate. For some people, this means they are victimized repeatedly.

When some individuals are repeatedly victimized while others of similar status are not, there is a larger problem at hand. One could argue that Mr. Jones in the opening story is never struck by a car because he is luckier, smarter, or somehow better than the injured pedestrian. But this explanation does not seem plausible. A more realistic explanation is that some force is working against the pedestrian but not against Mr. Jones. In that sense, the pedestrian is a selected victim.

Racism in Counseling and Therapy

Mental health clients who are members of minority groups are selected victims. They are victims of racism in the mental health care delivery system. This type of victimization is an almost unbelievable irony, in that many minority clients experience abuse, neglect, and mistreatment at the hands of counselors who should be helping them. Further, the ethical codes of the mental health professions hold that all clients deserve equitable treatment, regardless of their backgrounds. Counselors should be the most unlikely professionals to victimize their clients.

Unfortunately, racism in mental health care delivery systems is not new, nor has it been dealt with adequately since coming to society's attention during the civil rights movement of the 1950s and 1960s. The history of racism in U.S. mental health care dates back to the nation's early years. Thomas and Sillen (1972) examined the history of racism in psychiatry. They focused primarily on the experiences of African American patients, but their findings appear to be applicable to the mistreatment of racial minority patients in general. Two quotes from their book capture this despicable legacy:

> Thus a well-known physician of the ante-bellum South, Dr. Samuel Cartwright of Louisiana, had a psychiatric explanation for runaway slaves. He diagnosed their malady as *drapetomania,* literally the flight-from-home madness, "as much a disease of the mind as any other species of mental alienation." Another ailment peculiar to black people was *dysaesthesia Aethiopica,* sometimes called rascality by overseers, but actually due to "insensibility of nerves" and "hebetude of mind." (p. 2)

> Actually, most asylums in the North excluded blacks—for example, the Indiana Hospital for the Insane did not take Negroes on the ground that they were not legal citizens of the state. . . . In the few asylums that sometimes admitted Negroes the ratio was one to several thousand white patients. Dr. John S. Butler, superintendent of the Hartford Retreat, attributed the small number of blacks in his institution to their constitutional cheerfulness, which made them less vulnerable to insanity. The Northern psychiatrists "did not seem to see the contradiction in ascribing the lack of Negroes in their hospitals to their alleged general immunity to the disease and at the same time admitting that hospitals did not ordinarily admit Negroes." (p. 18)

Studies from the mid-20th century onward have documented the enduring pattern of racism in mental health care delivery systems. Researchers have examined the effects of racism on members of various racial minority groups, including African Americans, Asian Americans, Hispanics, and Native Americans. Scholars also have reported on racism in a variety of treatment settings, including inpatient and outpatient facilities. Table 1.1 lists citations of representative publications devoted to the topic of racism in counseling and mental health care delivery. Several of these studies date back to the 1950s.

This research, an accumulation of more than a half century of scholarly inquiry, yields a clear, unavoidable conclusion: Racism exists in mental health care delivery systems across the United States. Of course, not all professionals or practice settings are racist, and not all behave in consistently racist ways. Indeed, some investigations of this issue have produced no evidence pointing toward racism in mental health care, and others have generated mixed or inconclusive results (e.g., Broman, 1987; Goodman & Siegel, 1978; Neighbors et al., 1992; Warner, 1979). These findings are exceptions rather than the rule, however. As Table 1.1 reveals, more than 175 separate studies and commentaries have uncovered racism in American mental health care delivery systems. Professionals cannot dismiss racism as an anomaly in the face of such an overwhelming body of literature attesting to its pervasiveness. When counselors ignore racism, they not only jeopardize the well-being of minority consumers of mental health care but also threaten the very foundation of counseling, which holds the ideals of social justice and equality at its core. Thus, for the welfare of consumers and the integrity of the field as a whole, mental health professionals must confront racism and work to overcome it.

In 1978, the President's Commission on Mental Health produced an important publication that documented the continuing problems encountered by minority clients:

> Racial and ethnic minorities . . . continue to be underserved. . . . It makes little sense to speak about American society as pluralistic and culturally diverse, or to urge the development of mental health services that respect and respond to that diversity, unless we focus attention on the special status of the groups which account for the diversity. . . . Too often, services which are available are not in accord with their cultural and linguistic traditions. . . . A frequent and vigorous complaint of minority people who need care is that they often feel abused, intimidated, and harassed by non-minority personnel. (pp. 4–6)

Five years later, Jackson (1983), who has written extensively on race and psychotherapy, poignantly described racism in counseling. Two of her comments highlight the problem:

Table 1.1   Representative Publications Reporting Racism in Mental Health
                  Delivery Systems

Acosta (1979)	A. B. Goodman & Hoffer (1979)
P. L. Adams (1970)	J. A. Goodman (1973)
W. A. Adams (1950)	Graham (1992)
Adebimpe (1981, 1982)	Grantham (1973)
Adebimpe & Cohen (1989)	Greene (1994a, 1994b)
Adebimpe, Gigandet, & Harris (1979)	Grier & Cobbs (1968, 1992)
Adebimpe, Klein, & Fried (1981)	Griffith (1977)
Armstrong, Ishiki, Heiman, Mundt, &	Griffith & Jones (1978)
Womack (1984)	Gross, Herbert, Knatterud, & Donner
Babigian (1976)	(1969)
Baskin (1984)	Gurland (1972)
Baskin, Bluestone, & Nelson (1981)	Guthrie (1976)
Bell & Mehta (1980, 1981)	Hall (1997)
Blake (1973)	Hampton & Newberger (1985)
Blazer, Hybels, Simonsick, & Hanlon	Hanson & Klerman (1974)
(2000)	Hoffman (1993)
Bond, DiCandia, & MacKinnon (1988)	Hollingshead & Redlich (1958)
Boyd-Franklin (1989)	Hu, Snowden, Jerrell, & Nguyen (1991)
Brantley (1983)	Jackson (1973, 1976)
Brody, Derbyshire, & Schleifer (1967)	Jackson, Berkowitz, & Farley (1974)
Butts (1969, 1971)	Jaco (1960)
Calnek (1970)	Jenkins-Hall & Sacco (1991)
Carter (1979, 1983)	A. Jones & Seagull (1977)
Casimir & Morrison (1993)	B. E. Jones & Gray (1983, 1986)
Cervantes & Arroyo (1994)	B. E. Jones, Lightfoot, Palmer,
Coleman & Baker (1994)	Wilkerson, & Williams (1970)
Collins, Rickman, & Mathura (1980)	D. L. Jones (1979)
J. E. Cooper et al. (1972)	E. E. Jones & Korchin (1982)
P. D. Cooper & Werner (1990)	Kadushin (1972)
S. Cooper (1973)	Karno (1966)
Corvin & Wiggins (1989)	Katz (1985)
Cuffe, Waller, Cuccaro, Pumariega, &	Keefe & Casas (1980)
Garrison (1995)	Korchin (1980)
d'Ardenne (1993)	Kramer (1973)
DeHoyos & DeHoyos (1965)	Lasser, Himmelstein, Woolhandler,
Dreger & Miller (1960)	McCormick, & Bor (2002)
Edwards (1982)	Lawson, Hepler, Holladay, & Cuffel
Fernando (1988)	(1994)
Flaherty & Meagher (1980)	Lefley & Bestman (1984)
Flaskerud & Hu (1992a, 1992b)	Lindsey & Paul (1989)
Garb (1997)	López (1989)
Gardner (1971)	Loring & Powell (1988)
Garretson (1993)	Lu, Lim, & Mezzich (1995)
Garza (1981)	Malgady, Rogler, & Costantino (1987)
Geller (1988)	Manderscheid & Barrett (1987)
Gerrard (1991)	Manderscheid & Henderson (1998)

Table 1.1 (Continued)

Manly (2001)
Mass (1967)
Masserman (1960)
Maultsby (1982)
Mayo (1974)
McNeil & Binder (1995)
Melfi, Croghan, Hanna, & Robinson (2000)
Mercer (1984)
Mollica (1990)
Mollica, Blum, & Redlich (1980)
Mukherjee, Shukla, Woodle, Rosen, & Olarte (1983)
Neighbors, Jackson, Campbell, & Williams (1989)
Neighbors et al. (1999)
Pavkov, Lewis, & Lyons (1989)
C. A. Pinderhughes (1973)
E. Pinderhughes (1989)
President's Commission on Mental Health (1978)
Priest (1991)
Prudhomme & Musto (1973)
Rendon (1984)
Richardson, Anderson, Flaherty, & Bell (2003)
Ridley (1978, 1984, 1985b, 1986c, 1989)
Rogler et al. (1983)
Rollock & Gordon (2000)
Rosado & Elias (1993)
Rosen & Frank (1962)
Rosenfield (1984)
Sabshin, Diesenhaus, & Wilkerson (1970)
Sager, Brayboy, & Waxenberg (1972)
Scheffler & Miller (1991)
Segal, Bola, & Watson (1996)
Shervington (1976)
Simon, Fleiss, Gurland, Stiller, & Sharpe (1973)
Smedley, Stith, & Nelson (2003)
Snowden & Cheung (1990)
A. Solomon (1992)
P. Solomon (1988)
Spurlock (1985)

Stack, Lannon, & Miley (1983)
Stevenson & Renard (1993)
Strakowski et al. (1995)
Strakowski, Shelton, & Kolbrener (1993)
Strauss, Gynther, & Wallhermfechtel (1974)
D. W. Sue (1978)
S. Sue (1977)
S. Sue & McKinney (1975)
S. Sue, McKinney, Allen, & Hall (1974)
S. Sue & Zane (1987)
Sutton & Kessler (1986)
Sykes (1987)
Takeuchi & Uehara (1996)
Taube (1971)
Teichner, Cadden, & Berry (1981)
A. Thomas & Sillen (1972)
C. S. Thomas & Comer (1973)
C. W. Thomas (1973)
Thompson & Jenal (1994)
Thompson & Neville (1999)
Tinsley-Jones (2001)
Toch, Adams, & Greene (1987)
Townsend (1995)
Trierweiler et al. (2000)
Turner & Kramer (1995)
Uba (1982)
U.S. Department of Health and Human Services (1999, 2001)
Wade (1993)
Warren, Jackson, Nugaris, & Farley (1973)
Watkins, Cowan, & Davis (1975)
Whaley (1998a, 1998b)
Willie, Kramer, & Brown (1973)
Willie, Rieker, Kramer, & Brown (1995)
Windle (1980)
Worthington (1992)
Yamamoto, James, Bloombaum, & Hattem (1967)
Yamamoto, James, & Palley (1968)
Young, Klap, Sherbourne, & Wells (2001)

NOTE: The term *racism* does not appear in every publication cited in this table. However, the discussions found in all of these publications imply dynamics that are consistent with the definition of racism used in this book.

> In the psychotherapy relationship, characterized by close interpersonal interaction, aspects of racism may intrude readily. Differential experiences and effects of racism have not changed appreciably historically even though attention has been called to inequities in practice delivery and therapy process, . . . and even though new concepts in treatment delivery have been proposed and partially implemented. (p. 143)

> Race has been identified as a major factor in treatment involvement and treatment process. . . . Prevalent differences as associated with race have been found as it pertains to diagnosis disposition, therapy process and outcome. (p. 144)

Although the work of Jackson and many others has made it obvious that racism is a continuing problem in mental health care service delivery, professionals have made little progress in dealing with it. Fernando (1988) sheds additional light on the problem of racism in service delivery:

> Discriminatory practices result from ways in which the services are organized—selection procedures, points of comparison for promotion, etc. (in the case of staff) and diagnostic processes, selective criteria for types of treatment, indicators of "dangerousness," etc. (in the case of patients). Racism may have direct advantage for the dominant (white) population in that, for example, the exclusion of black staff from management, and the easing out of black patients from time-consuming types of "sophisticated" treatment modalities or their labelling as (psychiatrically) dangerous, allows white society to continue its dominance. (p. 147)

The most compelling case attesting to racism's continued existence in the American mental health care system appears in a recent special report from the Office of the Surgeon General of the United States. Based on the findings of a previous report, Dr. David M. Satcher acknowledges that Americans do not share equally in the benefits of mental health care. He notes that he commissioned "a supplemental report on the nature and extent of disparities in mental health care for racial and ethnic minorities and on promising directions for the elimination of these disparities" (U.S. Department of Health and Human Services, 2001, p. vii). The introduction to this report, which is titled *Mental Health: Culture, Race, and Ethnicity,* states:

> This Supplement to *Mental Health: A Report of the Surgeon General* (U.S. Department of Health and Human Services [DHHS], 1999) documents the existence of striking disparities for minorities in mental health services and the underlying knowledge base. Racial and ethnic minorities have less access to mental health services than do whites. They are less likely to receive needed care. When they receive care, it is more likely to be poor in quality. (p. 3)

What exactly are the nature and extent of the disparities noted in this report? Specifically, how are minority consumers victimized by the mental health system? Compared with White clients, minority clients are more likely to have unfavorable experiences in many aspects of counseling, including the following:

- *Diagnosis:* Minority clients tend to be misdiagnosed more often than White clients. Their misdiagnoses usually involve more severe psychopathology than their symptoms warrant, but they occasionally involve less severe psychopathology.
- *Staff assignment:* Minority clients tend to be assigned to junior professionals, paraprofessionals, or nonprofessionals for counseling rather than to senior and more highly trained professionals.
- *Treatment modality:* Minority clients tend to receive low-cost, less preferred treatment consisting of minimal contact, medication only, or custodial care rather than intensive psychotherapy.
- *Utilization:* Minority clients tend to be represented disproportionately in mental health facilities. Specifically, minority clients are underrepresented in private treatment facilities and overrepresented in public treatment facilities.
- *Treatment duration:* Minority clients show a much higher rate of premature termination and dropout from therapy, or they are confined to inpatient care for much longer periods than are White clients.
- *Attitudes:* Minority clients report more dissatisfaction and unfavorable impressions regarding treatment than do White clients.

Factors Contributing to Counselor Racism

Many counselors are well-intentioned professionals with strong humanistic values. They are motivated to help people who are hurting, and they get personal fulfillment from their work. Moreover, most counselors prioritize the ethical principle of client welfare (American Counseling Association, 1995; American Psychological Association, 2002). If counselors have such lofty human ideals, why is there so much racism in counseling? Part of the answer is that many counselors do not really understand racism. Racism is what people *do,* regardless of what they think or feel. It is a complex social problem, and to understand racism fully, counselors must analyze race-related issues carefully. One part of the problem is that many counselors cling to oversimplified explanations of racism. The other part lies in factors predisposing counselors to racist practices. I describe five such factors below: good intentions coupled with bad interventions, traditional training, cultural tunnel vision, blaming the victim, and either/or thinking.

Good Intentions/Bad Interventions

As a popular cliché notes, "Good intentions are not good enough." Counselors often assume their good intentions automatically make them helpful. This notion implies that only their bad intentions make them unhelpful. As much as good intentions are important, however, counselors need more if they are going to help minority clients. Consider the fact that good intentions sometimes lead to good results and sometimes do not. Also consider the fact that bad intentions often lead to bad results, but not always. Fernando (1988) puts these observations into perspective:

> Racist practices in the context of "bad practice" are easier to detect than those within seemingly "good" practice. Ordinary services carried out by ordinary, honest and decent people can be racist, . . . and it is assumed that "good practice" is automatically non-racist. (pp. 152–153)

Counselors should not be content with knowing only that their intentions are good. They also must know that what they are doing is indeed helpful to their clients. With this in mind, they also should evaluate their interventions. The effectiveness of their interventions matters more than their intentions. If, after taking a good hard look at themselves, counselors find they are not as helpful as they thought, they should admit it. Then they should change their behavior so their clients do benefit from counseling. Counselors should update their knowledge and not continue to behave in particular ways just because they always have.

Traditional Training

Some counselors assume they are prepared to counsel clients of any background. This assumption is embedded in the philosophy of traditional clinical training, which holds that existing counseling theories and techniques are appropriate for all people, regardless of race, ethnicity, or culture. Traditionally trained counselors tend to believe they are competent to adapt to any differences among their clients and thus serve their clients' best interests (Larson, 1982).

For many years, the traditional form of training was the only option available to counselor trainees. The assumption of "equal applicability" of techniques to clients from diverse populations went unchallenged, and changes in training were deemed unnecessary. Over time, however, strong voices arose among professional counselors who began questioning the adequacy of traditional training (Casas, 1984; Ridley, 1985a; Sue & Sue, 1977; Wrenn, 1962). They argued that traditional training does not equip counselors with the skills or competencies they need to be effective with ethnic minority clients. Scientific evidence lent credence to their arguments.

Fortunately, counselor training in multicultural competencies has found its way into the curricula of most graduate programs (Ridley, Mendoza, & Kanitz, 1994). However, there remains considerable variability in the quality and content of such training (Hills & Strozier, 1992; Ponterotto & Casas,

1987). In addition, many clinicians practicing today received their graduate degrees before multicultural training became available. Sue and Zane (1987) describe the deficiencies of traditional training, which was the norm when they conducted their research:

> Most therapists are not familiar with the cultural backgrounds and life-styles of various ethnic-minority groups and have received training primarily developed for Anglo, or mainstream, Americans. . . . [They] are often unable to devise culturally appropriate forms of treatment, and ethnic-minority clients frequently find mental health services strange, foreign, or unhelpful. (p. 37)

Traditionally trained counselors need to accept the inadequacy of their preparation for service delivery. In some respects, their training is a liability. Counselors who have not benefited from multicultural training may mistakenly believe they are qualified to counsel individuals from minority populations.

Cultural Tunnel Vision

Many counselors are ineffective with minority clients because they fail to see the "big picture." That is, they overlook societal factors that influence the behavior and adjustment of these clients. Corey, Corey, and Callanan (2003) describe these counselors as having cultural tunnel vision: "They have had limited cultural experiences, and in many cases they unwittingly impose their values on unsuspecting clients, assuming that everyone shares their values" (p. 321). These authors' point is in keeping with research findings on counseling and values, which indicate that counselors generally do not remain value neutral even when they intend to do so (Kelly, 1990).

Counselors need to broaden their field of vision to include the realities of the ethnic minority experience. Jones and Gray (1983) point out that the intrapsychic conflicts of minorities are amplified by external stresses such as racism, economic pressures, and educational disadvantages. Without a broader field of vision and an ability to bracket their biases, nonminority counselors are prone to expect their minority clients to act like them. YAVIS is the handy acronym often used to describe the type of person many counselors prefer as a client—it stands for young, attractive, verbal, intelligent, successful (Schofield, 1964).

Blaming the Victim

Blaming the victim is a basic human tendency; we often attribute victimization to victims' own actions or behaviors while overlooking its real causes. Typically, this process involves shifting the blame from the perpetrator to the victim. As William Ryan (1971) has noted, blaming the victim "so distorts and disorients the thinking of the average concerned citizen that it becomes a primary barrier to effective social change" (p. xv). This basic misattribution of blame not only pervades society but also infiltrates the counseling profession. Most counselors, however, are scarcely aware of their tendency to blame victims. Ryan contends that victim blaming "is not a process of intentional distortion although it does serve the class of interests of those who practice it" (p. 11).

In the counseling profession, blaming the victim takes many forms. Much victim blaming is subtle, hiding behind the veil of clinical judgment and psychological diagnosis. Sometimes it appears in the labeling of minority clients as "resistant" or "untreatable." Whatever form it takes, mental health professionals must stop blaming victims. Counselors and therapists must understand that it is always wrong to victimize and then blame the victim. They must realize that their distorted views of minority clients are a significant element of the racism pervading the mental health field.

Either/Or Thinking

Either/or thinking is the predominant mode of thought in the Western worldview. This kind of thinking also underlies the conceptual basis of race relations in the United States (Dixon, 1971). The either/or framework advances the idea of discrete categories: Everything falls into one category or another, and nothing can belong to more than one category at the same time. The either/or framework has its roots in the logic of Aristotle (1952):

> It is impossible for the same thing at the same time to belong and not to belong to the same thing and in the same respect; and whatever other distinctions we might add to meet dialectical objections, let them be added. This, then, is the most certain of all principles. (p. 68)

This philosophy is based on several axioms: (a) the law of identity, which states that A is A (e.g., an apple is an apple); (b) the law of non-contradiction, which holds that something cannot be both A and Non-A (e.g., something cannot be both an apple and a nonapple); and (c) the law of the excluded middle, which states that something is either A or Non-A, or neither A nor Non-A (e.g., something is either an apple or a nonapple, or neither an apple nor a nonapple).

Either/or thinking is a legitimate philosophical perspective. However, the theory underlying such thinking can be misconstrued, and several false premises derived from it can be applied erroneously to race relations. The first of these false assumptions is the notion of mutual exclusivity. This idea involves a dichotomizing process. In its extreme form, it assumes that racial groups have nothing in common. Separation of the races is the logical outflow of this assumption. For instance, although segregation is illegal, many Whites do not permit minorities to enter their social spaces. This separation may be depicted as follows:

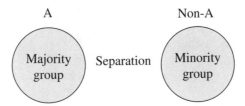

The second assumption is a subtle extension of the first. It adds the notion of group superiority and involves a dehumanizing process. Members of the dominant cultural group devalue members, cultures, and customs of minority groups. This assumption—although lacking scientific credibility—allows the dominant group to view any deviation from its values as inherently inferior. Tajfel (1978) points out that Whites tend to perceive their values, mode of thinking, and behaviors as superior to those of people they deem inferior. A counselor might regard a minority client's value of collectivism as inferior to the value of rugged individualism, for example. Of course, members of minority groups may hold superior attitudes as well. They might regard Whites or other minorities as inferior. An example of the devaluing process is illustrated as follows:

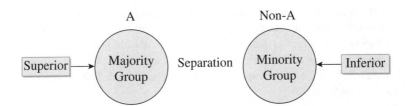

The third assumption is group supremacy. It involves an oppressing process whereby the dominant group overpowers and controls the subordinate group. For example, a counselor who considers rugged individualism a superior value may express this belief by pathologizing a minority client who values collectivism. The counselor may then expect the client to yield his or her collectivist orientation in favor of the counselor's preferred individualist orientation. Research findings suggest that counselors tend to judge increased conformity to the counselors' values as therapeutic change (Kelly, 1990). A's control over Non-A is depicted as follows:

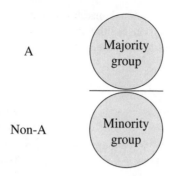

In many respects, either/or thinking is so deeply embedded in Western culture that it goes both unnoticed and unchallenged. Mental health professionals' failure to critique either/or thinking affects their behavior toward minority clients, however. Counselors engage in a host of activities without considering the assumptions that underlie them. Although they desire to help their minority clients, their own implicit assumptions can interfere with the quality of service delivery.

Chapter Summary

In this chapter, I have described minority clients as victims of racism in mental health care delivery systems in the United States. Racist practices in mental health care delivery are documented in early writings, and the current literature indicates that minority clients still report adverse counseling experiences. The chapter concludes with a discussion of five factors that predispose counselors to racism. This discussion should provoke counselors to examine and evaluate their own behaviors and counseling practices. In Chapter 2, I set forth 15 propositions that support the definition of racism used in this book.

Note

1. Currently, there is some debate over the use of the term *victim* versus the term *survivor.* Professionals often speak of persons as survivors of sexual abuse, of trauma, and so on, rather than as victims. I acknowledge this debate but choose not to attempt to resolve the issue of such terminology in this volume. I prefer to use the term *victim* here because many members of minority groups are still being victimized in mental health care delivery systems in the United States.

2

Fifteen Propositions

Racism is a polemical topic—that is, it is a topic that provokes considerable discussion and controversy. In contrast, as Miles (1989) notes, much of the everyday usage of the word *racism* is uncritical. Therefore, a well-substantiated definition of racism is essential to the integrity of any discussion of this topic. Such a definition, like the definition of any abstract concept, should rest on a set of constituent propositions, or statements that affirm the concept. These propositions are conceptual building blocks, and they function much like a foundation that supports the weight of a building.

It follows that the strength of a concept, much like the structural integrity of a building, depends on carefully formulated supporting propositions. Any concept that does not have a sturdy foundation eventually will collapse under its own weight. A rigorous intellectual test only will hasten its demise. It is disturbing that few professionals stop to reflect on the propositions supporting their ideas. All too often, the propositions are unidentified and unexamined, leaving the concepts they are assumed to support especially vulnerable to collapse.

In this chapter, I lay the groundwork for defining and elaborating on racism. The concept of racism needs a crisp and accurate definition, and to achieve this end, I offer and critically examine 15 supporting propositions. This examination is intended to channel the reader's thinking and dispel unfounded notions about racism.

Propositions

Proposition 1: Racism Is Reflected in Human Behavior

The most important thing to say about racism is that it is *behavior*— what a person actually does. Any definition that excludes this basic premise is incomplete. It is more accurate to say racism involves motor behavior, technically known as *operant behavior.* This class of behavior is voluntary. Running, typing, and washing windows are all operant behaviors. Such behaviors are distinguished from involuntary or respondent behaviors, such as eye blinks and knee jerks. This proposition implies that individuals can voluntarily control their racist behavior. Even the most blatant bigots can change when made aware of their racism. However, they first must decide that they want to change.

Several features characterize operant behavior. First, behavior is *observable.* For example, a counselor can be observed conducting an intake interview or writing a psychological report. This characteristic distinguishes behavior from nonbehavior, which cannot be observed. Unless people in the behavior setting have visual disabilities or have their field of vision blocked by physical barriers, they can readily observe racist behavior.

Second, behavior is *repeatable.* Once a behavior has occurred, it can occur again. If a person has learned to ride a bicycle, he or she can repeat cycling behavior. The exception to the repeatability of a behavior is when a physical limitation or outside force interferes. A cyclist who breaks a leg or rides into a hurricane probably cannot continue cycling. If such interference is not present, the cyclist can more than likely repeat the behavior. Any act of racism can be a onetime event or a recurring behavior, depending on the degree of freedom the individual has to continue the racist behavior and whether or not he or she chooses to do so.

Third, behavior is *measurable.* Astute observers can count how often particular behaviors occur. All they need to do is decide what behaviors they want to measure and then place themselves in a position where observation is possible. If they could observe a therapy session, they might count the psychologist's open-ended questions, reflections of feelings, paraphrases, and interpretations. If they were to install a hidden camera in the counseling office, they could measure the counselor's behaviors unobtrusively.

Proposition 2: Racism Is Not the Same as Racial Prejudice

Numerous terms are used to describe race-related dynamics. Many people use the terms *racism* and *racial prejudice* interchangeably, but this creates confusion. Although both refer to some form of bias, the concepts these terms represent involve different dynamics. This confusion over terminology is a major problem because it hinders efforts to understand and resolve racial tensions. Some clarification is in order here.

Prejudice is a preconceived judgment or opinion that is formed without justification or sufficient knowledge (Axelson, 1999). This judgment can be positive or negative. A counselor may have a prejudice in favor of young, attractive, verbal, intelligent, successful (i.e., YAVIS) clients (Schofield, 1964) and a prejudice against religious fundamentalists; these prejudices lead the counselor to lump the members of these groups together without considering the merits of each individual. As Locke (1998) notes, everyone uses some prior knowledge in their urgency to categorize other people; thus everyone is prejudiced in one way or another.

An assertion of *racial prejudice* usually carries a negative connotation. Schaefer (1988) defines racial prejudice as negative attitudes, thoughts, and beliefs about an entire category of people. Along similar lines, Davis (1978) defines racial prejudice as an attitude that includes the expression of unfavorable feelings and behavioral intentions toward a group or its individual members. "Behavioral intentions" are not actual behaviors; rather, they are dispositions toward behaving in certain ways.

The major difference between racism and racial prejudice may be summarized as follows: Racism always involves harmful behavior, whereas racial prejudice involves only negative attitudes, beliefs, and intentions. That is, racism is behavioral, and racial prejudice is dispositional.

Proposition 3: Although Racial Prejudice Involves Unfavorable Attitudes and Intentions, It Does Not Necessarily Translate Into Racism

It is widely held that to be a racist, one must be racially prejudiced. As Lum (2004) notes, however, the idea that prejudice always precedes racism is a misconception. Although some social scientists, such as Leigh (1984), propagate this point of view, their logic has a flaw. This conventional perspective assumes a causal relationship in which racial prejudice is the presumed underlying cause and racism is the effect. This relationship can be illustrated as follows:

CAUSE	⟶	EFFECT
Prejudice		Racism
Nonprejudice		Nonracism

There is an assumed corollary in this logic: Without the presence of prejudice, there can be no racism. This means that people who are not prejudiced do not behave in racist ways. Implicit here is the more deeply embedded assumption that nonracists do not have harmful behavioral intentions.

This argument sounds logical. Deviant acts are typically associated with people who have moral, ethical, or character flaws. Well-known deviants such as Jeffrey Dahmer and other serial killers reinforce the belief among the general public that only bad people do bad deeds. But, for a variety of reasons, well-intentioned people do sometimes harm others. For example, they may be misinformed or unaware of the potential harmful consequences of their behavior. Their ignorance does not make the consequences of their actions any less detrimental, however. As Smedes (1984) observes, sometimes people hurt others with their good intentions:

> Sometimes people hurt us even when they mean to do us good. Their well-meant plans go awry, maybe through other people's knavery, maybe by their own bungling. No matter how, what they do to help us turns out to hurt us. (p. 11)

The work of Ignaz Semmelweiss, a Hungarian obstetrician known as the "savior of mothers," dramatizes the seriousness of unintentional harm. In 1847, Semmelweiss noticed that women in Vienna who gave birth at home had a much lower mortality rate than did women who delivered in the hospital. This problem interested him, and he went on to discover that a fatal puerperal infection was transmitted by obstetricians who failed to clean their hands prior to examining the women in labor. Although 19th-century medical practices seem primitive when measured against modern standards, Semmelweiss's discovery underscores an important reality: Even professionals with the best of intentions can be dangerous, and their harmful behavior may not necessarily be coupled with any malicious intent.

Conversely, people who have malicious intentions are not necessarily harmful. Their potential to harm others may be prevented by forces more powerful than they are, such as the behavioral sanctions enforced by society or the strong counteractions of their intended victims. This means that even if someone is racially prejudiced, he or she may temporarily refrain or be restrained from acting like a racist.

Proposition 4: Anyone Can Be a Racist, Including Members of Racial Minority Groups

Widely held stereotypes of racists include White supremacists and ignorant bigots. Ku Klux Klan members, skinheads, and Archie Bunker fit these stereotypes. Some of the most heinous acts of racism are indeed committed by members of hate groups, and many of their notorious deeds have been well publicized. Many people believe that to be a racist, an individual must match one of these profiles.

Are White bigots really the only ones responsible for racism? Before answering this question, consider that members of minority groups sometimes victimize members of their own and other minority groups. Racism practiced by minorities is real—as real as incest, in which the victim and perpetrator are both members of the same family. Racist behavior of one minority group member toward another may be intentional or unintentional. But racism practiced by members of minority groups does not end there. Minorities also can behave in racist ways toward Whites. A gang of African American adolescents might assault an unsuspecting White passerby in a city park, for example. Although the idea that minorities can be racists may not be popular, a counselor never should discount anyone's potential to be a racist simply because of the person's skin color. If we use race as the basis for deciding who is a racist, we are likely to discount the more important issue—that it is actions that make a racist. More daunting is the hindrance this viewpoint poses to the broadscale elimination of racism. It is impossible to eliminate racism without first acknowledging all of its perpetrators.

Proposition 5: The Criteria for Determining Whether Racism Has Occurred Lie in the Consequences of the Behavior, Not the Causes

Intentions are not the appropriate criteria for determining whether or not a behavior is racist. As I have noted above, racial prejudice does not always cause racism. Even when prejudice does motivate racism, the prejudiced person's intentions do not indicate whether the behavior is racist. This proposition is not to discount the occurrence of visible bigotry and racially motivated acts of violence and vandalism. Behavioral intentions constitute a valuable area to explore, given that such intentions convey a great deal about why people behave as they do. Yet intentions are not the real problem. As Semmelweiss's work illustrates, it may be more beneficial to focus on the consequences of behavior.

To usher in a better way to evaluate racism, I propose the topology for the classification of behavior shown in Figure 2.1. As the figure shows, the consequences of behavior can be divided into two categories: adverse and nonadverse. People are either victimized by the behaviors of others or not victimized. The motivations underlying behavior also can be divided into two categories: prejudiced and nonprejudiced. People either do or do not judge others negatively without justification.

Combinations of the two categories of behavioral consequences and underlying motivation yield four possible types of individual: (a) a prejudiced person who is racist, (b) a prejudiced person who is not racist, (c) a nonprejudiced person who is racist, and (d) a nonprejudiced person who is not racist. According to this typology, the presence of racism is determined by the adverse consequences of a person's behavior. Whether or not a racist person is prejudiced is of secondary importance, for it is possible to not be prejudiced and yet unintentionally act like a racist. Thus a useful way of determining whether racism is present is to look at behavioral consequences

Fifteen Propositions

Behavioral Consequences

		Adverse	Nonadverse
Underlying Motivation	Prejudice	1 Racism	2 Nonracism
	Nonprejudice	3 Racism	4 Nonracism

Figure 2.1   Behavior Typology for Classifying Racism and Nonracism

first and motivation second. Regardless of a counselor's motivation, his or her actual clinical behavior is what affects a client.

Proposition 6: A Person Needs Power to Behave Like a Racist

It takes more than malicious intent for a prejudiced person to behave like a racist. Some people are too powerless to harm others. Even the imperial wizard of the Ku Klux Klan cannot behave like a racist if he is stripped of his power. He may hate African Americans and people of Semitic heritage, but he cannot personally carry out hate crimes if he becomes severely disabled.

It takes power to behave like a racist. Power in this context may be defined as the ability to control oneself and others (Leigh, 1984). Counselors, for example, control access to goals that are of interest to minority clients. Counselors select treatments, make diagnoses, and refer clients to other agencies. These actions can have far-reaching consequences. If counselors are misguided in their actions, they can do their clients tremendous harm.

In U.S. society, minorities in general have considerably less power than do Whites. In the mental health field, this power imbalance is reflected in the tremendous underrepresentation of ethnic minorities among practicing professionals (Ridley, 1985a). For example, ethnic minorities are estimated to represent only 5% to 6% of all psychologists in the United States (American Psychological Association, 1997; Johnson, 2001). White professionals overwhelmingly compose the largest group of service providers. Given that racism is pervasive in mental health care delivery systems, it follows that White professionals account for a large share of the problem. In 1993, in testimony given before a subcommittee of the U.S. House of Representatives, Esteban Olmedo stated that a shortage of ethnic minority mental health professionals is one of the major barriers keeping disadvantaged and minority clients from receiving high-quality service (Moses-Zirkes, 1993).

Proposition 7: Failing to Combat Racism Is a Form of Racism

Most discussions of racism focus on the direct and deliberate acts of racists. Consider another perspective, however—a focus on indirect racism. Suppose one has the ability to rescue a drowning child but does nothing. The consequence of that inaction could be fatal. In fact, such inaction could lead to the same consequence as the action of pushing the child into deep water: The child drowns.

Racism—like the drowning of a child—can occur directly through action or indirectly through inaction. In the former situation, the person does something to bring about the fatal consequence. In the latter situation, the person does nothing, and that failure to act results in the same fatal consequence. In both situations, the person has the ability to influence the outcome.

Direct forms of racism, such as violence and vandalism, are usually easy to challenge for what they are. Indirect forms of racism, on the other hand, are more elusive. Whether racism is direct or indirect, however, the failure to combat it is not just a simple act of racism; it is a perpetuation of racism, especially when the bystander has the power to prevent it. A well-known adage popularized during the civil rights movement of the 1950s and 1960s aptly describes those who participate in indirect racism: If you are not part of the solution, you are part of the problem.

Counselors cannot easily dismiss their responsibility to combat racism. Even counselors who are not bigots participate in a larger system that victimizes minorities. Ineffective interventions, misdiagnoses, and the imposition of biased cultural expectations are among the many ways in which the system victimizes minority clients. No client deserves such mistreatment. Certainly, mental health professionals face great challenges concerning racism, but they must understand that if they do not at least try to stop it, they are actually behaving in a racist manner by allowing it to continue.

Proposition 8: Although Racism Is Observable, Racist Behavior Is Not Always Observed

Behavior is either public or private. Observers can usually see public behavior, but private behavior, for the most part, cannot be seen. Private behavior typically occurs behind the scenes and out of the viewing range of other people. In the privacy of his or her office, a counselor can misinterpret test data and case history information. The counselor then can write up his or her misinterpretations in a psychological report without anyone else ever examining the original source of the data. This unobserved activity can have detrimental consequences for the subject of the counselor's report.

Whether it is observed or not, racism is still racism. It harms its victims. Private racism, however, poses an additional threat because it is more difficult to change than public racism. People usually cannot change what they do not know exists, and they usually do not know something exists unless they first see it. Many acts of racism occur in private, making these behaviors unavailable for public scrutiny. This situation interferes with efforts to eliminate racism. Only those change agents astute enough to recognize the consequences of unobserved racism can detect it; even then, they have to infer its existence.

Proposition 9: Racism, Like Other Operant Behaviors, Is Learned

Racist behavior differs from nonracist behavior in one way: in its impact on the victim and the larger social community. In every other respect, these two kinds of behaviors are fundamentally alike. Both reflect the individual's learning history, and both are based on the same general principles of learning. Moreover, both belong to the operant class of behavior.

Learning can be defined as "a relatively permanent change in potential performance or behavior as a result of experience" (Mancucella, 1985, p. 1). This definition includes two critical elements. The word *potential* indicates that learned behavior is not always manifested. Under certain conditions, a more powerful force may interfere with the display of the learned behavior. A novice counselor, taking a traditional textbook approach and using outdated norms, may conclude that a minority student who has marginal test scores is intellectually deficient. A competent supervisor may recognize the counselor's antiquated understanding of assessment, however, and overrule that evaluation.

Second, nonlearning influences on behavior are excluded from the definition. Not all changes in behavior are the result of learning. Some changes are temporary, such as when a person's behavior is influenced by drugs or fatigue. Hence the definition includes the phrase *relatively permanent.* Other changes are permanent, resulting from physical factors such as the aging process and illness. Thus the definition includes the word *experience.*

Proposition 10: Because Racism Is Operant Behavior, It Can Be Changed

The elimination of racism is a major social concern in the United States. Most Americans agree that racism is wrong and understand that it constitutes a violation of human rights. Racism also is inconsistent with the democratic principles on which this country was founded. Widespread agreement that racism is wrong and the development of actual solutions to this problem are two different matters, however.

To be successful, attempts to eliminate racism must be rooted in a basic understanding of the psychology of behavior. No one is *born* a racist; racism is learned, as is any other operant behavior. This fact implies that no one has to behave as a racist.

The question to ask is not, Can racism be eliminated? It can. There are more important questions: How can racism be eliminated? and Will racism be eliminated? To answer these questions, counselors need to understand the laws of behavior change and make a commitment to the process of change. The elimination of racism in counseling depends on the willingness of counselors to learn and practice new patterns of behavior.

Proposition 11: Consciousness-Raising Is an Inadequate Method of Combating Racism

Spurred by the civil rights and women's movements, U.S. society has witnessed a tremendous growth in the emphasis on consciousness-raising. During the past several decades, activists have initiated numerous efforts to promote the equality of minorities and women. In doing so, they have employed the power of persuasion, the clarification of societal injustices, and appeals to morality. Despite their persuasive messages, however, such attempts at consciousness-raising have yielded disappointing results. Major inequities continue to exist.

Proponents of consciousness-raising as a method for eliminating racism correctly recognize the problem of inequality, but they flounder as change agents. They tend to aim their efforts at presumed underlying causes rather than at racist behavior itself. Of course, their attempts to examine behavioral intentions such as prejudice are important, but their priority should be to change problem behavior. This lack of attention to behavior is what proponents of consciousness-raising often overlook and why they fail to produce significant change.

Moreover, even when proponents of consciousness-raising propose behavior change, they often describe the behavior they are addressing in the most general terms. For example, they might say that counselors need to become "culturally sensitive," yet they provide no clue as to what it means to be culturally sensitive and how this differs from being culturally insensitive. Although they advocate change, proponents of consciousness-raising as a method to address racism in counseling offer only vague guidelines concerning proper counselor behavior.

Proposition 12: To Eliminate Racism, We Must Begin by Identifying Specific Racist Behaviors

As long as counselors are unaware of the harmful effects of their behavior, they probably will not recognize the need to change. Counselors cannot provide equitable and fair treatment for minority clients unless they first determine whether or not their behavior is racist. To accomplish this task, counselors should attempt to locate where their actions fit in the behavior typology presented in Figure 2.1.

Counselors may classify their behavior as either racist or nonracist. In attempting to classify their behavior or the behavior of others, they may make any of four possible decisions: correctly identifying behavior as racism, correctly identifying behavior as nonracism, incorrectly identifying behavior as racism, and incorrectly identifying behavior as nonracism. Two of these decisions are correct, and two are incorrect. Unfortunately, people do not always recognize racism when they see it. Their misidentification stems from their inadequate definition of racism and their lack of knowledge concerning the appropriate criteria for judging behavior. To change racist behaviors, one must be able to identify specific behaviors as racist or nonracist. Unless counselors take this course of action, they are unlikely to overcome their racism.

Proposition 13: Racism Tends to Resist Change

Behavior change is seldom automatic. Human beings are creatures of habit. Their patterns of behavior are well established and supported by long histories of reinforcement. Attempts to eliminate racism—like attempts to change any well-established behavior—are typically met with resistance.

The encounter with resistance has two important implications. First, changing racist behavior is a serious challenge. It demands careful attention and commitment based on the scientific principles of behavior change. Counselors must meet this challenge head-on if they are to overcome racism in counseling and therapy. Second, counselors can overcome their racism. They can acquire empowering behaviors that will help them serve their minority clients better.

Proposition 14: To Prevent Relapse Into Racism, Individuals Must Acquire, Reinforce, and Carefully Monitor Nonracist Behaviors and Fair Practices

Overcoming racism is one accomplishment; maintaining equitable practices and preventing the recurrence of racism is another. The science of human behavior distinguishes behavioral assets from behavioral deficits.

Behavioral assets are socially appropriate and self-enhancing behaviors. Behavioral deficits are socially inappropriate and self-destructive behaviors. A counselor's attributing pathology to a minority client who exhibits mannerisms unfamiliar to the counselor could be described as a behavioral deficit. The counselor's simply stopping his or her destructive behavior does not mean that he or she has developed a behavioral asset, however. To develop a behavioral asset, the counselor must acquire skills in multicultural assessment.

One of the best ways to prevent relapse into racism is to reinforce behavioral assets that replace racist behaviors. Two competing behaviors cannot coexist. Counselors cannot engage in racist behavior and nonracist behavior simultaneously. In the language of behaviorism, preventing relapse involves the differential reinforcement of other behavior. As applied to this discussion, it involves the reinforcement of equitable practices that are incompatible with racist practices. For example, if counselors are reinforced for conducting good multicultural assessments, they will not do poor assessments. To ensure their change to equitable treatment endures, counselors need clear descriptions of helpful behaviors, methods of evaluating the consequences of these behaviors, and methods for observing and measuring the frequency of these behaviors. Without an effective system for monitoring their behavior, counselors are likely to drift back into racist practices.

Proposition 15: Combating Racism in Counseling Is the Responsibility of Every Mental Health Professional

Earlier in this chapter, I noted that no race has a monopoly on racism. Anyone is capable of behaving as a racist. Moreover, racism has a long and pervasive history in mental health care delivery service. Therefore, all counselors—regardless of race—should be involved in combating their own racism and the racism of other professionals. This stance echoes that of Ponterotto and Pedersen (1993), who also conclude that racism and prejudice transcend all peoples. If racism is to be eliminated in mental health systems, counselors must begin to take personal responsibility for the way things are rather than claiming, "It's not my problem."

It could be argued that counteracting racism in counseling ought to be an ethical mandate. Current ethical standards in the mental health professions are ineffectual in promoting the welfare of minority consumers. These standards have several shortcomings: They fail to reflect the state of knowledge regarding diversity, they show a bias toward Eurocentric values, and they emphasize the prevention of harm but not the provision of benefits to minorities (Ridley, Mendoza, & Kanitz, 1994). Counselors should explore these issues and search for ways to make professional ethics more responsive to minority consumers.

Chapter Summary

In this chapter, I have presented 15 propositions that support the concept of racism used throughout this book. Most prominent among these is the proposition that racism is operant behavior. Racism is what people *do,* and that means it can be observed, repeated, and measured. The other propositions emanate from this central theme. In Chapter 3, I build on the foundation developed in Chapters 1 and 2 to elaborate on the definition of racism used in this book.

3

What Is Racism?

Many definitions of racism have been proposed. One need only read several discussions on the topic of racism to discover the variety of ways this concept has been defined. Even social scientists and human relations experts seldom agree on a uniform definition. In fact, the definitions they use often contradict one another. This lack of a clear definition is confusing for the average person. In all likelihood, the contradictions that exist among definitions of racism hinder advances in racial understanding.

In this chapter, I attempt to erase the confusion and move the reader beyond polemics by proposing a coherent definition of racism. This definition is grounded in the 15 propositions presented in Chapter 2. After I define racism, I offer a behavioral model that separates the construct into its various component behaviors.

Racism Defined

Racism is any behavior or pattern of behavior that tends to systematically deny access to opportunities or privileges to members of one racial group while allowing members of another racial group to enjoy those opportunities or privileges (Ridley, 1989; Taborn, personal communication, February 1977).[1] This definition includes five key features: It emphasizes the variety of racist behaviors, the systematic nature of racist behavior, and the roles of preferential treatment, inequitable outcomes, and nonrandom victimization. To help the reader gain a better understanding of racism, I briefly discuss each of these features below.

The Variety of Racist Behaviors

When most people think about racism, they envision blatant and possibly sensational acts of bigotry. They may recall images they have seen on television of angry mobs of White people attacking civil rights demonstrators assembled in peaceful protest, or of hooded Klansmen burning crosses. Most people seldom see themselves as racist because their behaviors do not fit these images. In reality, however, racism is more—much more—than a few notorious acts of violence. Racism can be found in a wide variety of behaviors, many of which do not correspond to the average person's conception of racism.

In their professional lives, counselors engage in numerous kinds of behaviors, as the list presented in Table 3.1 illustrates. Among their many behaviors, counselors ask probing questions, take case notes, interpret client defenses, provide feedback to clients, and give clients homework assignments. These are only a few types of behavior that fall under the rubric of counseling, but even this brief list shows the immense possibilities for racism in the counseling profession. Suppose a counselor misinterprets an Asian client's deference toward the counselor. The client may be showing respect for authority, but the counselor may view the client as passive. In the chapters that follow, I will discuss many specific examples of racism in counseling situations.

The list of counselor behaviors in Table 3.1 reveals something else as well: Not every behavior of a counselor, even the most blatantly racist counselor, is racism. The racism most counselors exhibit occurs on a small scale in comparison with their total repertoire of professional behaviors. But even minuscule amounts of racism can have harmful consequences. In the aggregate, across many counselors, racism exists in incredible magnitude in the mental health care system. Counselors should strive not simply to reduce their racist behaviors, but to eliminate racism from their behavioral repertoires.

The Systematic Nature of Racist Behavior

Racism does not exist in a vacuum. It operates in larger social contexts where people interact with one another. General systems theory is useful for explaining human behavior. This theory is particularly helpful for examining racism, which can be seen as a problem of social systems. In the context of the theory, a system is a pattern of relationships that prevails over time. In their classic work on organizations, Katz and Kahn (1978) provide an insightful description of social systems:

> All social systems, including organizations, consist of the patterned activities of a number of individuals. Moreover, these patterned activities are complementary or interdependent with respect to some common output or

Table 3.1   Behavior Repertoire of Mental Health Professionals

Direct service delivery

  Counseling
  Assessing and diagnosing
  Writing case notes
  Writing psychological reports
  Making referrals
  Prescribing medications
  Terminating treatment
  Interpreting test data
  Consulting
  Addressing prevention issues

Training

  Teaching
  Conducting workshops
  Writing instructional materials
  Evaluating
  Supervising

Administration

  Delegating
  Organizing
  Planning
  Monitoring
  Hiring
  Firing
  Budgeting
  Scheduling appointments

Policy making

  Evaluating proposals for change
  Legislating policy
  Lobbying

Research and scholarly activity

  Describing the psychology of ethnic minorities
  Hypothesis testing
  Designing research
  Reviewing literature
  Selecting measurement instruments
  Interpreting data
  Writing proposals for research grants

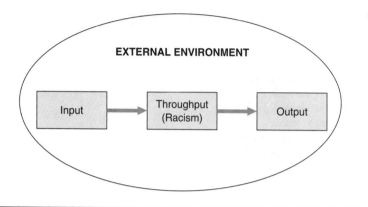

Figure 3.1   Racism as Social Systems Behavior

outcome; they are repeated, relatively enduring, and bounded in space and time. If the activity pattern occurs only once or at unpredictable intervals, we could not speak of an organization. The stability or recurrence of activities can be examined in relation to the energetic input into the system, the transformation of energies within the system, and the resulting product or energetic output. (p. 20)

Three important characteristics of open systems are embedded in this definition, and these are relevant to an understanding of racism. Figure 3.1 depicts racism as social systems behavior, consisting of input, throughput, and output.[2]

Input. Open systems import energy in some form from the external environment. Katz and Kahn (1978) use the example of the human body, which takes in oxygen from the air and food from the external world. To survive, social systems must similarly draw renewed supplies of energy from the larger external environment. Because no social system is entirely self-sufficient or self-contained, the survival of racism as a system depends on inputs in the form of such elements as money, personnel, attitudes, and mental paradigms. For example, government agencies may fund programs that disempower and foster dependence among minorities. Some professionals who enter the mental health field may have the attitude that minority issues are not important. Even minority clients may enter the sanctum of the counseling session with great suspicion. If clinicians fail to deal constructively with these types of inputs, the consequences are almost certain to be negative.

Throughput. Open systems that survive transform their energetic input. Katz and Kahn (1978) illustrate this point by noting how the human body converts starch and sugar into heat and action. Social systems create products, convert materials, change people, and offer services. Essentially, social systems change their inputs into qualitatively different outputs. Racism may be viewed as a process of systemic transformation—racist behavior and patterns of behavior transform minority clients into victims. In counseling, much of the throughput occurs through microinteractions between counselor and client. In addition to direct service delivery, counselors engage in training, administrative duties, policy making, and research and scholarly activities. All of these are system behaviors. Depending on its consequences, any counselor behavior in any of these categories may be racist.

Output. Open systems export products—transformed inputs—into the environment. Katz and Kahn (1978) use the example of the human body's export of carbon dioxide from the lungs. Racist outcomes are similarly linked to a system's input and throughput. When minority clients leave the mental health system prematurely, unhelped, misdiagnosed, or disenchanted, these racist outcomes are the outputs of systemic behavior.

The elements of input, throughput, and output suggest that racism is a function of social systems. Like the numerous survival activities that occur in the human body, racism is reinforced by larger social systems. Without this support and reinforcement, racism could not exist. Therefore, efforts to change racism—even the isolated behavior of individuals—must take a systems perspective into account.

Preferential Treatment

In a fair system, all participants have equal opportunities. No one is unfairly advantaged or disadvantaged. Racism, however, involves preferential treatment. Members of the preferred group have an unfair advantage over members of the nonpreferred group. Suppose that two 15-year-old boys agree to a wrestling match. The boys are of equal height, weight, strength, and intelligence. One boy has never wrestled, however, whereas the other boy has trained for a year under an Olympic team wrestling coach. Despite the many similarities between these two boys, one important difference between them gives one boy an advantage over the other.

In the mental health care system in the United States, Whites have advantages over members of minority groups. For example, as Leong (1992) notes, Asians sometimes encounter a particular disadvantage in group counseling:

> In many Asian cultures, there is a strong cultural value that involves
> humility and modesty in social interactions. This value is often expressed

> in the form of deferential behavior and not drawing excessive attention to
> oneself and one's personal concerns. . . . The group climate of open and
> free self-expression may then be experienced by these Asian Americans
> as an uncomfortable and culturally alien demand. (p. 219)

Leong argues that this conflict in values contributes to premature termination
of therapy among Asians. It is not unreasonable to surmise that in group
counseling, White clients have an advantage over Asian clients. Unless group
counselors are multiculturally competent, they are unlikely to facilitate the
group experience in ways that will maximally benefit Asian group members.
Racism denies equal access to opportunities and privileges to one race while
perpetuating the access that members of another race enjoy. No group of
people deserves to enter counseling with an unfair advantage or disadvantage.

Inequitable Outcomes

Racism typically confers benefits on members of the majority group
but not on members of minority groups. Such benefits may be psychological,
social, economic, material, or political. As a result, Whites consistently find
themselves in a one-up position over minorities. The inequitable outcomes
of racism may be illustrated as follows:

$$\text{Racism} \longrightarrow \frac{\text{Majority Group}}{\text{Minority Group}}$$

Evidence of consistent inequitable outcomes for minority clients can
be found easily in the mental health field. As noted in Chapter 1, less positive outcomes are apparent for minority clients, in comparison with majority clients, in the areas of diagnosis, staff assignment, treatment modality,
utilization, treatment duration, and attitudes toward treatment. As Rogler
(1993) has pointed out, the revised third edition of the *Diagnostic and
Statistical Manual of Mental Disorders* (*DSM-III-R;* American Psychiatric
Association, 1987) paid scant attention to the significance of culture, yet
the *DSM* is used cross-nationally more widely than any other system for
classifying mental illnesses. Rogler asserts that the taxonomy found in the
DSM-III-R had the potential to lead to diagnostic errors stemming from
practitioners' neglect of culture or misconceptions about culture.

Granted, as Smart and Smart (1997) explain, the *DSM-IV* marks a significant improvement over the *DSM-III* and *DSM-III-R*. The fourth edition of
the *DSM* includes five new features aimed at promoting cultural sensitivity:
(a) descriptions of culture-specific features of some disorders; (b) a glossary
of culture-bound syndromes; (c) an "Outline for Cultural Formulation" to
help practitioners assess the relative influence of client culture; (d) a revised
Axis IV that addresses a wide variety of psychological and environmental

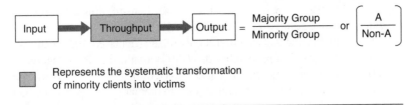

Figure 3.2   Mental Health Systems as Racist

stressors, including discrimination; and (e) V codes that account for accul-turation as well as religious and spiritual problems. Smart and Smart stress that, despite these additions, much work remains to be done to boost the *DSM*'s level of cultural sensitivity. They note the persistent Western cultural bias in the *DSM-IV*, which manifests itself in a glossary that, in excluding non-American syndromes, presents culture-bound disorders as "artificial and exotic." They also bemoan the manual's limited inclusion of cultural consid-erations for diagnosis, which appear in only 79 of 400 diagnostic descrip-tions. When such a powerful tool of the mental health system ignores culture, it is easy to see why minorities find themselves in a one-down position.

Figure 3.2 depicts the mental health system as racist and shows the inequitable outcomes that result. The outcomes depicted in the figure are reminiscent of those illustrated in Chapter 1. This implies that racism is tied inextricably to either/or thinking, which is deeply embedded in American culture. Professional paradigms and models often categorize people, and Western paradigms and models tend to favor individuals whose behaviors are consistent with traditional Western values. Such paradigms may very well contribute to unintentional racist outcomes in counseling, as many mental health workers are committed to professional business as usual.

Nonrandom Victimization

It is one thing to be a victim and be treated as just another statistic. It is much worse, however, to be victimized repeatedly. When members of par-ticular racial groups are consistently victimized, it is almost impossible to conclude that the victimizations are random events. Of course, one might argue that the adverse counseling experiences reported by the members of ethnic minority groups reflect nothing more than chance occurrences. This perspective implies the belief that neither the victims (i.e., ethnic minority clients) nor the social settings (i.e., counseling offices or clinics) are respon-sible for the repeated difficulties of minority clients in counseling. However, probability theory strongly suggests the presence of an influencing dynamic.

Consider a probability experiment. A barrel contains 100 balls, 50 of which are black and 50 of which are white. A blindfolded experimenter draws balls from the barrel; each ball is drawn individually and not replaced. The first 25 balls selected are tossed into the trash. Successive drawings are made until all of the balls have been drawn.

Assuming that the balls are thoroughly mixed (unbiased) before any are drawn from the barrel, a probability of 1/100 is assigned to the selection of each ball. That is, each ball has an equal chance of being selected. Although 100 possible outcomes exist, it is impossible to predict when a particular ball will be selected. During the experiment, an interesting pattern arises: The first 25 balls selected, all of which are thrown away, are black. Thus all of the white balls but only half of the black balls are retained.

The experimenter could conclude that white balls are luckier than black balls. The favorable selection of white balls over black balls is certainly possible, but, according to the laws of chance, such an outcome is highly improbable. With 100 selections, fairly proportionate numbers of black and white balls should be chosen. The chance occurrence or recurrence of an event or set of events in a given sample space (situation) is measured by the ratio of the number of cases or alternatives favorable to the event to the total number of cases or alternatives. It is statistically improbable that only black balls would be selected on the first 25 draws, all things being equal. But that is precisely the problem: In this case, all things probably are not equal. The most likely explanation for the experiment's results is that outside factors influenced the favorable selection of white balls.

In an equitable mental health care delivery system, the chance recurrence of minority clients' victimization is improbable. When minority clients repeatedly drop out of counseling prematurely, are assigned to junior professionals, or receive inaccurate diagnoses, it is difficult to explain these outcomes as random events. Systematic influence—the behavior operative in the mental health system—is a more plausible explanation. In this context, racism could be described as nonrandom victimization: the systematic denial of access to opportunities and privileges.

On various occasions, students and colleagues have asked me, "Isn't it true that White clients are also sometimes victimized in counseling?" My answer is an unqualified yes. Anyone may be mistreated by an incompetent counselor, and the victimization of a White client is no less serious than the victimization of a minority client. My point here, however, is that incidents of White client victimization tend to be random in nature. The consistent victimization evident in the treatment of minority clients often stems from racism, which is both nonrandom and predictable.

A Behavioral Model

To clarify the dynamics of racism further, I propose here a behavioral model that is based on the definition of racism used throughout this book. This model categorizes racism into its essential component behaviors.[3]

Each of the behavioral categories is a type or level of racism. No category of behavior in the model represents racism exclusively. The model is outlined as follows:

I. Individual racism
   A. Overt (always intentional)
   B. Covert
      1. Intentional
      2. Unintentional

II. Institutional racism
   A. Overt (always intentional)
   B. Covert
      1. Intentional
      2. Unintentional

The model classifies racism into two major behavioral categories: individual and institutional. *Individual racism* involves the adverse behavior of one person or a small group of people. A waitress who refuses to serve a minority customer in a restaurant is exhibiting individual racism. *Institutional racism* involves the adverse behavior of organizations or institutions (Sedlacek & Brooks, 1976). The Jim Crow laws in the South, which limited African Americans' access to public accommodations and included the requirement that they sit at the backs of buses, are an example of institutional practices of racism.

The major categories of racism can be subdivided into smaller units of behavior. *Overt racism,* which may be either individual or institutional, is always intentional. Overt racist behavior implies intentionality on the part of the perpetrator, leaving no room for doubt about the racist's underlying motive. When an African American man is lynched, malicious intent is unmistakably implied by the behavior. *Covert racism,* on the other hand, is more subtle. It is similar to overt racism in that it is reflected in the behavior of either individuals or institutions, and its adverse consequences are the criteria that make it racist. However, in covert racism, the motives underlying the behavior are hidden. Others are left to guess or hypothesize about the covert racist's motives. The only person who really knows the underlying motives is the person who performs the racist behavior. In fact, some racists are skillful in hiding or masking their motives. They might be the first to say, "There isn't a racist bone in my body!" They may even attempt to portray their behavior toward the victim as beneficent.

Covert racism may be either intentional or unintentional. Intentional covert racism involves malicious intent. The behaviors of intentional racists are consistent with their motives, even though others may be unable to identify those motives. Unintentional covert racism involves no malicious intent. The behaviors of unintentional racists result in consequences that often

Table 3.2   Examples of Racism in Mental Health Care Delivery Systems

	Individual Racism	*Institutional Racism*
Overt	A therapist believes that ethnic minorities are inferior and on this basis refuses to accept members of minority groups as clients.[a]	A mental health agency openly denies treatment to members of ethnic minority groups.[a]
Covert Intentional	A senior psychologist assigns a minority client to an intern because of the psychologist's own social discomfort but claims to have a schedule overload.	A mental health agency deliberately sets fees above the range most ethnic minority clients can afford, thus excluding them from treatment.
Unintentional	A therapist, functioning under the illusion of color blindness, erroneously diagnoses pathology in a minority client.	A mental health agency routinely uses standardized psychological tests without considering subcultural group differences and biases in test construction and interpretation.

SOURCE: Adapted from Ridley, C. R. (1989). Racism in counseling as an aversive behavioral process. In P. B. Pederson, J. G. Draguns, W. J. Lonner, & J. E. Trimble (Eds.), *Counseling across cultures* (3rd ed., pp. 55–77). Honolulu: University of Hawaii Press. Used by permission.

a. This practice is now illegal under federal civil rights legislation.

contradict their motives. Table 3.2 presents some examples of the various types of racism found in mental health care delivery systems.

Unintentional Racism: An Insidious Form of Victimization

As the preceding discussion clearly shows, racism is a complex social problem with many faces. Solutions to racism cannot be found until those who oppose racism agree on its definition and fully understand its component behaviors. According to the definition of racism applied in this volume, whether a given behavior is individual or institutional, overt or covert, intentional or unintentional, it is racism if the result is systematic victimization.

In general, overt forms of racism are the easiest to identify. This means they are also the easiest to overcome. Today, most forms of overt racism are illegal in the United States. For example, Title VII of the 1964 Civil Rights Act prohibits employers from discriminating in hiring, placement, and promotion of employees on the basis of race, color, sex, religion, ethnic background, or national origin. To a large extent, the legal system can monitor and enforce these practices. Although overt racism has not been totally eradicated, our society has come a long way in reducing the incidence of overt racist practices.

But what about other forms of racism? There is evidence that more subtle forms of racism have replaced blatant discrimination (Dovidio & Gaertner, 1986). Sedlacek and Brooks (1976) go so far as to argue that most racism is unknowing or unintentional:

> Most people do not know enough about the sources or effects of their behavior to realize how it damages someone of another race. It is even more destructive as a collective action of the majority society. For instance, if a white belongs to an organization that excludes blacks, formally or informally, then he or she is lending support to a racist organization, whether or not he or she realizes it or has the best intentions. The consequences are that blacks can't get in. (p. 43)

Unintentional racism is perhaps the most insidious form of racial victimization. Unintentional racists are unaware of the harmful consequences of their behavior. They may be well-intentioned, and, on the surface, their behavior may appear to be responsible. Because individuals, groups, and institutions engaging in unintentional racism do not wish to do harm, it is often difficult to get them to see themselves as racist. They are likely to deny their racism. Unintentional racists need to realize, however, that it is not necessarily the person wearing the white sheet and carrying a torch who poses the greatest threat to minority group members. Rather, cloaked in their sincerity and desire to do good, unintentional racists often do some of the greatest harm. Certainly, overt racism has not been completely eradicated in mental health care; sometimes counselors with bad intentions do harm minority clients. However, today covert racism is the more pervasive problem (see, e.g., Dovidio & Gaertner, 1986). The major challenge for counselors is overcoming unintentional racism to provide more equitable service delivery to minority clients.

Therapist Inaction as Racism

Therapist inaction—behaviors of omission—is an important element in the victimization of minority clients. Some mental health care professionals are so frightened of doing the wrong thing that they refuse to do or say anything when issues of race arise. Although they attempt to escape racism by doing nothing, they end up perpetuating the problem they seek to avoid by refusing to act. One form of therapist inaction surfaces in White professionals' delegation of responsibility for minority clients to minority professionals. White practitioners often assume that minority professionals are the exclusive experts on treating minority clients. This avoidance behavior is not only irresponsible, it also places an unfair burden on minority professionals—ironically, yet another act of racism.

White professionals are not the only ones guilty of therapist inaction, however. Some minority professionals are so confident they are "doing the right thing" for their minority clients that they are closed-minded. They assume they understand the dynamics of racism when they may not, and, in their attempts to attack racism, they sometimes end up "doing the wrong thing." In another version of therapist inaction, some minority professionals posture as experts on treating minority clients, but they avoid examining their own racism or fail to become truly competent in dealing with minority issues.

Most mental health professionals will encounter numerous opportunities to confront racism in their practices. They must not allow their fears or their unwarranted confidence to prevent them from doing the right thing for their clients. They must get involved, confront racism in themselves and others, and strive to make the mental health care system more equitable for all clients. They must understand that racism can surface in what they fail to do as well as in what they do. As Thouless (1974) explains, "So important is action that we can reasonably condemn as crooked thinking any device in thought which has as its purpose the evasion of useful or necessary action" (p. 166).

Chapter Summary

In this chapter, I have proposed a definition of racism that comprises five important features: It emphasizes the variety of racist behaviors, the systematic nature of racist behavior, and the roles of preferential treatment, inequitable outcomes, and nonrandom victimization. I also have presented a behavioral model that categorizes racism into its various component behaviors. Of the various forms of racism, unintentional racism is the most insidious. Unintentionally racist behaviors often go unnoticed, but their harmful consequences are far-reaching. The following chapters closely examine unintentional racism in the mental health system in the United States. I begin by examining the practices of individual mental health practitioners and showing how racism exists in many of their behaviors. Racism is a problem shared by many counselors, regardless of their racial backgrounds, therapeutic orientations, or years of professional experience. The discussion then broadens to include the policies and practices of mental health institutions. This examination reveals that minority consumers of mental health care services are the victims of both unintentional individual racism and unintentional institutional racism. Finally, with the goal of eliminating unintentional racism in mind, I propose some workable solutions and practical alternatives to current practices.

Notes

1. The exclusively behavioral definition of racism used in this book deviates somewhat from other definitions. More often than not, scholars have used racism to identify the presumption that apparent differences between minorities and Whites can be explained biogenetically (for other points of view, see Fairchild, 1991; Jones, 1972; Katz & Taylor, 1988; Miles, 1989, 1993). The classification of groups of people into races is often based on phenotypes, or observed physical characteristics. From this perspective, race is a sociological phenomenon that consists of a set of beliefs about people together with the behavioral consequences of those beliefs. Some professionals prefer to use the phrase *visible racial, ethnic group,* or *VREG,* to designate any group of non-White people in the United States (Cook & Helms, 1988). In this book, the term *race* takes on a social definition (Jones, 1992; van den Berghe, 1967). This application recognizes the power of phenotypes to provoke attitudinal and behavioral responses. John Griffin's classic book *Black Like Me* (1961) graphically illustrates the force of perceived physical characteristics and their sociological consequences. Although I take a sociological stance, I acknowledge that the concept of race is questionable. Even biological-evolutionary explanations of race are dubious (for excellent discussions of this topic, see Montagu, 1964; Yee, Fairchild, Weizmann, & Wyatt, 1993; Zuckerman, 1990). Many groups—including women in general, gays, and handicapped persons—experience systematic oppression and victimization in the United States. The behavioral definition of racism applied here also is helpful for improving our understanding of the mistreatment of these groups' members. However, scholarly integrity demands that separate social science analyses be conducted to ferret out the special dynamics of victimization for each oppressed group.

2. According to Katz and Kahn (1978), the open systems approach was developed to deal with the inadequacies of closed systems thinking. The most important problem with the closed system approach is that it fails to recognize fully that organizations are dependent on inputs from their environments. In this respect, no system is ever closed or self-contained. As I have noted in earlier work, organizations that pay homage to open systems theory without respecting their interdependence with the surrounding suprasystem are operating under an illusion (Ridley & Mendoza, 1993).

3. I want to acknowledge Dr. John M. Taborn for introducing me to the behavioral model of racism used in this book.

4

Models of Mental Health

Everyone uses yardsticks of one sort or another to size up other people. Sometimes we use such yardsticks unknowingly as we gauge human behavior and determine its appropriateness. When individuals measure up to society's mainstream cultural values, they are labeled *normal*. Those who do not measure up are labeled *abnormal* or *deviant*. Behind the use of every behavioral yardstick and the labeling that goes along with it lies a more basic purpose: to determine whether an individual should change and, if so, how much.

In the counseling profession, the yardsticks practitioners use to measure behavior are called *models* of mental health. These models provide the standards against which counselors judge the normalcy and deviance of their clients' behaviors. As Nietzel, Bernstein, Kramer, and Milich (2003) note, models of mental health aid counselors in three ways: (a) by helping them organize their thinking about behavior, (b) by guiding their clinical decisions and interventions, and (c) by allowing them to communicate with colleagues in a common, systematic language. Models of mental health are, in effect, the tools of the counseling trade.

In this chapter, I describe four prominent models of mental health: the deficit model, the medical model, the conformity model, and the biopsychosocial model. Despite the benefits of models, such as those that Nietzel et al. (2003) suggest, professional counselors also must recognize that each model of mental health has inherent limitations as well as the potential to be misused. Of special interest in the following discussion is how counselors unknowingly perpetuate racism through their application of these models.

The Deficit Model

The deficit model of mental health, as its name implies, views individuals who exhibit mental or emotional problems as flawed. When applied to members of minority groups, this model assumes predetermined deficiencies. As Thomas and Sillen (1972) observe, assumptions about the deficiencies of minority group members have been used historically in the United States to relegate minorities to inferior status. Further, mental health professionals often have used these alleged deficiencies to explain psychopathology in minority group members.

Two major variations of the deficit model are often applied to minority groups. The first of these is the *genetic deficit hypothesis,* which rests on the assumption that racial/ethnic minorities are deficient in desirable genes. According to this hypothesis, any differences between minorities and Whites reflect the groups' differing biological/genetic capacities (Atkinson, Morten, & Sue, 1998a). The genetic deficit hypothesis has a long history in the social sciences. Early support for this way of thinking can be found in the writings of such prominent scholars as Darwin (1859), deGobineau (1915), Galton (1869), Hall (1904), and Terman (1916).

The genetic deficit hypothesis can be further subdivided into two more specific hypotheses concerning intellectual and personality deficits. According to the *intellectual deficit hypothesis,* genetic makeup plays the predominant role in the determination of intelligence. This hypothesis asserts that ethnic minorities are born with brains inferior to those of Whites and so have limited capacity for mental development (Stanton, 1960). In the late 1960s and early 1970s, several proponents of this view espoused their own particular renditions of this theme, including Herrnstein (1971), Jensen (1969), Rushton (1988), Shockley (1971), and Shuey (1966). The *personality deficit hypothesis* describes ethnic minorities as abnormal in both character and behavior. Some proponents of this viewpoint have used it to explain criminal behavior on the part of minority group members.

The second variation of the deficit model is the *cultural deficit hypothesis,* which also can be divided into two more specific hypotheses. One of these, the *cultural deprivation hypothesis,* states that ethnic minority groups have inferior cultures or no culture at all. This theory shifts the blame for mental health problems to the lifestyles of ethnic minorities. The *cultural stress hypothesis,* in contrast, portrays minority group members as "wounded soldiers." This theory holds that minorities break down and become debilitated under the weight of societal oppression. A by-product of this debilitation is minorities' inability to compete effectively in society with their White counterparts.

Implications of the Deficit Model for Unintentional Racism

The deficit model is the most explicitly racist of all mental health models. Most people would assume that mental health professionals who believe their minority clients are somehow deficient are intentional racists, especially professionals who are proponents of the genetic deficit hypothesis. On closer examination, however, it becomes clear that professionals who embrace the deficit model also may practice unintentional racism. This possibility exists especially for professionals who embrace the cultural deficit hypothesis. As Sue, Arredondo, and McDavis (1992) comment on this subject:

> Ironically, it was well-intentioned White social scientists who were attempting to reject the genetically deficient model who talked about "cultural deprivation." Unfortunately, these social scientists were as much prisoners of their own cultural conditioning as those of an earlier decade. . . . The cultural deficit notion does not make sense because everyone inherits a culture. What proponents of this view were really saying was that racial and ethnic minorities do not possess "the right culture." (p. 479)

Counselors who believe minority clients have cultural deficits tend to make one of two treatment errors: They either lower their expectations for what the clients can accomplish or they set unrealistically high goals for their clients. As a member of a minority group myself, I have personally experienced both types of situations. When I was an inner-city high school student in Philadelphia, my guidance counselor advised me to attend the city community college. Despite my strong academic record and desire to attend a more competitive university in another state, she persisted in her advice. She probably would be surprised to learn that I now hold a Ph.D. from a prominent university. When I defended my doctoral dissertation, I encountered different expectations. Several members of my committee asked extremely difficult questions. My chairman later told me that my oral examination was one of the most rigorous he had ever witnessed. He believed the line of questioning was unreasonable. A well-known member of my committee, who seemed embarrassed when I saw him later, told me that I had really earned my degree.

Counselors' unrealistic expectations set minority clients up for failure. Treatment goals that are set too low can become self-fulfilling prophecies. Goals that are set too high may be impossible to achieve. Although some minority clients are assertive enough to challenge their counselors' expectations, many are not. The most damaging thing about a counselor's unrealistic expectations is their ability to generate failure in counseling, an experience that may reinforce the client's preexisting feelings of inadequacy. The deficit model of mental health, even in its less blatantly racist variations, is not suited to empowering minority clients.

The Medical Model

The medical model is the dominant framework that mental health professionals use to understand and treat psychological problems. This model is based on an assumed analogy between psychological disorders and physical problems (Turner & Cumming, 1967). Classical psychoanalysis, a major impetus behind the medical model, is unsurpassed in shaping the thinking and practice of mental health treatment. Sigmund Freud, the founder of psychoanalysis, was a neurologist. His medical orientation naturally influenced the development of his clinical theory and practice.

In the United States today, many mental health professionals and a large segment of the general population continue to accept the medical model, which has four key features. First, it focuses on illness. The model views psychological problems as diseases just like physical ailments. As Hersch (1968) notes, the terms *illness* and *disease* have been defined as the presence of symptoms. On this topic, Phares (1992) states, "Nowhere is this view better illustrated than by statements such as 'This patient is *suffering* from schizophrenia' or 'This patient has been *afflicted* by these phobias for many years'" (p. 133). By implication, mental health is a condition characterized by the absence of symptoms. According to the medical model, successful intervention for mental illness involves first diagnosing and then destroying the underlying disease.

Second, the medical model emphasizes the classical doctor-patient relationship. From this viewpoint, counseling professionals are regarded as experts and knowledgeable authorities. They are expected to be highly trained, skilled, and almost omnipotent. Clients, on the other hand, are regarded as needy recipients of counselors' services. They are expected to accept their counselors' diagnoses and to comply unquestioningly with treatment recommendations.

Third, the medical model of mental health emphasizes long-term treatment. Clients may be expected to spend months or even years in therapy because the real work of change is believed to require in-depth analysis. Short-term therapy is regarded as superficial and ineffective, or as a quick fix. According to this model, clients' deep conflicts accumulate over many years, and they cannot be treated adequately in a few sessions.

Finally, the medical model's approach to treatment involves a verbal endeavor. Beginning with Freud's notions of catharsis and free association, individual insight-oriented psychotherapy has long been the prevailing mode of mental health treatment. In fact, it has been called the "talking cure." Therapists ask provoking questions to get their clients to self-disclose. Therapists also interpret their patients' disclosures. For therapy to be successful, the client must be highly verbal and capable of discussing his or her intimate thoughts and feelings.

Implications of the Medical Model for Unintentional Racism

To explain exactly how mental health professionals' use of the medical model can result in unintentional racism, I first need to offer a brief review of Freud's theory of personality. This theory divides personality structure into three antagonistic systems: the id, the superego, and the ego. The *id* is the primitive, unconscious part of the personality. It is the storehouse of the libido, the person's psychic energy. The id constantly attempts to avoid pain and gain pleasure by discharging unrestrained sexual and aggressive impulses (Freud calls this the pleasure principle). The *superego,* which corresponds roughly to the conscience, represents the person's moral attitudes. The superego learns its ideas of right and wrong from family and society, and it attempts to guard the individual's moral values while also controlling the pleasure-seeking impulses of the id. The *ego* stands between the id and superego. It has two roles. Like a referee in a sports event, the ego mediates the conflicting demands of the other two systems (Freud calls this the ego's *synthetic function*). The ego also guides the individual as he or she meets the demands of the real world (Freud calls this the *executive function*).

All three components of personality get their energy from the id's instincts, and the supply of energy is limited. Thus the more energy the ego uses to perform its synthetic function, the less it has to perform its executive function. According to psychoanalytic theory, the synthetic role of the ego takes precedence over the executive role. If the ego expends too much energy performing synthetic activity, it will not have enough energy available for relating to the outside world. Freud (1940/1949) argues that excessive internal claims of the id and the superego weaken the ego's ties to external reality. When this happens, the person suffers from neurosis: a condition in which the ego is weakened by internal conflict and forced to adopt inappropriate coping strategies. Freud likens the conflict to a civil war. Ruch (1967) elaborates:

> Caught in this conflict, the ego usually resorts to some form of compromise which will at least partially satisfy both libido and conscience. Inability of the ego to make such a compromise leads to the appearance of neurotic symptoms. (p. 120)

Freud's method of therapy follows from his concept of neurosis. Because the patient's problems are rooted in the unconscious, the goals of analysis are to uncover repressed conflicts and raise those conflicts to the level of the preconscious mind, allowing the ego to return to controlling the id's drives and guiding effective relations to reality. To achieve these goals, the analyst must overcome the strategies the patient uses to repress material in the unconscious. Initially, the analyst takes over the role of the patient's superego, which scrutinizes all psychological material. Then the therapist interprets the material that the client has brought to consciousness through the techniques of free association or analysis of slips of the tongue and dreams. The therapist also traces the material back to its origins in the patient's childhood.

Mental health treatment based on the medical model features five characteristics that have important implications for unintentional racism in counseling. I discuss these characteristics briefly below.

Tendency to overpathologize. The medical model's persistent focus on illness allows counselors to overlook external explanations for behavior. As Reiff (1967) points out, many mental health professionals find it easy to associate disturbance with everyone and difficult to associate health or normalcy with anyone. As victims of racism, ethnic minority clients are more likely than White clients to be blamed for their problems and to be given a label of pathology. Professionals who are committed to the medical model tend to search for intrapsychic explanations of disturbing symptoms. When treating minority clients, they often overlook the possibility that the clients' puzzling behaviors may reflect social pathologies such as racism, discrimination, poverty, inadequate health care, and poor education. Labeling a minority client as pathological after such a superficial inspection of the situation is comparable to naming the individual identified as "acting out" in a dysfunctional family system as the primary source of the problem.

Limited social applicability. The pervasive influence of Freudian psychology has given rise to the psychiatric worldview (Kuriloff, 1970). That is, as Riessman and Miller (1964) observe, Western societies tend to evaluate all social problems, from political to educational, in intrapsychic, psychoanalytic terms. To some extent, the psychiatric worldview is helpful for conceptualizing individual problems, but it is inadequate for conceptualizing racism and other social pathologies. As Eisenberg (1962) states:

> Society is more than an aggregate of its individual members. When systems in the social organism go awry, it is absurd to attempt their correction by medicating the individuals whose aberrations are secondary or tertiary order consequences of the basic lesions. (p. 789)

The medical model has an indirect effect on minority mental health. It does not help counselors or other professionals analyze or change the social conditions causing much of minorities' distress. Actually, it does the opposite. By proffering causal rather than consequential explanations for racism, the medical model perpetuates the problem it seeks to overcome. When social reformers attack racism and other forms of oppression, they emphasize attitude change, often leaving insidious racist behaviors unchallenged.

Inaccessibility to minority clients. Because the goal of treatment in traditional psychotherapy is in-depth change, therapy tends to be a long-term undertaking. The expense and time involved in this type of treatment eliminates a large pool of potential patients, especially members of minority groups, who tend to be economically disadvantaged. And, as Kuriloff (1970) points out, such treatment is of limited value to those minority clients who do receive it because the public agencies serving these consumers "always employ it in a 'watered down' version. Professionals, unable to go either as 'deep' or as long as the treatment model prescribes, must compromise and seek shortcuts which are, by definition, inferior techniques" (p. 19).

Failure to teach coping skills. Psychoanalytic theory's preoccupation with synthetic ego functions over executive functions tends to ignore how members of minority groups manage and cope with reality. Even when minority clients successfully resolve intrapsychic conflicts, the model does not help them take the next step: learning to negotiate the stressful demands of reality. In many cases, the difficulties minorities experience stem from executive ego deficiencies rather than from intrapsychic conflict (Kuriloff, 1970). For example, a minority client may not have good job search or interviewing skills but still may be perfectly capable of maintaining gainful employment. The problem-analysis approach of the medical model is inadequate for meeting the problem-solving needs of many minorities.

Role confusion of therapeutic participants. The implicit expert role of the therapist and passive role of the client in the medical model create a paradox in multicultural counseling. In fact, this situation contradicts some of the real requirements for change. Many counselors do not understand the backgrounds or cultures of their minority clients, and they often use their counseling sessions with these clients to acquire cultural expertise. This means that minority clients are put in the position of educating "expert" counselors about their cultures, even though many counselors do not know what to do with the cultural information they gather.

The Conformity Model

The conformity (or sociocultural) model of mental health has evolved from the scientific tradition of the social sciences. It assumes a normal distribution of characteristics and behaviors throughout a population. Social scientists adhering to this model assert that many personality variables can be shown to be normally distributed once enough observations of those variables are made. The bell-shaped, symmetrical *normal curve* is a powerful statistical concept that is used to plot frequency distributions (see Figure 4.1).

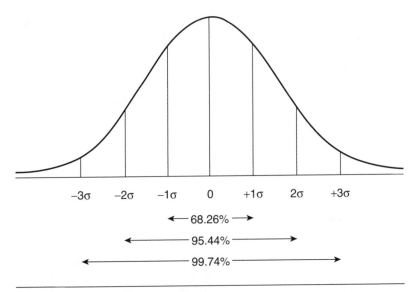

Figure 4.1   Bell-Shaped Curve

Under this model, interpretations of individual behaviors are referenced to the normative or standardization sample of a given population—that is, a group of representative members of the population. Theoretically, the sample provides a set of *norms* against which the behaviors of individuals are compared. Norms provide an external standard that permits observers to interpret behaviors as "good," "average," or "poor." Behaviors that occur in a population with high frequency are judged as healthy or normal, whereas behaviors that occur with low frequency are judged as deviant or abnormal. Wallace (1970) uses the concept of the *modal personality* to denote "any method that characterizes the personality typical of a culturally bounded population by the central tendency of a defined frequency distribution" (p. 152).

Two versions of the sociocultural model exist: the etic and the emic. The *etic* model is a culturally universal or generalized model of mental health. It defines behavior patterns on a fixed continuum from adjustment to maladjustment (Ridley, 1986a). This model promotes a standard of normalcy that spans cultural, ethnic, and racial lines. The criteria for interpreting behavior always remain constant, regardless of the cultural context or the persons being judged. That is, in the etic model persons are all judged against the same norms, whether they come from the South Bronx, Peking, Papua New Guinea, or Cairo, Egypt. Their respective backgrounds are not considered.

The *emic* model is a culturally sensitive or specific model of mental health. It assumes that, as Draguns (1989) and others have suggested, norms and expectations vary across cultures. This model construes mental health in terms of divergent attitudes, values, and behaviors that arise out of specific cultures. Similar overt behaviors may mean different things to people of different backgrounds. On the other hand, different behaviors may have similar meanings across various cultures. This model implies that the valid interpretation of behavior rests on individuals' indigenous cultural norms. As Chess, Clark, and Thomas (1953) note, behavior that is interpreted as pathological in one culture may be interpreted as healthy adaptation in another.

Implications of the Conformity Model
for Unintentional Racism

The major implication of the conformity model for unintentional racism lies in the model's imposition of majority group values on minority group members. Phares (1992) lists several problematic issues associated with the conformity model: (a) cutoff points (i.e., How deviant must a person be to acquire the magic designation of deviant?), (b) number of deviations (i.e., How often must a person not conform or show deviations from the norm to be considered deviant?), and (c) acute versus chronic behaviors (i.e., To what extent is maladjustment contingent on the acuteness or chronicity of behavior?). Counselors who take an etic stance, as opposed to an emic stance, are more likely to impose their own cultural values when interpreting the behaviors of minority clients.

Many counselors do not struggle with the questions Phares (1992) raises, let alone realize the implications of leaving them unanswered. In theory, they may acknowledge emic and etic distinctions, but in practice they often adopt a "pseudoetic approach" (Triandis, Malpass, & Davidson, 1973). That is, they generalize their own etic values and techniques across cultures as if this generalization is equally valid for all cultures. In so doing, they violate the principle of norm-referenced interpretation: An individual must be compared only with others who have characteristics that match those of the individual and who are randomly selected representatives of the target population. As Belkin (1984) observes, "Unintentionally and through ignorance counselors frequently impose their own cultural values upon minority clients" (p. 536).

The literature abounds with clinical case reports that illustrate the problems that occur when counselors overlook cultural influences on behavior (e.g., Lum, 2004; Martinez, 1988; Pinderhughes, 1989; Ramos-McKay, Comas-Díaz, & Rivera, 1988; Thompson, Blueye, Smith, & Walker, 1983). Thompson et al.'s (1983) discussion of a patient labeled a "crazy Indian" is one such case. The emergency room physician who made the initial diagnosis failed to account for the cultural and circumstantial dimensions of the patient's presenting problem. Likewise, the nurse saw the patient as impulsive and potentially violent. When a Native American psychiatric resident was summoned, the psychiatrist interviewed the patient and formed a different impression:

> In making my psychiatric assessment of this man's situation it was clear that I was not being asked to deal with "pure" psychopathology. . . . I knew that if this man had been seen by a doctor with no training in cultural psychiatry he might well have been diagnosed as psychotic and/or alcoholic, deemed dangerous to himself and others, and committed to a psychiatric ward. (quoted in Thompson et al., 1983, p. 271)

The Biopsychosocial Model

The biopsychosocial model of mental health is a relatively recent innovation, although its historical roots run deep. The early Greek philosophers, for example, first attended to the mind-body relationship. This model emphasizes the whole person. Unlike the almost exclusively intrapsychic focus of the medical model, the biopsychosocial model takes into account every major influence on human functioning, including physical health, interpersonal and social competence, and psychological and emotional well-being (Lewis, Sperry, & Carlson, 1993). Taylor (1990) describes the basis of the biopsychosocial model:

> Research in behavioral medicine and, correspondingly, in health psychology has taken the position that biological, psychological, and social factors are implicated in all stages of health and illness, ranging from those behaviors and states that keep people healthy to those that produce severe, long-term, and debilitating disease. (p. 40)

According to Engel (1977), the model is based on systems thinking. Sperry (1988) refers to the model's application to psychological intervention as *biopsychosocial therapy*. A major emphasis of treatment in such therapy is the changing of behavior to prevent or mitigate disease. Thus the biopsychosocial model is a health promotion model. Matarazzo (1980) argues that the field of psychology must play an increasing role in the promotion and maintenance of health, prevention and treatment of illness, and identification of factors involved in health and illness.

Krantz, Grunberg, and Baum (1985) describe three processes through which behavior influences health and disease:

- *Stress:* Chronic stress ultimately produces changes in body tissues, even when the individual does not engage in direct harmful behaviors.
- *Harmful behaviors and lifestyles:* Some behaviors cause illness. Among the more prominent of these are cigarette smoking, poor diet, insufficient

exercise, excessive alcohol consumption, drug abuse, and poor hygiene. Some harmful behaviors reflect cultural practices; others are idiosyncratic.

- *Reaction to illness:* Some people respond inappropriately to illness. They may deny the significance or severity of their symptoms, delay getting medical attention, or fail to comply with treatment or rehabilitation programs.

By understanding these processes, counselors can gain insight into their minority clients' behaviors and target problematic behaviors for intervention.

Implications of the Biopsychosocial Model for Unintentional Racism

The biopsychosocial model is not inherently racist. Because the model involves a comprehensive approach to understanding health and illness, it does not have a bias that could lead counselors to misinterpret the behaviors of minority clients. In that sense, it stands apart from the other models of mental health discussed above. When the biopsychosocial model is used appropriately, it is an effective tool for treating minority clients. Counselors using the model should be able to gather and integrate a broad range of information relevant to their clients' presenting problems.

Racism may occur when this model is misused or not used at all. Counselors' misuse or nonuse of the biopsychosocial model can lead to two important problems: the failure to treat clients holistically and the failure to promote client health.

Failure to treat clients holistically. One danger that counselors face in treating minority clients lies in disregarding all of the major influences on minority group members in U.S. society. A major criticism in the literature has been mental health professionals' tendency to overlook social factors such as racism, oppression, and other stressors. Psychology has been identified as the "handmaiden of the status quo" (Halleck, 1971, p. 30). Given poverty's negative influence on health, dietary deficiencies, poor access to medical treatment, low-quality education, and other social factors faced by many minorities, it is easy to see how counselors neglecting the biopsychosocial model unintentionally mistreat minority clients. Because they apply inappropriate models of mental health, they miss many opportunities to include such factors in their formulas for assessment and treatment planning. This problem is compounded by the fact that many practicing counselors were trained before the biopsychosocial model became a valued resource of the profession. In many training and practice contexts, the model remains an underutilized resource.

Failure to promote health. Most mental health services provided to minorities are rehabilitative; that is, they attempt to reduce the residual effects and adverse consequences of severe disturbance. Mental health professionals give limited attention to illness prevention and health promotion among minority populations, even though epidemiological studies report higher rates of major diseases in minority communities. For example, in the U.S. population, African Americans and Latinos are disproportionately represented among cases of HIV infection (Centers for Disease Control and Prevention, 1992). Counselors who do not emphasize illness prevention or teach minority clients positive health behaviors are perpetuating racism, regardless of their intentions. This problem is compounded by the general failure of the mental health profession to design outreach programs aimed at minimizing stress, harmful behaviors and lifestyles, and inappropriate reactions to illness in minority communities. Primary prevention of mental health problems is conspicuously unavailable to many minorities.

Chapter Summary

In this chapter, I have described four prominent models of mental health: the deficit, medical, conformity, and biopsychosocial models. As yardsticks for measuring normality and abnormality, these models are powerful tools for mental health professionals. I also have described in this chapter how the use, misuse, or lack of use of each of these models perpetuates unintentional racism. Counselors often do not adapt these models appropriately for use with minority clients. The most insidious problems probably occur when counselors use the medical model indiscriminately and when they neglect the use of the biopsychosocial model.

5

Judgmental and Inferential Errors

Clinical decision making is an integral part of counseling. In terms of serving clients' needs, counselors' judgment may be second in importance only to the counseling relationship. Dumont and Lecomte (1987) define psychotherapeutic counseling as an inferential process whereby counselors engage in clinical reasoning and make causal inferences based on information imparted by clients. Counselors are assumed to be skilled in logical reasoning and inference making, which suggests that their judgments are likely to be objective and impartial.

This chapter explores the complex and challenging process of clinical decision making, particularly the numerous judgmental and inferential errors counselors make regarding minority clients. Counselors' decision making is never simple, and it is further complicated by the nuances of meaning that arise from racial and cultural differences between themselves and their clients. As Westermeyer (1987) and other researchers have noted, misdiagnosis as well as overestimation, underestimation, and neglect of psychopathology are frequent problems when clinicians and their patients have different cultural backgrounds.

Why Is Clinical Decision Making Difficult?

Several factors combine to make clinical decision making difficult. First of all, people are complex. Each individual is a unique blend of many emotions, life experiences, values, attitudes, preferences, coping styles, and psychological issues. When clients show up for counseling, they exhibit their own complex features (Dumont & Lecomte, 1987). A counselor must sift through each client's many characteristics to figure that client out.

Aside from all individuals' complexity, many clients do not describe themselves or their experiences to counselors completely and coherently. Instead, their self-disclosures are often fragmented, incoherent, and emotionally charged. Because of their psychological pain and feelings of vulnerability, clients often omit or distort crucial information about themselves. When this happens, counselors often find it extremely difficult to sort out the pieces and separate those elements that are real from those that are clever distortions or distractions. Sue and Sue (1977, 2003) discuss at length the differences among verbal, nonverbal, paralinguistic, proxemic, kinesic, and contextual communication styles, all of which are operative in multicultural counseling. They also describe how generic characteristics of counseling are culture bound. Counselors who fail to attend to such cultural variables increase their chances of making judgmental errors.

Strohmer and Shivy (1992) describe the complexity of clinical decision making from the perspective of information processing:

> The counseling process is a massive information processing task in which the counselor is bombarded by a large volume of complex data. Cognitive psychology, as well as counseling experience, tells us that, as counselors, we are realistically unable to attend to all the information available in the counseling interaction. Counselors simply cannot process the variety of both verbal and nonverbal stimuli that make up a counseling session, and therefore must learn to attend selectively to the information presented. Perhaps what distinguishes talented and professional counselors from simple interviewers is the ability to identify, attend to, and adequately process the salient information a client provides. The complex nature of this information processing and decision making task must certainly test the counselor's skill, and make the counselor's ability to operate as a scientist/practitioner critically important. (p. 2)

In addition, counselors bring to their decision making their own biases and hidden agendas. Like all human beings, counselors are influenced by a host of factors that may impair their judgment. For example, the literature presents considerable evidence that, given ambiguous or complex material to judge, individuals' judgments are biased in the direction of preexisting stereotypes. Of course, counselors regularly encounter situations that are both ambiguous and complex. Therefore, they need to be alert not only to biases in judgment but also to their personal biases as judges. Counselors may be especially hindered in making appropriate judgments when they interact with clients of races and cultures other than their own, or when their clients hold worldviews that differ from theirs.

The Need for Judgmental Accuracy

Despite the difficulty inherent in clinical decision making, counselors are expected to have the skills necessary to form impressions and hypotheses about their clients from the information clients give them (Morrow & Deidan, 1992; Spengler, 1992). And these tasks are a mere sampling of the decisions counselors must make. Clinical decision making involves all of the activities requiring counselors to form impressions and hypotheses about clients. The following are just some of the many areas in which counselors must make decisions:

- Diagnosis
- Prognosis
- Referrals
- Treatment planning
- Selection of interventions
- Frequency of treatment
- Termination
- Medical therapy
- Reporting of abuse or neglect
- Duty to warn
- Involuntary commitment
- Importance placed on case history data
- Interpretation of test data

Clinical decision making is an inevitable part of a counselor's duties. It is not a matter of *whether* counselors will make clinical decisions; rather, it is a matter of what decisions counselors will make, how they will use client information in decision making, and how valid their decisions will be.

Obviously, counselors should strive to make valid clinical decisions. Their decisions should be impartial, each reflecting as accurate a picture of each client as possible (Dumont & Lecomte, 1987). If two skilled counselors were to treat the same client, they should formulate similar clinical judgments. Also, counselors' decisions should aim to serve the clients' best interests. Counselors should not allow their decisions to be biased by their own or their clients' backgrounds, or by the complexity or the nature of their clients' presenting problems (Ridley, 1986b).

Counselors must make accurate clinical decisions to ensure clients receive equitable and reliable service delivery. Inaccurate decision making results in poor service delivery. Gambrill (1990) points out some of the adverse consequences of poor clinical decisions:

> Errors in judgment may result in misattributing client problems to internal mental disorders; overlooking pathology; selecting weak or ineffective intervention methods; or predicting incorrectly suicidal potential, need for hospitalization, or future recurrence of violent acts. (p. 3)

Decision

		Unfavorable	Favorable
	Positive	False Negative (Incorrect Decision)	True Positive (Correct Decision)
Actual State of Affairs	Negative	True Negative (Correct Decision)	False Positive (Incorrect Decision)

Figure 5.1   Four Categories of Decisions

Four Types of Decisions

The many decisions that counselors make generally fall into four categories: true positives, false positives, false negatives, and true negatives (see Figure 5.1). The decisions classified into two of these categories are correct decisions; those classified into the other two categories are incorrect.

True positive. A decision that falls into the true positive category is a favorable decision or judgment that is correct. Smirnow and Bruhn (1984) provide an excellent example of such a decision in a case study involving sound diagnosis and treatment planning. Juan was a 7-year-old boy, the son of very poor, rural Hispanic immigrant parents. He was successfully treated at a community mental health center for encopresis (an eating disorder) and school phobia. The success of Juan's therapy, which lasted 21 sessions over an 8-month period, hinged on the therapist's ability to "distinguish pathology from subcultural beliefs and practices" (p. 24). This skill enabled the therapist to select appropriate interventions. It is important for mental health professionals to acknowledge that some clinicians do make good clinical decisions about minority clients.

False positive. A decision that falls into the false positive category is a favorable decision that is incorrect. Westermeyer (1987) describes the case of a 14-year-old Cambodian boy who was referred to his school counselor because of his disruptive classroom behavior. The boy had not undergone psychological assessment before being placed in the school, even though he had been withdrawn from school in Asia. There he had difficulty learning, and during his early childhood he had experienced a prolonged fever with a coma. When the boy underwent a physical examination after his referral to the school counselor, he showed "soft signs" of brain damage. Intellectual testing revealed mild mental retardation. The boy then was placed in a school program for children with mental retardation, and he did well. The original decision to place him in a regular classroom was a false positive. The decision maker had assumed the boy was functioning at a higher level than he was.

False negative. A decision that falls into the false negative category is an unfavorable decision that is incorrect. Westermeyer (1987) describes a 48-year-old Chinese woman who was placed on a regimen of antipsychotic and antidepressant medication. As a result of this treatment, she lost weight and hope and became increasingly immobilized. At the time of her original diagnosis, she had expressed a belief that her deceased mother, who appeared in her dreams, was attempting to induce the patient's own death and bring her to the next world. Clinicians later reinterpreted this symptom as a culturally consistent belief instead of a delusion, given that harbingers of death are common in the dreams of some Asian patients. The patient responded well to the discontinuation of antipsychotic medication, reduction in dosage of antidepressant medication, and reinstitution of weekly psychotherapy.

True negative. A decision that falls into the true negative category is a negative decision that is correct. For example, a clinical psychologist judged a Japanese American client to have suicidal potential and accordingly obtained involuntary commitment for the client. The client later somehow escaped from the psychiatric hospital and made an unsuccessful suicide attempt. In this case, the psychologist's judgment about the client was negative but accurate.

Prevalent Judgmental Errors

Counselors are constantly confronted with the need to make decisions in cases such as those described above. Competent counselors attempt to maximize their correct decision making and minimize incorrect decision making. That is, they attempt to make as many true positive and true negative decisions as possible while also making as few false positive and false negative decisions as possible. In this section, I discuss some of the most common decision errors that counselors make in regard to minority clients.

Fundamental Attribution Error

It is very common for counselors to overestimate the importance of personality or dispositional factors and to overlook situational variables in understanding the problems of minority clients (Batson, Jones, & Cochran,

1979; Dumont & Lecomte, 1987; Wills, 1978). Counselors readily attribute client problems to broad personal dispositions, expecting consistency of client behavior across dissimilar situations. They see client behaviors as freely selected, and they fail to consider situational factors that may lead to particular behaviors (Ross, 1977).

Goffman (1961) relates the following incident in discussing fundamental attribution bias in a clinical setting:

> I have seen a therapist deal with a Negro patient's complaints about race relations in a partially segregated hospital by telling the patient that he must ask himself why he, among all the other Negroes present, chose this particular moment to express this feeling, and what this expression could mean about him as a person, apart from the state of race relations in the hospital at the time. (pp. 376–377)

In this case, the therapist attributed the patient's problems to personal or dispositional traits. The therapist completely ignored the context in which the so-called problems occurred—a partially segregated hospital. More than likely, the therapist's blaming of the victim in this case resulted in unwarranted labeling of the patient.

Diagnostic Overshadowing

The term *diagnostic overshadowing* refers to many counselors' tendency to use one diagnosis to obscure or minimize the importance of another diagnosis. In such cases, counselors disregard certain types of assessment information in favor of others, with the result being underdiagnosis of psychopathology and minimization of clients' need for treatment. Counselors have been found to overshadow vocational problems with personal problems (Spengler, Blustein, & Strohmer, 1990) and psychopathology with intellectual functioning problems (Reiss & Szyszko, 1983).

Case Example

A Native American student went to the counseling center on her university campus. She was a sophomore and needed to select a major field of study. Although she had not completely adjusted to life off the reservation, she had made friends with a small group of other Native American students. Most of her friends were majoring in Native American studies, but she was interested in science. When the student met with a counselor, the counselor was intrigued by the young woman's Native culture and her struggle to adjust to life at a predominantly White university. The counselor preferred to work with the student on personal problems, and the counselor's interest in those problems overshadowed the student's pressing need to select a major. An unbiased counselor would have paid more attention to this student's quandary. Among the possible concerns such a client might have would be a feeling of guilt for not pursuing a major in Native American studies, uncertainty that she could be successful in a science field, and indecision about whether to major in chemistry or biology.

Confirmatory Bias

Confirmatory bias is the tendency to focus on information that confirms initial assumptions or hypotheses. Counselors who show confirmatory bias "find" evidence to support their suppositions even in the face of greater amounts of contrary evidence (Strohmer & Shivy, 1992). Meehl (1960) asserts that clinicians form "images" of their clients within the first 4 hours of treatment, after which they staunchly adhere to the beliefs, expectations, and hypotheses they have formed. According to Rosenhan (1973), clinicians usually expect to observe pathology, and most report it even when there is little evidence supporting their conclusions.

Case Example

David Lee, a Chinese American, was a successful architectural engineer. After experiencing intense headaches and lower back pain for 2 months, he went to his family physician, who gave him a thorough examination. The physician could not find any physical problems, so she referred David to a psychiatrist. The psychiatrist remembered reading that Asians do not like to discuss personal problems because this brings shame on their families, and the psychiatrist concluded that David was somaticizing and repressing his feelings. In the meantime, the psychiatrist dismissed the almost obvious likelihood that David's success as an entrepreneur was catching up with him. David had started a consulting business 7 months previously, and he was working 12 to 14 hours a day. Recently, he had won several impressive contracts. In addition, his wife had a busy career, and the couple was struggling to take care of their domestic responsibilities. David Lee was actually in a state of distress.

Judgmental Heuristics

Counselors often use quick decision rules known as judgmental heuristics. These rules serve as shortcuts through the decision-making process. Counselors use judgmental heuristics almost automatically, often without thinking through the nature of the resulting decisions. When counselors make snap decisions, they are not behaving as true scientist-practitioners, who, by definition, gather as much information as possible before formulating clinical hypotheses.

There are two kinds of judgmental heuristics: availability heuristics and anchoring heuristics. Judgments formed using availability heuristics are based on salient information. Counselors use relevant information that comes easily to memory. At the same time, they do not search for less salient, less consistent information. Judgments formed using anchoring heuristics are based on the chronology of information gathering. Counselors cling to initial information and downplay or ignore the importance of information acquired later. As Strohmer and Shivy (1992) explain, a counselor may anchor to salient client information early during an assessment and, as a result, disregard contradictory information that he or she might have found through skillful searching.

Case Example

Henry, a 35-year-old African American, was seen at the Outpatient Clinic of the Veterans Administration Hospital in Chicago. He had recently lost his job and appeared highly agitated. The clinical psychologist administered the Minnesota Multiphasic Personality Inventory, and the profile indicated an elevation on Scale 6, suggesting sensitivity, guardedness, and suspiciousness. The psychologist diagnosed Henry as paranoid. A more thorough investigation into Henry's life would have led to a judgment that contradicted the psychologist's, however. Elevated scores on Scale 6 of the MMPI are more common among African American males than among White males. Moreover, Henry worked in a factory where the employees' interpersonal relations were filled with subtle racial tension. When several White employees tried to set him up for a confrontation, he physically assaulted one of them. The factory manager fired Henry, asserting that he was "hostile and aggressive" and that there was no tangible proof anyone was bothering him. The diagnosis of paranoia ignored Henry's experience as an African American male who must deal with the reality of racism.

Reconstructive Memory

Sometimes people fill in gaps in their memories or alter their memories so they are consistent with their present experience (Loftus & Loftus, 1980; Snyder & Uranowitz, 1978; Wells, 1982). Bartlett (1932) first postulated the existence of this cognitive process more than 70 years ago. It is most likely to occur when an individual needs to create important categories, such as diagnoses. Wells (1982) suggests that people who reconstruct memories are less likely to remember specific information with accuracy. He also notes that people tend to be confident in their memories' accuracy even when they are actually recalling reconstructions rather than factual information.

Morrow and Deidan (1992) observe that documentation helps counselors avoid reconstructive memory errors:

> Case notes are vital because they are "the only record or documentation of what transpires between a counselor and a client." . . . Despite the significance of accurate records, we were unable to find any investigations of reconstructive memory in counseling. (p. 575)

Aside from the clinical value of accurate record keeping, Keith-Spiegel and Koocher (1985) note that counselors need to be aware of its ethical importance. Counselors' reconstructive memory can jeopardize the welfare of minority consumers.

Case Example

Phillip Greenwood is a psychology intern at a comprehensive community mental health center in Houston. The center serves a large Hispanic and African American clientele, and because of a severe economic recession and job layoffs at many local firms, the census at the center is high. During the past couple of weeks, Phillip has put off writing his case notes until the end of each week. Although Phillip is extremely bright and has a good memory, he has inadvertently included incorrect information in several case summaries. In one case, he wrote that a Hispanic female was a victim of assault. In actuality, the woman told him that she feared being assaulted because of the recent wave of crime and violence in her community. Philip also wrote that this client should consider joining a victims' support group.

Overconfidence

Some clinicians are overconfident about the accuracy of their clinical judgments (Arkes, 1981; Lichtenstein, Fischhoff, & Phillips, 1982). According to Holsopple and Phelan (1954), there is a negative relationship between clinicians' confidence in their judgments and their diagnostic accuracy. That is, the most confident clinicians tend to be the least accurate.

Numerous factors undoubtedly contribute to counselor overconfidence. Einhorn and Hogarth (1978) note that treatment effects constitute one factor. If a client improves for any reason, the therapist may attribute the improvement to the treatment. In certain situations, improvement results from placebo effects rather than the efficacy of interventions. Koriat, Lichtenstein, and Fischhoff (1980) suggest another reason for unwarranted confidence in general: People find it easier to generate support for their decisions than to generate evidence that contradicts those decisions.

Case Example

Rafic Ali is a 29-year-old Arab from Iraq. He has gotten into several heated conflicts with a neighbor. Both parties have legitimate gripes, but most of the problems between them have arisen from culture-related misunderstandings. Rafic became so upset by these conflicts that he went to see a therapist in private practice. Although Rafic is sympathetic to Arab causes, he is basically a peace-loving person. In fact, he has hesitated to return home since completing his MBA at an American university because he is not sure if he wants to live with unrest and Arab militancy. Unfortunately, the therapist Rafic consulted perceived him as a radical Arab and interpreted Rafic's conflicts with his neighbor as stemming from animosity toward Americans. For the therapist, the 2001 terrorist attacks in New York City and Washington, D.C., added weight to his confidence in his opinion of Rafic.

Attribution of Paranoia

Most forms of counseling encourage client growth through self-disclosure. This emphasis has its roots in the Freudian notion of free association and catharsis. One of the roles of counselors is to help clients explore and understand their feelings and behaviors. The assumption is that clients gain insight into themselves as they self-disclose and get feedback from their counselors.

Several scholars have described the reluctance of minority clients to self-disclose in therapy, especially when their counselors are White (e.g., Ridley, 1984, 1986c; Sue & Sue, 2003; Thompson, Worthington, & Atkinson, 1994; Whaley, 2001). Many members of minority groups in the United States have been conditioned to be cautious around Whites in general and mistrusting of White counselors. Harrison (1975) pinpoints this problem in his comments on African American clients:

> White society's traditional expectations of blacks have generated role behaviors that often contribute to a certain lack of openness, "gaming," and "telling the man what he would like to hear." Previous negative experiences with whites may cause blacks to develop both sensitivity and concealment of true feeling. Self-disclosure, which is basic to the counseling process, has been found to be greater among whites than blacks. . . . The hesitance of blacks to fully disclose themselves, often viewed as "playing it cool," suggests a cautiousness and initial lack of trust in the person to whom one is to disclose. Under such circumstances, establishing rapport with the counselee is more difficult, requiring sensitive and skillful counselor intervention in order to facilitate authentic communication. (p. 132)

By expecting minority clients to self-disclose, White counselors inadvertently create a paradoxical situation. One the one hand, minority clients may protect themselves by remaining tight-lipped about their problems. In so doing, they forfeit the potential benefits of counseling. On the other hand, when minority clients do choose to be open about themselves, they risk being

Functional Paranoia

		Low	High
		MODE 1 **Intercultural Nonparanoiac Disclosurer** • Disclosive to either ethnic minority or White therapist	**MODE 2** **Functional Paranoiac** • Nondisclosive to both ethnic minority and White therapist
	Low		
Cultural Paranoia		**MODE 3** **Healthy Cultural Paranoiac** • Disclosive to ethnic minority therapist • Nondisclosive to White therapist	**MODE 4** **Confluent Paranoiac** • Nondisclosive to both ethnic minority and White therapist
	High		

Figure 5.2   Typology of Ethnic Minority Client Self-Disclosure

SOURCE: Ridley, C. R. (1989). Racism in counseling as an aversive behavioral process.
In P. B. Pederson, J. G. Draguns, W. J. Lonner, & J. E. Trimble (Eds.), *Counseling across
cultures* (3rd ed., pp. 55-77). Honolulu: University of Hawaii Press. Reprinted by permission.

misunderstood by their counselors. Thus minority clients sometimes find
themselves in a no-win situation (Ridley & Tan, 1986).

In my previous work, I have described two dimensions of interpersonal
functioning related to self-disclosure: cultural paranoia and functional paranoia (Ridley, 1984). Although my focus was on African American clients in
that discussion, the dynamics apply to clients of other minority groups as
well. *Cultural paranoia* is a minority group member's healthy reaction to
racism. The minority client who fears the White counselor and avoids self-
disclosure fits this category. *Functional paranoia,* in contrast, is an unhealthy
psychological condition. The minority client with a pervasive suspicion of
others fits this category. Such a client will not disclose to any counselor,
regardless of the counselor's race.

Figure 5.2 presents a four-mode typology that categorizes minority
clients according to these two dimensions. In Mode 1, the intercultural non-
paranoiac discloser is a client who is low on both functional and cultural

paranoia. This client typically will self-disclose to a counselor of any race. The inclusion of this mode acknowledges that some multicultural relationships are effective; however, counselors should be aware that this type of minority client is a rarity. In Mode 2, the functional paranoiac is a client who has a true clinical paranoid disorder. This client does not disclose to any counselors, including members of the client's own race. This client has unusual fears that he or she is being persecuted, spied upon, or followed. In Mode 3, the healthy cultural paranoiac is a client who attempts to protect him- or herself from racism and discrimination. Grier and Cobbs (1968, 1992), two African American psychiatrists, first described the phenomenon of healthy cultural paranoia. This client typically is nondisclosing to White counselors but open with minority counselors. Many minority clients seem to fall into this category. In Mode 4, the confluent paranoiac is a client who has both a strong reaction to racism and a traditional paranoid condition. This is the most difficult minority client to treat because of the complex interaction between cultural paranoia and functional paranoia. Like the functional paranoiac, this client does not disclose to counselors of any race.

Most minority clients exhibit appropriate reactions to racism. Ironically, many White counselors classify Mode 3 clients as functional paranoiacs (Mode 2). In such cases, the counselors arrive at their diagnoses independent of these clients' actual mental health status. Counselors' misunderstanding of minority clients' reluctance to self-disclose contributes significantly to the overrepresentation of minorities in pathological categories. Research evidence indicates, for example, that the diagnosis of schizophrenia, especially of the paranoid type, is often misapplied to minorities (Kleiner, Tuckman, & Lavell, 1960; Pavkov, Lewis, & Lyons, 1989; Steinberg, Pardes, Bjork, & Sporty, 1977).

Chapter Summary

Clinical decision making is an integral part of counseling. Counselors must make many different types of decisions during all phases of the counseling process. Despite the importance of objectivity and impartiality in such decision making, counselors make numerous judgmental and inferential errors. Racial and cultural factors further complicate the clinical decision-making process, causing multiculturally incompetent counselors to be particularly ineffective as decision makers. This chapter has highlighted some of the specific kinds of errors that counselors make, with particular emphasis on their misjudgments about minority clients.

6

Defensive Racial Dynamics

The counselor-client relationship is often regarded as the most important aspect of counseling. As the context of change, a good counseling relationship enables a client to self-disclose, explore intrapsychic conflicts, take risks, and work through personal problems. Gelso and Fretz (2001) suggest that an expert's application of techniques is less important than the relationship between the client and counselor. Highlen and Hill (1984) go even farther, calling this relationship the sine qua non of counseling.

A major obstacle to the development of a good counseling relationship is defensiveness, whether on the part of the client or the counselor. Sometimes both participants are defensive, creating a sort of therapeutic gridlock. Sigmund Freud (1926/1989), who originated the concept of defense mechanisms, asserted that people use such mechanisms to protect themselves when they feel threatened. Clark (1991) defines a defense mechanism as an "unconscious distortion of reality that reduces painful affect and conflict through automatic and habitual responses" (p. 236). This definition includes four important characteristics common to all defense mechanisms:

- *Unconscious motivation:* People are unaware of their own defensiveness and the motives that underlie their defensive behavior. They hide parts of who they are from themselves. The hidden sources of motivation usually reside in the region of the unconscious.
- *Distortion or denial of reality:* When people are defensive, they do not see reality objectively—the way it really is. Typically, they create an idealized picture of reality for themselves—the way they would like it to be. Then they relate to the world on the basis of their distortion or denial.
- *Reduction of emotional pain:* Defense mechanisms serve the important purpose of blunting emotional pain and intrapsychic conflict. In a sense, they are bandage solutions to emotional pain.

- *Automatic and habitual responsiveness:* Defensiveness quickly triggers behavior that expresses intrapsychic conflict. The behavior occurs automatically and in reaction to emotional pain.

Descriptions of the major defense mechanisms are available in many basic counseling textbooks (e.g., Corey, 2005; Gladding, 2004). A random survey of the literature reveals research reports and discussions about many different defense mechanisms. In this chapter, I focus on 10 race-related defenses. Although these defense mechanisms introduce important dynamics into the relationships between minority clients and their counselors, they often remain unacknowledged. Some of these defenses are employed by counselors and others by clients. When counselors exhibit such defenses or mishandle the defensiveness of their minority clients, they undermine the counseling relationship (Sandler & Freud, 1985) and perpetuate racism (Ridley, 1989). Counselors who recognize these defense mechanisms can take a better look at themselves and determine whether they are unintentional racists.

Ten Race-Related Defense Mechanisms

Color Blindness

Color blindness in this context is the counselor's illusion that minority clients are no different from nonminority clients. Several scholars have called attention to the erroneous assumption that the minority client is simply another client (e.g., Bernard, 1953; Block, 1981; Griffith, 1977; Thomas & Sillen, 1972). Color-blind counselors reveal themselves by using phrases such as "We're all the same"; "I don't see you as being a minority, just another human"; and "It is as though you are White."

Several factors can cause color blindness. It may result from counselors' strong need to appear impartial because they fear that deep down inside they are unconscious bigots. Counselors may feel uncomfortable discussing race because it is a sensitive topic, or they may have insecurities or unresolved personal issues about race. Some counselors may be overly protective of their minority clients; they choose to avoid hurting the clients' feelings. Other counselors may simply misunderstand minority clients; they avoid the subject of race because they fear appearing incompetent and exposing their ignorance.

Color-blind counselors attempt to relate to minority clients as though race is unimportant. In so doing, they disregard the central importance of race to these clients' psychological experience. These counselors tend to overlook the influence of racism and discrimination on the attitudes, feelings, behaviors, and personality development of minority clients. Color-blind White counselors also disregard the undeniable influence of their Whiteness on minority clients (Sager, Brayboy, & Waxenberg, 1972).

The most common adverse consequence of color blindness is misdiagnosis. Color-blind counselors automatically label deviations from White middle-class cultural values as psychopathology. White counselors who do not understand the cultures of their minority clients tend to view these clients' cultural values and idioms as inherently inferior to their own. For example, some minority clients come from cultures that place high value on group affiliation and collectivism. Counselors who understand only the mainstream American ideal of rugged individualism may misinterpret the behavior of such clients as codependency. Color blindness is a major reason behind the excessive pathological diagnoses assigned to minority clients.

Over the years, many mental health care professionals have consulted me about their work with minority clients, and I have found the defense mechanism of color blindness to be pervasive. Usually, I try to encourage professionals exhibiting color blindness to consider the implications of their so-called impartiality. I often use word pictures or analogies to illustrate the consequences of looking at an individual apart from that person's social reality. I might ask, "Would your interpretation of an acting-out client change if you knew she was a victim of brutal sexual assault?" As I provide examples concerning minority clients, most professionals are startled to realize that their color blindness leads to unintentional racism.

Color Consciousness

Color consciousness, the opposite of color blindness, is another illusion of many counselors. From the color-conscious viewpoint, all of minority clients' problems stem essentially from their minority status (Adams, 1950; Bernard, 1953; Block, 1981; Griffith, 1977; Thomas & Sillen, 1972). The color-conscious counselor places too much weight on the client's race while overlooking the client's contribution to the presenting problem. A counselor who concludes, "The reason you have an alcohol addiction is because you are Native American" may be color conscious.

This defense mechanism rests on a kernel of truth, but it is still a distortion of reality. Many members of minority groups have been subjected to oppression and discrimination; however, it clearly is erroneous to conclude that they all have developed an "irreversible mark of oppression" or have permanently crippled personalities (Kardiner & Ovesey, 1951). Most minorities successfully resolve their experiences with racism.

A major cause of color consciousness is White guilt. White counselors often harbor strong and painful feelings about the mistreatment of minorities in U.S. society. In some respects, they feel that they bear the burden of guilt for all White people, whether or not they are overtly racist themselves. They try to atone for their feelings of guilt about racism through the defense mechanism of color consciousness, even though they themselves may never have been directly responsible for any injustice.

The primary adverse consequence of color consciousness is misdiagnosis, but the misdiagnosis in this case is opposite to that found with color blindness. That is, color-conscious counselors often fail to identify the severity of psychopathology in minority clients because they place too much emphasis on the effects of racism. For example, my local Department of Children's Protective Services referred a 13-year-old African American boy to me for treatment. The boy, who came from a low-income family, had been in the CPS system for a long time. It is likely that before I saw him, color-conscious therapists had minimized the boy's condition and failed to provide him with the appropriate treatment. He was rebellious, antisocial, and unresponsive to adult authority, and I diagnosed him as a conduct disorder adolescent. After meeting with him for several sessions, I recommended that he be placed in a residential treatment facility.

As this case illustrates, counselors' color consciousness leads to the underestimation of psychopathology. Other professionals had overlooked this client's conduct disorder, and their misdiagnosis led to a second adverse consequence: inappropriate intervention. The first professionals who treated the boy should have placed him in a highly controlled therapeutic environment that consistently reinforced any prosocial behaviors he exhibited. This protocol is the recommended treatment for conduct disorder adolescents.

Cultural Transference

The work of Freud (1940/1949) provides some original insights into the nature of the counselor-client relationship. In speculating about how the dynamics of the relationship affect treatment, Freud developed the concept of transference. That is, clients tend to transfer to their therapists both positive and negative feelings and attitudes they hold about their parents or other significant people in their lives. According to Freud, clients' reactions to their therapists are reminiscent of the clients' earlier reactions to these important people.

As a psychology intern at a Veterans Administration hospital, I had the opportunity to observe the effects of transference firsthand. One afternoon, a fellow intern was conducting therapy with a young woman in an office across the hall from where I was working. Suddenly, I heard a loud commotion coming from that direction. The patient yelled, "You remind me of my father!" and then jumped out of her chair and physically assaulted my colleague. The psychoanalytic perspective would explain this incident in terms of the patient's transference to the therapist of her anger and hostility toward her father. Obviously, this is a particularly dramatic illustration; transference usually appears in more subtle forms. Every counselor should anticipate transference of some kind, however.

According to Freud, despite the distortions inherent in transference, the dynamic itself can benefit the therapeutic relationship. As clients reenact their emotions and experiences, counselors have a unique chance to facilitate therapy. They can clarify and interpret psychological material that otherwise would be inaccessible. Clients can benefit by gaining new insight into their unconscious conflicts and by understanding the effects of these conflicts on their behavior and attitudes.

Cultural transference is a special category of transference that occurs when a minority client transfers emotional reactions to a therapist of another race. Before entering therapy, the minority client may have had significant interactions with other members of the therapist's race, and some of these experiences may have left the client with deep feelings of resentment and hostility. At times, client reactions in counseling have nothing to do with the therapist's disposition. A minority client's negative feelings toward Whites may surface during counseling, for example, and the client may direct anger toward his or her White therapist. Ironically, the therapist may not be a bigot and may not have behaved in a racist way toward the client. The therapist in such a case should not take the client's anger personally; rather, he or she should understand its source and use it as a therapeutic opportunity.

Unintentional racism may arise from counselors' incompetence in dealing with cultural transference. Unskilled or uninsightful counselors may fail to recognize such transference for what it is, or, if they do recognize it, they may minimize its psychological significance. Sometimes counselors are intimidated when minority clients direct race-related hostility toward them, so they attempt to avoid dealing with it altogether. A counselor's failure to employ constructive interventions aimed at resolving the conflicts that underlie cultural transference compounds the client's problems and difficulties in the therapeutic relationship, regardless of the reasons behind that failure. An incident from my work in training counselors illustrates the concept: When a White female doctoral student in counseling psychology became overly nondirective with an African American male client who had erupted in anger toward her, I encouraged her to take advantage of the cultural transference instead of letting the client scare her.

Cultural Countertransference

Freud (1940/1949) also addresses countertransference, another dynamic that can have tremendous impact on the quality of therapy and its outcomes. In countertransference, the therapist projects his or her emotional reactions onto the client. These reactions are based on similar feelings the therapist previously has felt toward someone other than the client—a person outside of therapy with whom the counselor has had an intense emotional experience. According to Freud, the therapist's anxiety causes countertransference. When counselors fail to resolve their feelings, countertransference results in the therapist's misperception of the client.

Cultural countertransference involves the therapist's projecting race-related emotional reactions onto a client of another race. The client's mere presence may spark intense emotions in the therapist that are reminiscent of feelings the therapist has experienced in past interactions with members of the client's race. The client's mannerisms, idioms, expressions, and values also may provoke cultural countertransference, especially if the therapist considers these characteristics peculiar. Jones (1985) comments on cultural countertransference, specifically regarding White therapists and African American clients:

> Any client can invoke in a therapist an unhelpful emotional response; what is noteworthy for this discussion is that it appears that black patients may evoke more complicated countertransference reactions and more frequently. The reason for this seems to be that social images of blacks still make them easier targets for therapists' projections and that the culturally different client provides more opportunities for empathic failures. (p. 178)

Like others who are defensive, therapists are not conscious of these feelings. Although their projections are irrational, they are reinforced by members of the therapist's race who share similar feelings and attitudes. In this state of collusion, therapists ineffectively test reality. They believe their responses are rational rather than what they really are—distortions of reality.

Cultural countertransference causes counselors to inappropriately attribute psychological deficiency to minority clients. Distrust, sexual promiscuity, hostility, and Machiavellianism are prominent examples of culturally countertransferred characteristics. As Sabshin, Diesenhaus, and Wilkerson (1970) observe, many counselors tend to regard African American clients as "hostile and not motivated for treatment, having primitive character structure, not psychologically minded and impulse-ridden" (p. 788). Once a clinician develops such false perceptions, therapy begins to lose its appropriate focus. The emphasis switches to treating an unreal person.

Some minority clients accept their therapists' invalid assessments without question. Others do so reluctantly because the power differential in the client-counselor relationship makes them feel vulnerable and reluctant to challenge their counselors. Some minority clients, however, are both insightful and courageous enough to protest invalid assessments. Unfortunately, when they protest they often are further labeled as uncooperative or resistant.

Cultural countertransference places the minority client in a double bind. If the client accepts the counselor's projections, the client is stuck with an inaccurate assessment. If the client rejects the counselor's projections, he or she risks further negative labeling. Either way, the net effect is that the client's real presenting problems remain untreated.

Cultural Ambivalence

White counselors often have ambivalent motives in treating minority clients. On the one hand, they may have high power and dominance needs

(Jones & Seagull, 1977). These counselors attempt to keep a tight rein on the course and direction of therapy. These counselors' need for power in their relationships with minority clients is motivated by insecurity, intimidation, and perhaps the perception that such clients may seek reprisal for injustice. On this topic, Pinderhughes (1973) states:

> One problem area for many patients lies in the unconscious needs of many psychotherapists to be in helping, knowledgeable, or controlling roles. Unwittingly they wish to be initiators and have patients accommodate to them or to their style or approach. More Black patients than White perceive in this kind of relationship the basic ingredients of a master-slave pattern. (p. 104)

Vontress (1981) fittingly describes the power needs of some White counselors who work with minority clients as the "Great White Father syndrome." Power-oriented counselors are condescending, paternalistic, and enraging. They tend to reinforce learned helplessness and passivity in clients. Paradoxically, this outcome contradicts one of the primary goals of therapy: to help clients become more responsible and assertive. The real danger is that clients will leave therapy as inept in problem solving as when they began.

In addition, these same White counselors who work with minority clients may be motivated by high dependency needs. These counselors expend considerable effort in trying to gain their clients' acceptance or approval. Beneath this approval seeking lies these counselors' desire to be absolved of guilt, whether real or imagined, for being racist. Here again, the counselors are working on their own issues, not those of their minority clients. Jones and Seagull (1977) argue that some White professionals are motivated to counsel minorities almost completely out of their guilt about racism, a motivation that probably is of little help to their clients. In an earlier work, I placed counselor cultural ambivalence within the historical context of racism in the United States:

> This dynamic is traceable to the plantation during the antebellum period. The white master, otherwise addressed as "massa" or "massr," had a peculiar type of psychological involvement with the slave community. This involvement was characterized by both high power and dependency needs. The massa sought emotional comfort from the blacks, though relegating them to the lowest form of involuntary servitude. The blacks, in turn, catered to the massa, though bemoaning their depravity and despair in their private thoughts and gatherings. Alex Haley (1976) makes the point in *Roots* that white masters were happiest when they were around their slaves, even when they were beating them. (Ridley, 1984, p. 1239)

Counselor cultural ambivalence has profound implications for therapy. In attempting to gain their clients' approval, culturally ambivalent counselors resort to subtle manipulation. Their goal is to appear nonracist, so they attempt—often in subtle ways—to prove they are different from White bigots. Without knowing it, these counselors set themselves up for countermanipulation by their minority clients, who may be keenly aware of the counselors' emotional dependency (Ridley, 1984).

The consequences of counselors' cultural ambivalence harm clients. Because culturally ambivalent counselors are preoccupied with their own issues about race, they are not as attuned to their clients' psychological conflicts and unresolved issues as they should be. Although their clients may remain in counseling, much of the time in counseling sessions is wasted on nontherapeutic conversation designed to alleviate the counselors' anxiety. In that sense, therapy with a culturally ambivalent counselor is actually counselor centered rather than client centered.

Pseudotransference

Sometimes a minority client will respond to a therapist in a manner that appears to be defensiveness but actually is not. Such pseudotransference reactions are based in reality. The client reacts strongly to the counselor's racist attitudes and behavior, and the counselor misinterprets the client's behavior and subsequently labels the client as pathological (Thomas, 1962; Thomas & Sillen, 1972). It is not unusual for White therapists to ignore the possibility that minority clients' critical reactions to them are grounded in reality. As Thomas (1962) explains:

> Disturbed, unhealthy responses of the patient in the therapeutic situation cannot, however, be assumed to be necessarily transference phenomena. They may be "pseudo-transference" responses to unhealthy attitudes or behavior of the therapist, and therefore not an accurate reflection of the patient's neurosis. The well-known counter-transference phenomena caused by an unhealthy pattern of individual origin in the therapist can produce such pseudo-transference reactions. (p. 899)

Thomas also suggests that minority clients may be especially sensitive to stereotyping, as they often encounter such behavior in their everyday lives. Further, minority clients may react strongly because they feel vulnerable, given that therapists are in a powerful one-up position (Ridley, 1985b).

Behaviorally, pseudotransference may be depicted by a simple operant paradigm. Here antecedent (controlling) events act as discriminative stimuli (S^D) for consequent events (R), and reinforcing stimuli (S^R) increase the probability of R when they are present. In the following interchange sequence, S^D represents the counselor's racist behaviors, R represents the reaction of the client, and S^R represents the counselor's negative evaluation of the client's behavior:

White Counselor:

Minority Client:

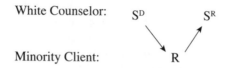

A hypothetical example illustrates the paradigm. During therapy, a White counselor remarks to his client, a young African American woman, "Why, we have a very fine African American psychologist from Harvard on our staff." This behavior is the S^D. Even though the counselor has "good" intentions, the remark is racist because it implies White superiority. The client has another interpretation of the remark: Minorities have to be super-human to achieve parity in the White world. In reaction to the counselor's comment, the client becomes visibly annoyed but does not disclose her intimate thoughts and feelings. This behavior is the R. The client probably perceives the counselor as patronizing. Stimulus generalization also may occur, because the client has heard similar comments from Whites outside of therapy. The counselor takes careful note of the client's behavior and erroneously concludes that the client has a psychological disorder. The labeling of the client's behavior is the S^R.

The interaction between the counselor and the client in such a case is actually much more complex than the above sequence indicates. The S^R also can acquire the S^D function, resulting in an ongoing interaction in which the behavior of each participant is both a stimulus and a response:

White Counselor:

Minority Client:

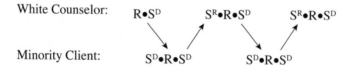

Within this "interlocking paradigm" (Skinner, 1957; Strong, 1964), each response of the counselor and client is both a reinforcing (or punish-ing) stimulus for the immediately preceding response and a discrimina-tive stimulus prompting the next response. The interchange sequence is a "chain" in terms of both its sequential properties and its stimulus properties (Reynolds, 1968). The response of either participant increases or decreases the frequency or probability of certain responses by the other participant, depending on whether the response serves as a reinforcing or discrimina-tive stimulus or as a punishment. Of equal importance is the fact that both participants may have no conscious awareness of their responses. The out-come of this interaction is that the counselor mistakenly assigns a patho-logical diagnosis (e.g., anxiety disorder, adjustment disorder, schizoid disorder) to the client even though the client's responses are justified in a scientific, "behavioral" sense.

The literature contains many reports of White counselors' cultural stereotyping of minority clients. In a study published in 1968, Bloombaum, Yamamoto, and James found that Mexican Americans were the most frequent targets of stereotyping by practicing psychotherapists in the United States, followed by African Americans, Jews, Chinese Americans, and Japanese Americans, in that order. Of the therapist responses examined in the study, 79.2% indicated subtle stereotypical attitudes. Bloombaum et al. concluded that the attitudes they found among therapists reflected American culture in general. Therefore, psychotherapists should not deem themselves immune to cultural stereotyping just because they are trained as helping professionals.

Word, Zanna, and Cooper (1974) have demonstrated the power of self-fulfilling stereotypes in interracial interviews. In one study, they found that White interviewers displayed more grammatical and pronunciation errors with African American respondents than with White respondents. The interviewers also spent less time and showed less immediacy with African American respondents than with White respondents. Essentially, they were less friendly, less outgoing, and more reserved with African Americans. In another study, the researchers had White confederates conduct interviews while behaving in either the immediate or the nonimmediate style observed in the first study. They found that White interviewees who were subjected to the nonimmediate style were more nervous and performed less adequately than did those exposed to the immediate style. Snyder (1982) interprets these findings:

> Apparently, then, the blacks in the first study did not have a chance to display their qualifications to the best advantage. Considered together, the two investigations suggest that in interracial encounters, racial stereotypes may constrain behavior in ways that cause both blacks and whites to behave in accordance with those stereotypes. (p. 67)

Race-Based Misdiagnosis

A number of researchers have observed an enduring and disturbing pattern of misdiagnosis of minority clients, particularly African Americans (Bell & Mehta, 1980; Faris & Dunham, 1939/1967; Frumkin, 1954; Helzer, 1975; Jones & Gray, 1986; Malzberg, 1963; Mukherjee, Shukla, Woodle, Rosen, & Olarte, 1983; Prange & Vitols, 1962; Rosenstein, Milazzo-Sayre, MacAskill, & Manderscheid, 1987; Simon, Fleiss, Gurland, Stiller, & Sharpe, 1973; Snowden & Cheung, 1990; Strakowski et al., 1995; Taube, 1971). On the one hand, there is substantial evidence that African Americans are underrepresented among mental health clients diagnosed with affective disorders. Several epidemiological studies have revealed significant differences between African Americans and Whites in the rates of diagnosis of affective disorders. For example, when Johnson, Gershon, and Hekimian (1968) studied 3 years of admissions at Bellevue Psychiatric Hospital, they did not find a single case of an African American patient diagnosed with a manic depressive disorder.

On the other hand, research indicates that African Americans are overrepresented among mental health clients diagnosed with schizophrenic disorders. African Americans are diagnosed as schizophrenic on initial admission more than twice as often as White clients. A National Institute of Mental Health study conducted in the early 1970s found that African Americans were diagnosed with schizophrenia at a rate more than 65% higher than that for Whites. More recently, Snowden and Cheung (1990) analyzed a national data set on psychiatric hospitalizations and found that the diagnostic bias extends to Hispanics as well as to African Americans:

> For all types of inpatient organizations, schizophrenia was diagnosed more frequently among Blacks than among Whites. The rate of diagnosis of schizophrenia was sometimes almost twice as great among Blacks as among Whites. However, this pattern was almost exactly reversed in regard to affective disorders. Hispanics also were diagnosed more frequently than Whites as schizophrenic at all types of organizations except VA Medical Centers. Similarly, affective disorders were diagnosed at a lower rate among Hispanics, but with less of a discrepancy among Whites than was true for Blacks. (p. 349)

This pattern may well be the result of the substitution of one diagnosis for another. As Simon et al. (1973) put it, "This hesitancy to diagnose blacks as affectively ill is more than compensated for by a strong tendency to diagnose blacks as schizophrenic more frequently than whites" (p. 511). These researchers challenge the validity of this pattern of diagnosis. After finding the same pattern in hospital diagnoses, they conducted an investigation using independent project personnel and found no race-based pattern of illness. In other words, in reality, Whites do not have more affective disorders than do African Americans, and African Americans do not have more schizophrenic disorders than do Whites. Helzer's (1975) research corroborates Simon et al.'s findings, with the exception of illness related to alcoholism in paternal relatives of African American men.

Overwhelmingly, research findings suggest that racial bias in diagnosis is pervasive in the U.S. mental health system. As Garb (1997) points out, race bias exists "when the *accuracy of judgments* varies as a function of client race, . . . not when *judgments* vary as a function of race" (p. 99). The consequences of this pattern of misdiagnosis are serious (Bell & Mehta, 1980). Clients who are misdiagnosed receive inappropriate psychotherapy and medication, which means they not only fail to receive the benefits they would have gained from appropriate treatment but also suffer the adverse effects of inappropriate psychopharmacological therapy. Furthermore, when hospitalized patients are misdiagnosed, they are more likely to return to the hospital later as they become victims of a vicious cycle of misdiagnosis.

Bell and Mehta (1980) note that there are several reasons for race-based errors in diagnoses, including the complexity of clients' problems and the dynamics of patient care. However, they place the greatest blame on covert racism in psychiatry:

> There are obviously other factors leading to the misdiagnosis of black manic depressive patients. It is a common belief that manic depressive illness is clustered in higher socioeconomic patients. This belief tends to support the notion that black patients (frequently at the bottom of the socioeconomic totem pole) do not get affective illnesses. The authors believe that these myths significantly contribute to the misdiagnosis of a patient exhibiting euphoria, pressured speech, poor interpersonal relatedness, hyperactivity, and a lack of personality deterioration as schizophrenic, chronic undifferentiated type. It is further felt that these myths are rooted in a pervasive, covert form of racism which has been institutionalized in psychiatry to the point that low prevalence and incidence of manic depressive illness in blacks is a given. (p. 145)

Keisling (1981) uses a real-life incident to illustrate the typical pattern of race-based misdiagnosis:

> Mr. B was a 53-year-old black man, who was a former construction worker and received a VA pension. He had a 20-year history of admissions to the hospital and experienced long hospital stays with each admission. Mr. B was always described on admission as "agitated, hostile, hyperactive, and hallucinating," and he frequently was secluded for many days—and sometimes weeks—before his behavior was under control. Mr. B was diagnosed as having chronic undifferentiated schizophrenia, and he was always treated with high doses of neuroleptics. Eventually he would become stable and could be placed in a boarding home, but his stay in these homes would usually be terminated due to agitated, hostile, and aggressive behavior. During the period of our study, Mr. B was admitted to the ward after becoming agitated and destructive at his boarding home. According to the landlady he was unable to sleep; he was aggressive and hyperactive and broke a window at the home. He was treated with 80 mg/day of fluphenazine hydrochloride, but he showed little response. He reported to the nursing station every few minutes with many demands, and he was unable to sleep. After Mr. B began taking 600 mg of lithium carbonate orally t.i.d., dramatic results occurred: he became calm, coherent, and rational and within a few days he was able to sleep. He was discharged on a maintenance dose of only lithium, and he has since found his own apartment. Mr. B has kept his outpatient appointments and has maintained a stable mental status. (p. 673)

Avoidance of Race

On the surface, avoiding discussions of race and culture may seem like a responsible way for counselors to keep from offending or arousing discomfort in minority clients. Behind such avoidance, however, other issues may be at work, and deleterious consequences for clients may ensue. Many theorists have argued that it is important for counselors to address culture in general and race in particular with minority clients (e.g., Atkinson & Lowe, 1995; Helms, 1994; Pinderhughes, 1989; Sue & Sue, 2003). According to Atkinson and Lowe (1995), the counselor should "acknowledge the existence of, show interest in, demonstrate knowledge of, and express appreciation for the client's ethnicity and culture" and "place the client's problem in a cultural context" (p. 402). Ultimately, such a culturally responsive counselor uses what he or she learns about the client's culture and race to understand the client's psychological presentation and facilitate the process of therapy.

A number of benefits derive from cultural responsiveness in counseling. Minority clients have been found to perceive culturally responsive counselors as more credible and competent than other counselors (Atkinson, Casas, & Abreu, 1992; Gim, Atkinson, & Kim, 1991; Pomales, Claiborn, & LaFromboise, 1986); they also achieve greater satisfaction from counseling and return for more sessions when counselors are culturally responsive (Wade & Bernstein, 1991). In one study, Thompson, Worthington, and Atkinson (1994) found that female African American pseudoclients made more intimate self-disclosures when counselors inquired directly about their experiences as African American women on a predominantly White campus. According to Fuertes, Mueller, Chauhan, Walker, and Ladany (2002), White counselors who directly address racial issues with minority clients early in counseling can establish strong therapeutic relationships with those clients.

Despite the evidence that counselor cultural responsiveness is beneficial, many counselors still avoid addressing race with their minority clients. This avoidance can lead to frustration and exasperation among these clients, especially when the clients raise racial issues in counseling and their counselors persist in avoiding discussion of those issues (Thompson & Jenal, 1994). In a study of African American and White psychologists, Knox, Burkard, Johnson, Suzuki, and Ponterotto (2003) found that the African American therapists in their sample routinely addressed race with clients of color and with clients whose race was part of their psychological presentation, but the White psychologists felt uncomfortable discussing race and normally avoided mentioning racial issues with their clients.

As Greene (1994a) notes, clients also may sometimes avoid discussing race in an effort to keep from offending or alienating their therapists, or from making the therapists anxious. Greene also suggests that therapists should take responsibility for introducing discussions of race with their minority clients if the clients do not bring the subject up themselves.

When a counselor avoids discussing racial issues with a minority client, the integrity of the therapeutic relationship is compromised. The avoidance of race can lead to misunderstandings that contribute to the minority client's dissatisfaction with the counseling process, eventually resulting in the client's decision to discontinue counseling. Most counselors who avoid the topic of race do not mean any harm to their minority clients. They simply are uncomfortable talking about race, and so they don't. However, in satisfying their need for comfort, they are contributing to their clients' discomfort and dissatisfaction.

The following example illustrates some of the negative consequences of counselors' avoidance of race-related issues in their work with minority clients. Imagine that you are a young African American woman who has left your family and friends in the African American community to attend a pre-dominantly White university (see Thompson & Jenal, 1994). You might be the only minority student in some of your classes, and you have few African American role models on campus. You have had experiences on campus with negative racial overtones, or you know other minority students who have had such experiences. At the same time, you have observed firsthand the taken-for-granted privilege of many White students. Then, when you meet with a counselor to talk about personal issues, the counselor avoids engaging in any discussion of race. How would you feel? Wouldn't you likely conclude that counseling will not be beneficial for you? Would it be any surprise that you develop mistrust in the counselor and the counseling process?

Overidentification

The problems of defensiveness about race and mishandling of minority clients are not limited to White counselors. Minority counselors also hurt minority clients by acting defensively. Overidentification is one of the key defense mechanisms that minority counselors employ.

To understand overidentification, one first must understand identification, a commonly used defense mechanism (Clark, 1991). Identification involves expressing admiration for and exhibiting some degree of behavioral similarity to idealized persons or groups (Bieri, Lobeck, & Galinsky, 1959; Lazowick, 1955). In identifying with others, an individual gains a sense of prestige, recognition, and acceptance based on his or her perceived association with the idealized others.

Minority counselors often have much in common with minority clients. They may come from similar backgrounds and may share similar interests and cultural values. They likely face some of the same challenges, such as those associated with racism, discrimination, and prejudice. Because of this similarity, minority counselors are in a beneficial position to identify and empathize with minority clients. When a minority client who is a student expresses frustration about being the only minority student in a physics class, the minority counselor may easily relate to the client's experience. Perhaps the counselor knows what it is like to be the only minority professional in the counseling center.

Minority counselors may sometimes overidentify with their minority clients, however. They may get caught up in the clients' negative experiences with racism and fail to conceptualize the clients' presenting problems in their context. In much the same way color-conscious White counselors tend to attribute minority clients' problems to their minority status, overidentifying minority counselors tend to develop narrow problem definitions.

Counselors who overidentify with minority clients may encourage excessive discussion of race issues. These counselors provide a safe haven for minority clients to unload rage about White people and the racist system. Although this catharsis is appropriate to a certain extent, counselors may take it too far. They may get personal gratification from allowing minority clients to unload. They also may use counseling sessions as opportunities to unload their own race-related anger, leading them to self-disclose inappropriately.

Overidentification is one result of minority counselors' unresolved issues surrounding race. For example, a minority counselor may resent the fact that he or she is more qualified than White peers who have the same professional status. Such a counselor may be angry about having to report to a supervisor who has limited knowledge about counseling minority clients. A minority counselor also may have unresolved racial issues stemming from the belief that he or she is being assigned all of the counseling center's difficult minority cases.

The most important negative consequence of overidentification is misdiagnosis. The counselor colludes with the client in attributing the client's problems primarily to racism. In so doing, the counselor denies the client's intrapsychic conflicts, which may be only remotely related to the client's race. For example, a client may be the identified patient in a family seeking therapy. The client has deep feelings of inadequacy that lead to self-defeating behaviors and prevent him from making full use of his potential. Yet the client blames his personal difficulties on racism—an easy scapegoat. A more accurate interpretation might be that the client's symptoms are an expression of a dysfunctional family system. When the counselor both overidentifies with the client and blames racism for the client's problems, the underlying pathology remains unrecognized and untreated.

I once counseled a young African American man who was a veteran of the Vietnam War. From the outset of counseling, we hit it off—partly because I am African American and partly because a special chemistry existed between us. We talked extensively about racism, both in civilian life and in the military. In retrospect, however, I realize that I was not very helpful to this young man. Our sessions could best be described as "White establishment bashing." Months later, when I ran into my former client, he appeared to be as confused as he was when I first began to counsel him. It was then that I realized what really had happened in our counseling sessions. Although he had been a victim of racism, he had other deep-seated issues that were never resolved. He used racism as a smoke screen, and by colluding in his denial, I hindered his progress in therapy.

Identification With the Oppressor

Some minority counselors who have difficulty dealing with their own race-related pain adopt the defense of denying their minority status and identifying with White people. Some scholars have likened this tendency to the psychoanalytic concept of the Oedipus complex, whereby a boy attempts to resolve his feelings of powerlessness by becoming like his father. This is the psychology of, "If you can't beat them, join them."

Minority counselors who identify with the oppressor harbor an underlying hostility. They feel self-hatred and hatred toward other members of their race. For these individuals, the pain of minority group membership is so intense that they avoid identification with their race. Atkinson, Morten, and Sue (1998c) would say that such counselors are in the conformity stage of the minority identity development model.

Among the negative consequences of minority counselors' identification with Whites is these counselors' tendency to place unrealistic expectations on their minority clients. It is important for counselors to have high expectations for their clients, of course, but these counselors take it too far. They judge minority clients harshly for not measuring up to White standards. They expect minority clients to make rapid therapeutic gains and penalize them for holding on to the values and customs of their racial/ethnic groups. The racism of such counselors can be more harmful to minority clients than the racism of White counselors. They counsel by the axiom, "If I can be successful in the White world, so can you." The problem is that they define success in overly narrow terms, disregarding the fact that all individuals are not created with equal ability or potential.

I once worked with an African American psychiatrist who acted as if he hated to treat minority patients. The few African American patients he treated seemed to hate the experience of having him as a therapist. In one case conference, I watched as this psychiatrist grilled an older African American man. I do not remember ever seeing him be as harsh with a White patient. Incidentally, the psychiatrist had no rapport with any of his African American colleagues.

Chapter Summary

In this chapter I have highlighted the importance of a good relationship between the counselor and the minority client. This relationship provides the context in which the counselor can help the client achieve positive therapeutic outcomes.

Numerous race-related defense mechanisms can prevent the development of a working therapeutic alliance between counselor and client; I have discussed 10 such defenses here. Counselors who are defensive about race or who fail to handle the race-related defensiveness of minority clients have been found to perpetuate racism.

This chapter concludes Part I of this book. The chapters in Part II build on the solid conceptual foundation provided in the preceding chapters on the nature, dynamics, and complexity of unintentional racism in counseling and therapy. In each of the following five chapters, I discuss a particular strategy counselors can use to overcome unintentional racism. The emphasis in Part II is on translating theory into practice. With that objective in mind, I describe a variety of practical interventions in each chapter.

Part II

Overcoming the
Counselor's Unintentional Racism

7

Counseling Idiographically

Each client is unique, a mixture of characteristics and qualities that make him or her unlike anyone else. Even clients of similar backgrounds are different from each other. Although they may have much in common, in the context of counseling their differences outweigh their similarities. When clients arrive for counseling, they bring their personal stories, and each has a different story to tell. Because each client is unique, counselors should not attempt to counsel all clients in exactly the same way.

Counselors should be aware that their effectiveness depends first and foremost on their ability to understand each client as an individual. To be really helpful, a counselor must tune in to the client's personal experiences. This idiographic perspective should guide the entire counseling process.[1] Jones (1985) underscores the importance of this perspective in counseling with minority clients, noting, "The point is that the concept of race is far too general and is not tailor-made for what is idiographically more significant to the development of a particular person" (p. 175).

In this chapter, I discuss the idiographic orientation—both what it is and how counselors should use it in their work with minority clients. I begin with a brief discussion of five principles that underlie the idiographic perspective and then present a case example. The chapter concludes with 12 guidelines aimed at helping counselors apply the idiographic approach to counseling.

Five Principles

Five guiding principles underlie the idiographic perspective in counseling. By keeping these principles in mind, counselors can serve minority clients more effectively.

Principle 1: Counselors should attempt to understand each client from the client's unique frame of reference. Carl Rogers (1961), the founder of person-centered therapy, was a leading proponent of this principle. In describing the helping relationship, he characterizes the effective counselor as one who becomes acquainted with the private world of the client

> by an acceptance of this other person as a separate person with value in his own right; and by a deep empathic understanding which enables me to see his private world through his eyes. When these conditions are achieved, I become a companion to my client, accompanying him in the frightening search for himself, which he now feels free to undertake. (p. 34)

Sometimes counselors think they understand their clients when they really do not. To avoid misunderstanding a client, a counselor needs to be empathic; he or she needs to see the client's inner world from the client's point of view. As my colleagues and I have observed, "The major assumption underlying the idiographic approach is that all hunches about a client that are based on prior knowledge must be considered tentative until the counselor obtains information directly from the client that either confirms or disconfirms the hunch" (Ridley, Mendoza, & Kanitz, 1994, p. 243)

Principle 2: Nomothetic, normative information does not always fit particular individual clients. The nomothetic perspective, in contrast to the idiographic perspective, focuses on the prominent characteristics of the group to which an individual belongs. Although the nomothetic view yields information about the typical or average member of a group, any individual within the group may deviate from that group's norms. A strictly nomothetic approach regards the deviant person as abnormal. The idiographic perspective, however, recognizes that deviation from the norm implies neither that a person is abnormal nor that he or she is exceptionally healthy. The person may simply differ from other group members. Thus normative data may be useful but not sufficient for understanding a particular client. Counselors should be aware of group norms, but they should not expect to understand any given client fully without exploring that individual's unique perspective.

The idiographic approach underscores the counselor's need to understand the personal meaning that the client holds as a *particular person*, not simply as a representative of certain groups.[2] Ibrahim (1991) argues that when counselors apply normative information to "idiosyncratic individuals," they violate their clients' right to individuality; this practice may even be considered a form of "cultural oppression" (p. 14). Many multicultural scholars have written about the importance of valuing minority clients' individuality. Table 7.1 displays the comments of a few mental health professionals regarding clients of a variety of races.

Table 7.1   Comments of Mental Health Professionals on the Individuality of
                  Minority Clients

African Americans

The question "How to treat the black client?" is naively and simplistically
phrased. It is as if one were asking how do we treat the narcissistic character disorder
or the depressed patient. But black clients do not constitute a particular clinical or
diagnostic type. Knowing that a patient is black fails to inform adequately about his
views of psychotherapy, about his personality and psychological conflict, and about
his aspirations and goals in therapy, let alone about educational level, social
background, or environmental context. There is enormous within-group variability.
The question is not how to treat *the* black client, but how to treat *this* black client.
(Jones, 1985, pp. 174–175)

Asian Americans

It is essential to acknowledge that Asian Americans represent a diverse group
of people with considerable between-group differences. There are over 29 distinct
subgroups represented among Asian Americans. Each of these subgroups has distinct
traditions, customs, and languages. Included in this population are recent immigrants
and refugees from various Asian countries (e.g., China, Korea, Vietnam) as well as
individuals who have been born and socialized in the United States (e.g., American-
born Chinese). In addition, there are considerable within-group variations in each of
the subgroups. For example, an American-born Chinese who is raised in one of the
many Chinatown communities tends to be less acculturated to Western culture and
values than an American-born Chinese who is raised in a rural, Midwestern town.
Such differences can have significant implications for treatment. (Moy, 1992, p. 359)

Hispanic Americans

Each woman's choice expresses something about who she is as an individual as
well as what her cultural values are. Superficial knowledge of Hispanic culture may
lead the therapist to accept as a cultural norm what might only be the client's
expression of her individuality. Conversely, a behavior that conforms to strict cultural
norms or violates them at a high personal cost can be interpreted by an unknowing
therapist as strictly an individual choice with no cultural implications. Cultural
norms may be used inaccurately by either client or therapist to explain or excuse a
woman's restricted behavior and thus prevent the exploration of other factors in the
individual's life history. (Espin, 1985, p. 169)

Native Americans

The Native American population is extremely varied, and it is impossible to make
general recommendations regarding counseling that apply to all Native Americans.
No only do various tribes differ from each other, but any one individual may differ
greatly from other members of the same tribe. . . . A major variable is the degree of
traditionalism of an individual versus the degree of acculturation to mainstream U.S.
society. The continuum stretches from the very traditional individual born and reared
on a reservation, who speaks the tribal language, to the Native American reared
in a city who speaks only English and may feel little identification with a tribe.
(Thomason, 1991, p. 321)

Principle 3: People are a dynamic blend of multiple roles and identities. The notion that any given person has only one racial or cultural identity overlooks the fact that each unique person has multiple identities. A minority client is not merely a representative of a single racial or ethnic group. He or she is a member of a variety of groups, with group identities overlapping to create a blend that is unique and special to that individual. Pedersen (1990a) asserts that one person may be a part of more than 1,000 cultures at any given time, taking on many different roles at once. To understand a particular client thoroughly, a counselor must explore how the client's multiple roles and identities intersect to give the client unique meaning.

Principle 4: The idiographic perspective is compatible with the biopsychosocial model of mental health. The most comprehensive understanding of any individual comes only through an examination of the person's integrated biological, psychological, and sociological experiences. Each of these contexts contributes to an understanding of the individual, but no single one is sufficient to produce comprehensive understanding. The more counselors know about their clients, the more likely they are to be able to help them. Unlike the medical model of mental health, which focuses primarily on the exploration of internal psychological dynamics, the idiographic perspective is concerned with a holistic view of persons. The biopsychosocial model is well suited for this purpose.

Principle 5: The idiographic perspective is transtheoretical. A focus on the individual is not constrained by a single therapeutic orientation. Rather, counselors who take an idiographic approach are free to adopt any therapeutic orientation and to use a wide range of specific interventions. For such a counselor, the most important rule is to select an intervention that specifically addresses the client's problem areas, as determined by an idiographic appraisal. In this sense, individualized treatment planning is the hallmark of the idiographic perspective in counseling.

The Case of Ricardo Garcia

The fictitious case of Ricardo Garcia illustrates the principles of counseling from an idiographic perspective. Ricardo, a 32-year-old Mexican American, lives in East Los Angeles. He and his family immigrated to the United States from Mexico 3 years ago in hopes of creating a better life. Ricardo's wife, Teresa, is 31 years old. She does not work outside the home, and she spends most of her free time watching Spanish-language television programs and socializing with other Hispanic women in the neighborhood. Ricardo and Teresa have two children: Their son, Manuel, is 13 and attends junior high school; their daughter, Selma, is 10 and in the fourth grade. Both of the children have been in bilingual classes since they arrived in Los Angeles.

Two months after he and his family came to Los Angeles, Ricardo found a job as an apprentice to an automobile mechanic. The mechanic liked Ricardo because of his dedication and his willingness to work hard. He taught Ricardo the trade, and within a year Ricardo had become an expert mechanic himself, soaking up everything his boss taught him. During Ricardo's second year in the United States, he began to take formal steps to learn English. He enrolled in an evening course in English as a second language, and he showed the same drive to succeed there as he did in learning to become a mechanic. As he became increasingly proficient in English, his interest in doing things "the way Americans do" also increased. Teresa, in contrast, showed little interest in branching out beyond the Hispanic community.

Gradually, Ricardo and Teresa have begun to have serious problems in their relationship. They have frequent heated confrontations, mostly over Ricardo's long hours away from home and their different perspectives regarding mainstream American traditions versus the traditions they brought from Mexico. In addition, their sex life has become dissatisfying.

To make matters worse, their children are having difficulties. Manuel is showing interest in being accepted by the members of a local Hispanic gang. One of his teachers recently called his parents at home to tell them about a change she has noticed in Manuel's attitude. Selma, who used to be outgoing, has become quiet and reserved, and nobody else in the family can tell what she is thinking.

As Ricardo's problems at home have escalated, he has begun spending even more time away from his family. After his evening class, he often stays and talks with Alba, a young Hispanic woman who also is learning to speak English. He knows there is an attraction between them, but because of his strong Catholic beliefs, he so far has avoided becoming more involved with Alba.

An Idiographic Conceptualization of Ricardo

After an intake interview with Ricardo, his counselor initially feels overwhelmed by the complexity of his story. The counselor then asks herself a number of questions about the case, including the following:

- How typical are Ricardo's problems among Hispanic males?
- To what extent are Ricardo's problems attributable to his cultural adjustment, racism, or his own psychological issues?
- Does a counselor need specialized training to counsel this type of client?
- Are particular interventions more suited than others for this type of client?
- How can one effectively assess Ricardo?

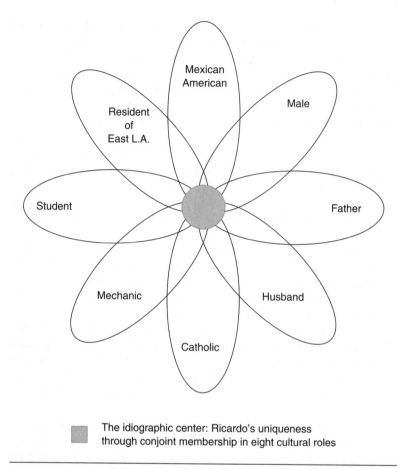

The idiographic center: Ricardo's uniqueness through conjoint membership in eight cultural roles

Figure 7.1   An Idiographic Approach to Client Conceptualization: The Case of Ricardo Garcia

To begin to answer these questions, the counselor must look at Ricardo idiographically. The case material suggests that currently Ricardo is playing at least eight cultural roles: He is a Mexican American, a man, a father, a husband, a Catholic, a mechanic, a student, and a resident of East Los Angeles. By determining Ricardo's various roles, the counselor can begin to form an idiographic picture of him. Figure 7.1 presents an idiographic conceptualization of Ricardo.

Given Ricardo's many different roles and identities, the counselor has many possible ways to attempt to understand him. She might look at Ricardo predominantly as a Mexican American or as a resident of East Los Angeles, for instance. But if she examines each role separately, she will gain only a limited view of what it means to be Ricardo as a unique person. The counselor can try to understand Ricardo as he appears in his various roles, but to see the total picture, she must explore Ricardo's unique frame of reference, which is a product of his conjoint membership in all of his roles.

To gain greater insight into Ricardo, the counselor decides to focus on Ricardo's idiographic experience (depicted at the center of Figure 7.1). This "indivisible intersection" (Robinson, 1993) of Ricardo's many life roles is the source of Ricardo's uniqueness as a person. Viewed from this perspective, Ricardo's idiographic experience distinguishes him from every other Mexican American, man, father, husband, Catholic, mechanic, student, and resident of East Los Angeles. His counselor knows she should not overlook any of Ricardo's roles because each contributes in some way to her understanding of him.

Possible Interpretations of Ricardo

A counselor initially hearing Ricardo's story might arrive at several different idiographic interpretations of Ricardo. Any one of these interpretations may be accurate or inaccurate. The following three possible interpretations of Ricardo illustrate how multiple counselors might view the same client and case material and yet arrive at different conclusions. These possibilities also demonstrate how counseling idiographically can help counselors better understand their clients.

Interpretation 1

Ricardo is fed up with his marriage and family responsibilities. He feels that he has worked hard to improve his life, and his reward for all his hard work has been nothing but trouble. He resents Teresa because she is lazy and unmotivated to help the family get ahead. He also blames her for their children's problems. He believes Teresa wastes too much time watching TV and visiting with friends when she could be helping their kids. He enjoys talking to Alba because, unlike Teresa, Alba wants a better life, as Ricardo does. He also thinks that if Teresa would put her religion into practice, she would be more motivated.

Interpretation 2

Ricardo is scared and feels guilty. His mother always wanted him to be a priest. In the poor Mexican village where he grew up, the priest was the person everyone turned to for help. Although being a mechanic is a good way to earn a living, Ricardo believes his job is not as important as being a spiritual guide and helping people. He now wonders if his problems are punishment for his not entering the priesthood. He feels he has let down a lot of people—first his mother and now his wife and children—as well as

God. He also feels guilty because he has been talking with Alba about his problems even though he realizes he should be talking to Teresa instead.

Interpretation 3

Ricardo is confused and ambivalent. On the one hand, he always has been a devout Catholic. Because of his strong Catholic faith, he has tried to take care of his family, attend Mass regularly, and be faithful to his wife. He even detests the macho stereotype of Hispanic males. On the other hand, Ricardo is struggling with some new attitudes. He doesn't like feeling "trapped at home." He questions the value of religion because it "doesn't work anymore," and now he is sexually attracted to Alba. And although he likes life in the United States, he wonders whether he is "selling out." Ricardo feels like he is being pulled in opposite directions. The only thing in his life right now that doesn't bother him is his job as a mechanic.

Guidelines for Counseling Idiographically

To counsel clients idiographically, counselors need to keep in mind the following 12 guidelines, each of which I discuss in turn below.

1. Develop cultural self-awareness.

2. Avoid imposing one's values on clients.

3. Accept one's naïveté regarding others.

4. Show cultural empathy.

5. Incorporate cultural considerations into counseling.

6. Avoid stereotyping.

7. Determine the relative importance of clients' primary cultural roles.

8. Avoid blaming the victim.

9. Remain flexible in the selection of interventions.

10. Examine counseling theories for bias.

11. Build on clients' strengths.

12. Avoid protecting clients from emotional pain.

Developing cultural self-awareness. Most people have strong cultural biases, values, and expectations, and counselors are no exception. Yet most counselors do not realize that their own culture-based feelings and attitudes affect their work, especially as they attempt to understand clients of different races or cultures. All counselors must become culturally self-aware. Unless they take a good hard look at themselves and examine their personal agendas, they are likely to ignore, distort, or underemphasize their minority clients' idiographic experiences.

The topic of race is a sensitive one, and it often arouses strong feelings. Counselors should look inward and examine themselves for hidden attitudes or biases that might limit their objectivity when they deal with particular clients. As Rosen and Frank (1962), two psychiatrists, have observed, few people are free of racial prejudice. Many scholars have argued that counselor self-awareness is an important element of effective multicultural psychotherapy (e.g., Wintrob & Harvey, 1981). Indeed, as Jones (1985) suggests, counselors' cultural self-awareness may be the only factor that can prevent counselors' personal reactions to minority clients from intruding negatively into their work.

One way in which counselors can develop cultural self-awareness is by seeking personal counseling of their own. According to Rogers (1961), counselors must be congruent if they are to be helpful. Congruent counselors are consciously aware of their feelings, attitudes, and perceptions. Because of their self-awareness, congruent counselors can manage their own issues without projecting those issues onto their clients.

In earlier work, I have suggested that a counselor who works with minority clients should seek counseling from a therapist of another race—especially one who is skilled in multicultural counseling (Ridley, 1989). Ideally, the counselor's therapist should be of the same race as the major client population the counselor serves because this is the racial group most vulnerable to the counselor's countertransference. The purpose of such counseling is to help the counselor identify and work through his or her own biases and prejudices and therefore reduce the likelihood of countertransference. As Axelson (1999) notes, the counselor's growing awareness of his or her own hidden prejudices is the first step in promoting an open-minded counseling relationship.

Avoiding imposing one's values. In addition to identifying their own biases, counselors must be careful not to impose their own cultural values on their clients. Therapist neutrality is widely cited as a therapeutic ideal. As Freud (1912/1963) describes this concept, the neutral analyst serves as a blank screen onto which the client can transfer intense emotions and reactions. According to Coonerty (1991), psychoanalysts generally believe the therapist's true identity and values are of negligible influence on the client.

A number of scholars have questioned seriously the possibility of complete therapist neutrality. Katz (1985) notes that therapy, instead of being value free, is always connected to the social, political, and historical realities of the counselor's culture. Along similar lines, Draguns (1989) argues that culture is an invisible and silent participant in counseling. Many counselors may not recognize the inevitable presence of culture, however. Wrenn (1962,

1985) coined the now common term *cultural encapsulation* to describe the disposition of counseling students and faculty who are unaware of their cultural biases.

So what role do counselors' values play in their counseling efforts? Kelly (1990), who conducted a review of the literature on values in counseling, concludes that counselors tend to impose their values on clients even when they do not intend to do so. In addition, counselors tend to judge their clients' progress in counseling according to how much the clients subscribe to the counselors' values. The implication of such findings for multicultural counseling is serious: Counselors unknowingly expect their minority clients to become like them.

Counselors must make a conscientious effort to avoid imposing their values on clients. To accomplish this feat, they first must identify what their values are. Edward Hall (1973) describes the following 10 basic categories of values that exist in every culture; all counselors should become familiar with this list:

- Language (verbal message systems, communications)
- Temporality (time, routines, schedules)
- Territoriality (space, property)
- Exploitation (methods of control, use, and sharing of resources)
- Association (family, kin, community)
- Subsistence (work, division of labor)
- Bisexuality (differing modes of speech, dress, conduct)
- Learning (observation, modeling, instruction)
- Play (humor, games)
- Defense (health procedures, social conflicts, beliefs)

Counselors should isolate their personal values in each of these categories and compare their values with those of their clients. When the counselor holds values similar to his or her client's, the counselor is unlikely to impose these values on the client. However, just because a counselor's values are similar to the client's, the counselor is not exempt from examining his or her own biases. A counselor may agree with a client on a particular value (e.g., *machismo* vs. *marianismo*), but that does not mean the counselor can fail to question the client's adherence to the value, which might not be functional in certain contexts. When counselors know their values are different from their clients' values, they should take extra care in determining whether or not the client should change values.

Accepting one's naïveté regarding others. Counselors are highly trained professionals who are regarded as psychological experts. They are skilled in client assessment and intervention planning. A few also are multicultural experts, skillful in counseling clients from races and cultures other than their own. No counselor, however, is initially an expert on any other individual.

Counselors must get to know their clients before they can help them. During the early phases of treatment, a counselor may get hunches or formulate hypotheses about a client, but such hunches and hypotheses are often wrong. Counselors always should proceed with caution when working with clients of other races. In these cases, counselors should replace the automatic information-processing style they employ when interacting with members of their own race with a more cautious style that lets them consider each client's unique cultural makeup. Even experienced counselors should analyze carefully how well their hypotheses fit each individual client.

Many counselors find that maintaining a naive posture is not easy, especially because they have been socialized to play the role of expert. They must commit themselves to this posture, however, and work at proceeding cautiously with each client. Only when counselors accept the limits of their own expertise are they likely to interpret their clients' problems and needs realistically.

Showing cultural empathy. Counselors who are culturally empathic can understand their clients' concerns from the clients' cultural perspectives (Ridley, Mendoza, & Kanitz, 1994). Cultural empathy has two dimensions: understanding and communication. Culturally empathic understanding involves getting at the heart of the client's idiographic meaning. Counselors must eliminate cultural bias from their perceptual filters to achieve this level of understanding. Culturally empathic communication involves conveying to the client the counselor's understanding of the client's idiographic experience. The counselor achieves such communication by using language that is meaningful to the client.

Counselors can demonstrate cultural empathy in several ways. First, if a counselor is unsure about what a client is trying to say, the counselor should ask for clarification. The counselor never should feign understanding of the client. Minority clients may use numerous expressions and idioms that nonminority counselors may not understand. Counselors should not expect to be familiar with every word or phrase that clients of different races or cultures might use. Therefore, they should not hesitate to seek clarification when they do not understand a client. For example, a counselor might ask for clarification by saying something like this:

Counselor: You have used the phrase "something, something" several times. Could you please give me an example of what you mean by this?

Second, counselors should invite their clients to ask for clarification if they need to. Sometimes counselors use professional language that is unfamiliar to laypersons, and minority clients especially may be embarrassed to admit they do not know what their counselors are talking about. A counselor should set the stage early in the counseling process by welcoming the client to ask for clarification at any time. The counselor might say something like this:

Counselor: We counselors sometimes use professional language that our clients don't understand. Because counseling is a new experience for you, feel free to ask for clarification if I use a word that is unfamiliar to you. This should help us both better understand each other.

Or the counselor might take this approach:

Counselor: You seem puzzled by something I've said. Tell me what I said that was puzzling, and I'll try to be more clear.

Third, counselors should ask clients to provide examples from the clients' cultural experience that illustrate the issues the clients want to address in counseling. Sometimes minority clients have difficulty expressing themselves to counselors from other cultures, and they might find it easier to communicate their idiographic experiences by giving real-life examples. A counselor might facilitate communication by using one of these two approaches:

Counselor: Describe the most vivid situation you remember when you felt like you were out of place with both Whites and other African Americans.

Counselor: Tell me about a time when you were trying to figure out if Whites really accepted you or just needed you around as the token minority.

Incorporating cultural considerations into counseling. Many counselors behave as though the cultural backgrounds and experiences of their minority clients are irrelevant to the counselors' understanding of these clients as unique persons. However, the failure to include culture in the therapeutic formula has been shown to affect many aspects of counseling adversely. Several scholars have noted the value of exploring cultural issues in treatment, especially when the client's concerns are related to racism and discrimination (Atkinson, Thompson, & Grant, 1993; Casas, 1984; Thompson, Worthington, & Atkinson, 1994; Vargas & Koss-Chioino, 1992).

Regarding the value of incorporating cultural considerations into counseling, my colleagues and I have noted:

All therapy is culturally contextualized, and positive therapeutic outcomes depend on the skillful incorporation of cultural considerations into the basic design of counseling intervention. Conversely, behaving as if culture is irrelevant is countertherapeutic. Such behavior results in an inadequate understanding of individuals and an inability to maximally assist them in achieving therapeutic goals. (Ridley, Mendoza, Kanitz, Angermeier, & Zenk, 1994, p. 128)

It is our argument that attention to cultural variables promotes an increase in therapeutic leverage, opening up greater opportunities for counselors to understand the needs, concerns, personal goals, and adjustment of clients.

A case from my training experience illustrates the importance of tailoring counseling interventions to the cultural experiences of minority clients. A counselor on our campus asked a young Japanese woman who had come in for counseling many questions concerning dating patterns and male-female relationships in Japan. This questioning was extensive and time-consuming, yet after the counselor finished this line of inquiry, he continued to counsel the student as though the discussion had never happened. The woman did not return for another session.

The counselor in this case made two mistakes. First, he did not personalize the cultural information he was seeking to the client; that is, he asked about Japanese women in general but not about this client in particular. The counselor should have been interested in learning whether dating patterns and male-female relationships in Japan had any impact on the client's life as a student at an American university. Second, the counselor did not translate his quest for information into therapeutic goals or interventions for the client. He simply wasted time, as he did not use the information he gathered to help the client.

Counselors must be purposeful in gathering and incorporating culturally relevant information. They must be alert to cultural data during all phases of counseling and incorporate cultural considerations into every therapeutic activity, whether it is problem identification, diagnosis, goal setting, treatment planning, termination, or referral. Otherwise, they may end up with clients who are puzzled and disappointed and who terminate counseling early, as did the Japanese student in the case related above.

Avoiding stereotyping. A stereotype is a simplified, generalized label applied to a group of people. Snyder (1982) lists several common stereotypes: Italians are passionate, African Americans are lazy, Jews are materialistic, and lesbians are mannish in demeanor. Stereotyping in general can be distinguished from racial prejudice, which is a special category of stereotyping. Racial prejudice implies bigotry, but whereas prejudiced people always stereotype, people who stereotype are not necessarily prejudiced. Brown (1965) argues that stereotyping is an inevitable and necessary coping mechanism that allows people to avoid cognitive overload. That is, stereotyping or overgeneralizing helps people package the large variety of stimuli they face daily into a manageable number of categories. Although many stereotypes are inaccurate, others contain a "kernel of truth."

McCauley, Stitt, and Segal (1980) point out that stereotypes have negative repercussions when people use them to make predictions about others but do not attempt to gain more information before making these predictions. Stereotyping is particularly harmful when it involves assigning certain characteristics to people because they are assumed to be inferior, when it leads to self-fulfilling prophecies, and when it is used by people who are dogmatic and unwilling to open themselves up to new information that might contradict their beliefs. Once rigidly formed, stereotypes are highly resistant to change (Axelson, 1999).

Counselors who work with minority clients should attempt to identify the culture- and race-related stereotypes that infiltrate their own thinking. For example, Atkinson, Morten, and Sue (1998b) cite the stereotype of Asian Americans as high achievers who experience few emotional and social problems, and point out how holding this positive stereotype might affect high school counselors in their work with Asian students. A counselor might assume that a particular Asian student needs academic and career counseling but not personal counseling, for instance. Without exploring other dimensions of the student's experience, the counselor might decide what is important for the student based on the counselor's erroneous preconceptions. The student may in fact need to work through some emotional issues unrelated to career and academic concerns, but the counselor may not see that because it does not fit the counselor's stereotype of an Asian student.

Gerrard (1991) quotes an African American student who found that she was stereotyped by her high school guidance counselor:

> He just took one look at me and it's just like, "Great, not only is she a girl but she's Black. Everyone knows like it's hard enough to find smart Black people, let alone smart Black girls." Basically, that was the assumption he was working under. (p. 562)

This student based her impression of the counselor's thoughts on several factors, including his attitude toward her, his tone of voice, and his comments that she could not go into medicine or get a scholarship—conclusions for which he offered no reasons. His body language also communicated lack of interest, the student said. "He was just sort of sitting there as if bored out of his skull, waiting for me to say something" (p. 562). Gerrard suggests that this is not simply a case of a pragmatic counselor attempting to be realistic with a client. He points out that the counselor at least could have said something like "Here are the barriers. Are you prepared to overcome them to get what you want?" (p. 562). Instead, he stereotyped the client based on her sex and race.

Determining the relative importance of the client's primary cultural roles. It is essential for the counselor to understand the client's idiographic center, or personal frame of reference. The counselor's failure to understand the client as a unique person precludes the possibility that the counselor will be able to help the client in the most appropriate manner. Counselors who do not understand their clients as unique individuals are likely to select inappropriate interventions.

Counselors must examine each client's various cultural roles and evaluate how each of these roles contributes to that particular client's idiographic experience. A few roles may be heavily influential for one client, whereas for another many roles have more equal influence. It is impossible for a counselor to know how a client's multiple roles uniquely contribute to his or her idiographic experience without first getting to know the client.

Effective counseling involves intense therapeutic work, and counselors cannot expect to understand their clients quickly and easily. Counselors must examine and reexamine their clients' cultural roles, taking care not to overemphasize or underemphasize the contribution of any one role. In the case of Ricardo Garcia, for example, it would be premature for his counselor to assume, given only the information presented above, that Ricardo's being Mexican American is any more or less important to his idiographic experience than his being a Catholic or a mechanic. Although his Mexican Americanness may be very important to understanding him, it is only one of many dimensions of his experience. With this in mind, Ricardo's counselor should strive to determine the relative importance of his various roles by asking him about them directly.

Avoiding blaming the victim. Being a victim in a racist society is tragic, but being victimized by racism twice—first in society and again in counseling—is worse. Counselors who strictly subscribe to the medical model and disregard the biopsychosocial model are almost certain to blame minority clients for their own problems. These victim-blaming reactions result from such counselors' "tunnel vision" (Corey, Corey, & Callanan, 2003).

Counselors need to educate themselves continually, no matter how long they have been in practice. To overcome the tendency toward victim blaming with minority clients, counselors should take the following steps:

- *Review all assessments of minority clients.* Periodically—every quarter or half a year—counselors should reexamine the case notes they have made on these clients to see if they can discern any pattern in their clinical judgments, such as diagnosis of psychopathology. By examining the factors that influence their assessments, they can judge whether their decisions are based on intrapsychic factors, environmental factors, or a combination of the two.
- *Compare assessments of minority clients with those of White clients.* Counselors should determine whether there are differences in the types of judgments they make about the two groups of clients. If such differences do exist, they should examine their case notes to find out what factors are involved in their decisions about clients from each group.

- *Get feedback on minority clients' cases.* Counselors should ask their supervisors or other professional colleagues who have multicultural expertise to help them review their minority clients' cases. From time to time, they should present minority clients' cases at conferences so colleagues can examine their assessment and treatment planning in these cases.
- *Examine minority clients' cases for instances of cultural countertransference.* Counselors should be aware that their own unresolved racial issues may lead to victim blaming with minority clients. They should be on the alert for their own hostile feelings and sexual idiosyncrasies, which are common projections among counselors who culturally countertransfer. They may want to seek personal counseling for help with this step.

Remaining flexible in the selection of interventions. Because each client is unique, counselors need to be flexible regarding the interventions they employ. They should be careful to avoid using the same interventions repeatedly just because those interventions fit their favorite counseling orientations. Rather, they should select interventions that are suited to the unique needs and problems of particular clients. If counselors put the needs of clients first, they will find that sometimes they must forgo their favorite interventions.

Some counselors believe they should use the same interventions with their minority clients that they use with nonminority clients in order to maintain "fairness." They wrongly assume that equal treatment means equitable treatment. D. W. Sue (1977) was probably the first scholar in the mental health field to recognize and challenge this assumption. Sue argues that equal treatment in counseling might actually mean discriminatory treatment and that differential treatment does not necessarily imply discriminatory treatment. Because the real issue is equal access and opportunity for all clients, Sue favors the use of differential techniques that are nondiscriminatory. This position makes a great deal of sense if one accepts the definition of racism proposed in this book.

Several scholars have suggested that counselors can achieve flexibility in treating minority clients by using multimodal therapy (e.g., Ponterotto, 1987; Ridley, 1984). As Lazarus (1989) explains, multimodal therapy encompasses a variety of techniques without allying itself with any specific therapeutic orientation. Lazarus identifies six modalities that constitute human personality: behavior, affect, sensation, imagery, cognition, and interpersonal relationships. He also identifies a seventh, nonpersonality, modality: drugs (or medication). (Lazarus refers to these modalities using the acronym BASIC ID.) Counselors who use multimodal therapy can systematically employ a broad repertoire of interventions. They are not confined to interventions that may be inappropriate or unhelpful for their particular clients. Instead, they can select interventions that address their clients' needs in each modality.

Ponterotto (1987) describes a hypothetical case that provides a good illustration of the use of multimodal therapy. Francisco, a Mexican American male, presents with a number of problems; Ponterotto matches each problem to one of the BASIC ID modalities and proposes a specific treatment. For example, Ponterotto identifies Francisco's lack of assertion at a local city agency as a behavior problem and then proposes treatment that includes assertiveness training, role playing, and self-as-a-model. Ponterotto adds another problem area to the regular profile, which he calls "interaction with oppressive environment." One of his proposed interventions for this problem area is to develop a plan of action to pressure the city agency to hire Spanish-speaking employees. Table 7.2 displays Francisco's modality profile. This case demonstrates why counselor flexibility in the selection of interventions is one of the most important requirements for effectiveness with minority clients.

Examining counseling theories for bias. Like all theories, counseling theories are predicated on assumptions and presuppositions. Most of today's major theories of counseling and psychotherapy originated in Eurocentric ideology, and a number of scholars have questioned seriously the relevance of such theories to counseling with minority clients. Holiman and Lauver (1987) describe the counselor's theoretical orientation as one of several "filters" that can distort the counselor's perception of the client.

To use traditional counseling theories beneficially with minority clients, counselors first must evaluate the assumptions contained in these theories for cultural bias. Pedersen (1987, 1994) identifies 10 assumptions that reflect cultural bias in counseling:

- A common measure of "normal behavior"
- Emphasis on individualism
- Fragmentation by academic disciplines
- Dependence on abstract words
- Overemphasis on independence
- Dependence on linear thinking
- Neglect of client's support system
- Focus on individual versus system change
- Cultural encapsulation
- Neglect of history

Using Pedersen's 10 assumptions, Usher (1989) evaluated client-centered theory for its cultural relevance and found that several assumptions underlying the theory are culturally biased: an emphasis on individualism and independence, a here-and-now time orientation, a minimal focus on external influences, abstract constructs that are meaningless or offensive to minority clients, and a narrow theoretical foundation. Usher's critique of Rogerian

Table 7.2   Francisco's Modality Profile

Modality	Problem	Proposed Treatment
Behavior	Lack of assertion at local city agency	Assertiveness training Role playing Self-as-a-model
	Behavior directed by what others (city agency) might think or say	Rational disputation Counselor modeling
Affect	Strong feelings of anger, frustration, guilt, and worry	Counselor support Anger management Rational discussion
Sensations	Tension headaches and stomach pains	Relaxation training Biofeedback Abdominal breathing exercises
Imagery	Images of uncomfortable scenes at city agency	Desensitization Positive imagery
Cognitions	Negative self-talk and self-blaming	Rational disputation and corrective self-talk Thought stopping
Interpersonal relations	Negative family interactions	Preventive rational discussion Substitution of coping behavior training
Interaction with oppressive environment	Oppressive environment influences	Counselor's *acknowledgment* of oppressive environment Joint development by client and counselor of an organized plan of action to pressure city agency to hire a member of the Spanish-speaking community Counselor's exploration (through referral contacts) of other options (e.g., Are there comparable Spanish-speaking agencies that could handle the client's financial concerns?)
Drugs/biology	Tension headaches and stomach pains	Physician consult if symptoms persist

SOURCE: Adapted from Ponterotto, J. G. (1987). Counseling Mexican Americans: A multimodal approach. *Journal of Counseling and Development* 65(6), 308–312. Copyright © American Counseling Association. Used with permission of the publisher.

theory is an excellent model for examining cultural bias in other theories. Her critique is particularly noteworthy in light of Rogers's strong leaning toward the idiographic perspective. If cultural bias can be found in his theory, mental health professionals certainly should question the relevance of other theories to their work with minority clients.

Ivey, Ivey, and Simek-Morgan's (1993) book examining the major theories of counseling and psychotherapy from the multicultural perspective is a helpful source of information for counselors who want to critique these theories. In addition, my colleagues and I have suggested a technique for examining theories for cultural relevance that involves identifying the key issues and assumptions of these theories (Ridley, Mendoza, & Kanitz, 1994). Counselors can use their analyses to develop their own multicultural theories of counseling.

Building on clients' strengths. A major criticism aimed at counselors who work with minority clients is that they often concentrate almost exclusively on these clients' weaknesses. Certainly, many minority clients have serious presenting problems, but they also have many strengths and tremendous potential. While vigorously looking for psychopathology in these clients, counselors often miss opportunities to help the clients identify their assets and use these assets advantageously. All clients need to realize that they have assets.

Counselors can help clients build on their strengths in several ways. First, they should look for the positive side of so-called dysfunctional behavior. As previously demonstrated, not all behaviors that counselors may initially judge as problematic are actually dysfunctional. In an early article on race in therapy, Rosen and Frank (1962) describe how a counselor can reframe certain behaviors positively:

> The Negro's position as a member of a minority group subjects him to experiences which differ from those of the white of corresponding socio-economic status, and the therapist must evaluate the patient's history with this in mind. Intermittent school attendance or frequent change of job may indicate not emotional instability but the effort to survive. Nor need a jail sentence have the same implications for a Negro as for a white patient. (p. 459)

If, for example, a client frequently changes jobs, the counselor should affirm the client's motivation and effort to survive instead of characterizing him or her as unstable. Perhaps the client's best attempt to cope with racism, poverty, and inadequate education has required moving from one menial job to another. The counselor should focus on the client's motivation to work and persistence in seeking gainful employment rather than on the erratic work history. Once the counselor reframes this behavior as an asset, he or she can try to figure out how to help the client make better use of this personal resource.

Second, counselors should identify their clients' past accomplishments. Some minority clients, especially those from economically disadvantaged backgrounds, may underestimate their potential. Sensitive counselors affirm the achievements of their minority clients, even when these clients initially might discount them as achievements or regard them as small or insignificant. I once worked with an African American teenager who was a member of an inner-city gang. He was streetwise and influential among his peers, but he knew right from wrong. His dream was to become a lawyer, and I saw tremendous potential in him. I encouraged him and assisted him in getting into college. Although he did not complete the education needed to reach his original goal, he still achieved a great deal: He became a police officer who works with inner-city youth. His savvy and experience, coupled with the confidence he gained by going to college, enabled him to excel at his job.

Third, counselors can teach their minority clients new behaviors or encourage them to get training in specialized areas. Vocational training, marriage enrichment, and assertiveness training are examples of areas in which clients might acquire new skills. Whatever the area, counselors can start by helping clients determine their existing level of functioning and then encouraging them to cultivate other skills for personal enhancement.

Avoiding protecting clients from emotional pain. Most clients are motivated to seek counseling by a desire to get relief from emotional pain. Pain relief is their number one priority, even at the expense of making constructive changes. Minority clients are no different from other clients in this respect. Counselors sometimes become so involved in their clients' quest for pain relief that they also make this the priority of counseling. What counselors and clients both may fail to realize is that healing always is accompanied by pain.

Some counselors are extremely sensitive to the pain of minority clients. They know these clients face racism and discrimination in addition to other social problems, and because of their genuine concern, they try to make counseling as painless as possible. Despite their good intentions, however, these counselors make the tactical error of choosing interventions that will cause the least pain rather than those that are most appropriate for helping their clients.

One of my clients was a very attractive African American woman in her mid-30s. She was a successful corporate executive, but she was unsuccessful in dealing with her emotional pain. Her personal life was like a terrible drama in which she moved from one abusive relationship to another. When I asked her what she gained from choosing men who abused her, she initially denied any responsibility and shifted the blame to the men in her life. As I continued to press her, we discovered that in her childhood she had received very little attention and approval from her father. In adulthood, she had come to perceive any attention she received, even if it was negative, as rewarding. In her eyes, negative attention was better than no attention. She had never come to terms with the pain she felt as a result of her father's emotional abandonment. We facetiously referred to her numerous forays with men as the "replacement strategy." It was a reminder of her dysfunctional way of dealing with emotional pain.

Pain inevitably accompanies healing. As Melzack and Wall (1982) note, pain can be a signal that helps prevent either serious injury or further injury where some injury already has occurred, or it can set limits on a person who has been seriously injured. Counselors do their clients a disservice when they try to protect them from therapeutic pain. They must employ interventions that work, even if those interventions make their clients uncomfortable. Counselors should adopt this motto: Effective interventions first and client comfort second.

Chapter Summary

Counselors must treat their minority clients as individuals and not simply as members of particular races or cultures. This chapter has emphasized that although minority clients' races and cultures are important, counselors must develop an idiographic understanding of each client, examining the client's multiple cultural roles and identities to comprehend that individual's unique personal meanings. I have presented 12 guidelines that are intended to increase counselors' effectiveness in treating each minority client as an individual.

Notes

1. The terms *idiographic* and *nomothetic,* first proffered by Wilhelm Windelband, were popularized by Gordon Allport (1946). The idiographic and nomothetic approaches to the study of personality are widely used in psychology; they are not limited to counseling and psychotherapy.

2. Studies in differential psychology have demonstrated consistently that within-group differences are larger than between-group differences. This finding applies to a variety of behavioral, personality, and cognitive variables. For authoritative discussions on this topic, see Atkinson, Morten, and Sue (1998c), Bronstein and Quina (1988), and Zuckerman (1990).

8

Setting Culturally Relevant Goals

The success of counseling ultimately depends on counselors' setting goals for their clients that are tailored to the clients' specific needs. Clients benefit most from counseling when they can achieve the goals their counselors set; thus goals must be realistic and attainable. The worst scenario occurs when the counselor sets no goals at all. Although goal setting does not guarantee success, it increases the chances that counseling will be successful. Goal setting also allows counselors to evaluate the outcomes of counseling. That evaluation, in turn, enables counselors to change their strategies when necessary—again improving the chances of successful counseling. Cormier and Hackney (1993) offer a helpful perspective on the importance of goal setting in counseling:

> Goals give direction to the therapeutic process and help both counselor and client to move in a focused direction with a specific route in mind. Without goals, it is all too easy to get sidetracked or lost. Goals help both the counselor and client to specify exactly what can and cannot be accomplished through counseling. (p. 103)

Counselors set two types of goals for clients: process goals and outcome goals. Both are critical to the success of counseling. *Process goals* are concerned with therapeutic movement and the conditions necessary for clients to change. Typically, they involve interaction between counselor and client. *Outcome goals* clarify the changes that clients are expected to make as a result of counseling. These include changes in behavior, attitudes, and feelings. The idiographic perspective demands that counselors determine a unique set of outcome goals tailored to each client.

This chapter focuses on culturally relevant counseling goals—both process and outcome goals—for minority clients. When working with minority clients, counselors must add the culturally relevant goals described here to any other goals they might set. The process goals discussed in this chapter should be incorporated into every counseling case, but the outcome goals addressed here may not be equally relevant to every minority client. Counselors should determine which goals are appropriate on a case-by-case basis.

The Need for Collaboration

Although it is clear that someone must take responsibility for goal setting in counseling, opinions vary as to who should shoulder that responsibility. Some professionals hold that counselors should set the goals because they have the psychological training and expertise to determine what goals will best serve their clients' interests. Others believe clients should set their own goals because they are experts on themselves and therefore capable of determining what goals will serve them best.

Both arguments have merit, but they also overlook the serious drawbacks attached to goal setting by either counselors or clients alone. Counselors may know psychological theory and how to apply clinical interventions, but they are not experts on any individual client at the beginning of the counseling process. Their lack of expertise concerning minority clients compounds the problem. Clients, on the other hand, know themselves better than anyone else, but when they present for counseling many are caught up in dysfunctional behavior, pain avoidance, and the pursuit of secondary gains. Because of their unhealthy status, they usually cannot discern how to receive counseling's full benefits and thus are incapable of setting appropriate goals by themselves. Therefore, to maximize the assets and minimize the liabilities of both participants in the counseling relationship, counselors and clients should approach goal setting as a joint effort. In short, they should collaborate.

Collaborative goal setting has particular advantages for counseling with minority clients. Clients often gain a sense of empowerment and ownership of the counseling process when they participate in their own goal setting. This sense is important for minority clients because they often enter counseling feeling powerless, and counseling cannot be successful if clients do not own their goals. In addition, collaboration can lend counselors early insight into their minority clients, a difficult achievement for some practitioners.

The best way for counselors to establish collaboration with their clients is by asking them directly to participate in goal setting. Some minority clients will respond readily to this request, whereas others will be more reluctant, especially if they are unfamiliar with counseling. Still others will blatantly resist collaboration. Counselors should explain to all minority clients how vital their input is to the success of counseling.

The Counselor's Unstated Goal

Every counselor's first priority should be to achieve equitable outcomes with all clients. Equitable outcomes also should be the most important criterion that counselors use to measure their success in overcoming racism. As counselors improve their service delivery, parity between minority and White clients should become increasingly evident in the areas of diagnosis, staff assignment, treatment modality, utilization, treatment duration, and client attitudes toward treatment. From an open systems perspective, the change from inequitable to equitable outcomes can be depicted as follows:

$$\frac{\text{Majority Group}}{\text{Minority Group}} \implies \text{Majority Group} = \text{Minority Group}$$

It may be difficult for counselors to achieve equitable outcomes across all racial groups. This difficulty is understandable given that multicultural counseling is a complex process. Nevertheless, counselors must work through the complexity. They must make every reasonable effort to provide fair and equitable service delivery to all their clients, to monitor their work, and to revise their interventions when necessary to meet the needs of minority clients.

Process Goals

In working with minority clients, counselors should be concerned with the following three process goals: establishing a working alliance, exploring the racial dynamics between counselor and client, and obtaining a counseling agreement.

Establishing a Working Alliance

The most important process goal is the establishment of a working alliance between the counselor and the minority client. Every counselor, regardless of therapeutic orientation, should make this goal a priority. Unless this goal is met, counseling cannot move forward. Gelso and Carter (1985) define the working alliance as the alignment or joining together of the client's reasonable or observing side with the counselor's working or "therapizing" side. This definition could be reframed to suggest that the client and counselor are both observers of the counseling process as well as active participants in change. The stronger the working alliance, the greater the likelihood that counseling will benefit the client.

The quality of the working alliance reflects the effort and commitment of both counseling participants. Clients must be permitted to "stand back" and reasonably observe what is happening within the counseling relationship and within themselves. They also must be able to experience their emotions, including negative feelings toward their counselors. Counselors must commit themselves to working wholeheartedly in the interest of their clients. They must conduct themselves professionally, abide by ethical principles, and employ scientifically based interventions.

As Gelso and Fretz (2001) observe, trust is the client's most important contribution to the working alliance. But trusting counselors, or the counseling process itself, is often difficult for minority clients. Many scholars have found a common theme of mistrust of White counselors among African Americans, Asian Americans, Hispanics, and Native Americans (Everett, Proctor, & Cartmell, 1983; Gomez, Ruiz, & Laval, 1982; Sue & Sue, 2003; Vontress, 1981; Whaley, 2001). Sometimes minority clients do not even fully trust minority counselors because they feel these professionals have sold out to the White establishment and, in effect, have compromised their commitment to minority causes.

Overcoming the client's mistrust is the greatest contribution the counselor can make to the working alliance. To overcome mistrust, counselors must always be authentic in their relationships with minority clients, and they must be alert to themes of concealment, suspicion, and disguise. They must seize every opportunity to demonstrate their dedication to their clients. When a client makes a therapeutic gain, for instance, the counselor can show strong affirmation. When a client is really struggling, the counselor can send a note of encouragement between sessions.

Exploring the Racial Dynamics Between Counselor and Client

Closely related to the establishment of a working alliance is the goal of determining the client's attitudes about race and how those attitudes might affect counseling. Ethnicity has been equated with sex and death as a subject that arouses deep, unconscious feelings in most people (McGoldrick, Pearce, & Giordano, 1982). Added to an already complicated process, racial dynamics present a major challenge to counselors working with minority clients. How can counselors sift through all the psychological nuances in a session to understand their clients' attitudes concerning race? How can they distinguish distortions caused by cultural transference from clients' realistic reactions?

First, counselors should realize that many minority clients enter counseling with a certain amount of fear and anxiety. To some of these clients, White counselors represent societal oppression. Some see minority counselors as people who no longer can relate to the minority experience. Counselors should remember that deep-seated fears and hostilities underlie these attitudes.

Counselors must accept their clients' anxieties and encourage clients to express their feelings openly. Counselors never should discourage or penalize clients for disclosing threatening information. It is a contradiction to encourage clients to be open and then penalize them when they are. Accepting clients' anxieties means that counselors first must accept their own anxieties, including those provoked by their clients. Counselors must be honest with themselves about their apprehension and discomfort. While being congruent about their feelings, they should be sensitive enough to avoid provoking more anxiety in their clients. Counselors should remember that the counseling setting is inherently threatening to many minority clients.

Second, counselors should explore their clients' racial attitudes early in treatment (Spurlock, 1985; Sykes, 1987). Some minority clients are not bothered by race differences between themselves and their counselors, whereas others are deeply troubled by such differences. If race is not a major issue for a given client, the counselor should move on to other issues. If the counselor senses that racial dynamics are important to the client, however, the counselor and client should explore these issues in depth together at the beginning of the counseling process. Jones and Seagull (1977) and Jones (1979) have found that race differences between counselor and client probably have their greatest impact early in treatment, particularly during the first session. The failure to explore these issues can block progress in therapy as well as minimize the possibility that the client will be receptive to positive interracial experiences in the future (Ridley, 1984).

Counselors who sense that racial dynamics might influence the counseling process should address race directly with clients. A counselor might introduce the topic to the client by saying something such as the following:

Counselor: Many clients who come to counseling for the first time do not know exactly what to expect. Some are threatened by the situation. The fact that you and I are of different races may make you even more uncomfortable or make you question whether I can really help you. If you have these feelings, let's try to get them out in the open. We can make better progress that way.

Another approach is to mention something specific about the client that the counselor has noticed; for example:

Counselor: You stated on your intake questionnaire that you are having
conflicts in the residence hall, and you used the word *ignorant*
to describe some of the students. I know that your experience
growing up on the south side of Chicago is very different
from the experiences of many of our students who grew up in
suburban and rural communities. I feel bad that not everyone
is as sensitive as they should be. I think we should begin
counseling by talking about your recent conflicts and what it
means to you to be an African American student at a predominantly White university.

Exploring race is not easy. As Jones (1979) observes, minority clients
may try to test therapists. They may be wary of counselors in general and
want assurances that they will be accepted. Once again, counselors must
create a supportive environment. By giving support, counselors can demonstrate that it is safe for minority clients to be vulnerable with concerned
counselors of other races. Such positive experiences also may help minority clients overcome the tendency to generalize racism to all White people
(Ridley, 1984).

Third, when it is appropriate, counselors should share some of their
own feelings with their minority clients. As Egan (2002) points out, counselor self-disclosure has several benefits: It can serve as a form of modeling,
it can help to create intimacy between counselor and client, and it can send an
indirect message to the client that he or she, too, can self-disclose. Counselors
should not overburden clients with their own anxieties, but they should allow
clients to see that they too are vulnerable. Consider the following counselor
self-disclosure:

Counselor: I sense that talking about this issue might be difficult for you.
I want you to know it is not really comfortable for me to talk
about race either. This is a sensitive topic, and I don't want
to be misinterpreted. It is important, though, that we get
these issues out into the open. If we avoid talking about race
just because it is uncomfortable, we might not accomplish
our goals.

This type of counselor self-disclosure is crucial, but counselors should
be aware that sensitivity is required in such circumstances. Consider the
following example of an insensitive counselor self-disclosure in the context
of the clinical treatment of a nondisclosing African American client: "When
I was in elementary school, one of my best friends was an African American
boy named Ralph." In contrast, sensitive disclosures are authentic and reflect
interest in the client's concerns; for example, "I was unemployed for six
months after I finished my Ph.D.; I just couldn't find a job" (Ridley, 1984,

p. 1241). Sensitive counselor self-disclosures help create a climate of trust and often encourage minority clients to share their feelings, whereas insensitive disclosures can promote mistrust and shut down communication.

Obtaining a Counseling Agreement

Cavanagh (1982) suggests that counselors and clients must reach agreement in four areas: the practical aspects of counseling, roles, expectations, and goals. The practical aspects of counseling include the frequency of sessions, the length of sessions, policies regarding cancellations and missed appointments, and billing procedures. Roles include such issues as whether a counselor adopts a more directive or reflective counseling style and how much the client should focus on the past versus the present. Expectations include areas such as honesty, commitment, and effort to reach counseling goals; the priority placed on counseling; and doing homework assignments. Goals—as I discuss in this chapter—should be specific, measurable, realistic, attainable, and capable of being owned by the client.

The importance of counselor and client agreement in all of these areas becomes clear when one considers how the lack of structure in counseling tends to affect minority clients. As Sue and Sue (1972) point out, the counseling situation is intentionally ambiguous. The counselor listens empathically and responds only to encourage the client to talk more. Research has shown, however, that racial/ethnic minority clients frequently find this lack of structure confusing, frustrating, and even threatening (Haettenschwiller, 1971). Preferences for a directive counseling style over a nondirective style have been found among Asian American college students (Atkinson, Maruyama, & Matsui, 1978), Japanese American young adults (Atkinson & Matsushita, 1991), Native American high school students (Dauphinais, Dauphinais, & Rowe, 1981), Mexican American community college students (Ponce & Atkinson, 1989), and African American students (Peoples & Dell, 1975). Research with Southeast Asian refugees has shown the importance of clarifying treatment expectations with clients from this population (Gong-Guy, Cravens, & Patterson, 1991). Southeast Asians often associate mental health treatment with severe psychopathology that requires permanent institutionalization. Thus they tend to shun treatment or use it only after traditional healing regimens and medicines have failed. When they do come to counseling, they may expect to receive medication on the first visit and interpret the need for repeated visits as a sign of ineffective treatment.

Clearly, misunderstandings between counselors and clients about the style of counseling can hinder clients' progress. Counselors therefore must be vigilant in clarifying issues concerning roles and expectations with minority clients. I have found it helpful to begin each new counseling relationship with a *structuring introduction.* In many ways, this discussion sets the tone for therapy. In this introduction, I cover a number of topics, including my philosophy of healing and change, my orientation to counseling, legal and ethical considerations, and practical aspects of counseling. I invite the client to share his or her goals and expectations, and I also encourage the client to ask me for clarification of anything I've said. Finally, with a minority client, I try to find out how the client's cultural expectations match up with my usual counseling procedures. I have found that many clients appreciate my attempts to collaborate with them and take the mystery out of counseling.

The Case of Nor Shala

The following is an actual case illustration presented in the words of the client. The difficulties that Nor Shala (a pseudonym) experienced in an intake interview illustrate why it is important for counselors to attend to the three process goals discussed above: establishing a working alliance, resolving racial dynamics, and obtaining a counseling agreement.

> Somewhere in the first week of this semester, I decided to see a counselor at the health center. So, I called them and told them that I preferred a woman counselor. I was very apprehensive because I have never seen a counselor before in my whole life. Nevertheless, I gave myself a try because I was desperate to see someone who could help me with my problem.
>
> At the counseling center, a lady counselor somewhere in her late 30s introduced herself to me and brought me to her room. Before that, I had filled in a form asking information about my general background. In the room, the lady counselor asked me to sit in a chair while she was busy reading the form that I had just filled in. Then she asked me, "What is your problem and why are you here?" The minute I opened my mouth, she quickly wrote down something with her face facing downward but not at me. I thought she was not yet ready to listen to me, so I stopped talking. But, while holding her pen and looking downward at her paper, she told me to go on. I personally feel weird talking to someone who doesn't even look at my face. I feel like I am talking to the wall.
>
> I did not know where to start my story or what I should talk about in order for her to understand me. So, many times after talking to her for a few sentences, I stopped. The counselor did not ask for clarification of certain points or even indicate to me if she understood what I was saying. When I stopped, she asked me to go on. While writing down everything, she'd say, "Go on. I am taking down what you are saying so that I can figure out things here." I was hoping that she would stop writing and try to reword what I said and then give me her interpretations of what my problem is.
>
> Toward the end, she said, "I understand your problem. I know it is very stressful on your part. But, I don't know much about Muslim culture.

Just in the last two weeks, I read a short paragraph about Islam." At that point, I was feeling very ambiguous. She was not focusing specifically on my problem, which has nothing to do with me being a Muslim. I was telling her about the differences in the background between me and my husband. Although we are both Malaysian, I graduated from a university in the United States, but my husband graduated from a Malaysian university. So we hardly communicate with each other because of the different meanings/interpretations that we have on some issues that we discussed.

She told me to come again because she needed to hear more before she could figure out what is my problem. While she was telling me that, her eyes kept looking back and forth at the clock hanging on the wall behind my back. Her behavior prompted me to ask her this question, "How long should this session take?" Then, she quickly answered me, "Oh, it's 15 minutes." At that point, I realized that I had taken about 17 minutes. I apologized to her because I did not know. When I talked to my classmates in the multicultural counseling class, they told me it was only an intake session. I asked them, "What is an intake session?" Only then did I understand why the lady did not say much to me. My suggestion would be that she should have told me from the very beginning that this is only an intake session and that she needed to write down some of the information that I told her. In addition, she should have told me how long this session should take rather than "hinting" to me that the time was over. I felt embarrassed about the "time" incident. I feel no sense of sincerity on her part. To me, what was more important to her was time and the procedure rather than the content of the problem. I would suggest that she focus on my problem, not myself as a Muslim woman. In addition, she did not even realize that I am Asian. I also hoped she would comfort me by telling me in her words what my problem is and by convincing me that I need to talk more in a longer session in the future so that she can help me sort out my problem. There are a lot of technical problems here.

I will never go back to the counselor again because of my feeling of distrust in the counseling process. Actually, if someone really knew how to show that she is concerned, I think Asians would appreciate that. In my culture, we really appreciate someone who is willing to listen and help us. That person will be perceived like "part of us."

Outcome Goals

Three outcome goals should be of particular interest to counselors who work with minority clients: resolution of memories of racial victimization, bicultural competence, and antiracism assertion.

Resolution of Memories of Racial Victimization

Racial victimization leaves minorities with invisible wounds. Although invisible, such wounds are testimony to actual trauma. Steele (1990) considers the memory of racial victimization to be a particularly powerful wound:

I think one of the heaviest weights that oppression leaves on the shoulders of its former victims is simply the memory of itself. This memory is a weight because it pulls the oppression forward, out of history and into the present, so that the former victim may see his world as much through the memory of his oppression as through his experience in the present. (p. 150)

As Steele notes, unresolved memories of victimization have several debilitating effects. First, they cause victims to distort reality, sometimes with gross exaggeration. Victims of racism have a propensity to attribute any problems they have to racism. In this state of denial, even the most remote cue may trigger feelings of victimization "by connecting events in the present to emotionally powerful memories of the enemy" (pp. 153–154). For example, if a member of a minority group experiences conflict with an employer, he or she may automatically connect it to racism based on the past actions of a racist. The present conflict, however, may not have anything to do with racism.

Second, unresolved memories of victimization lead to reenactment of the victim role. Shackled by self-doubt, fear, and helplessness, many minorities forgo chances to exploit their potential and opportunities because they are reenacting their past victimization. The secondary gains these individuals realize from such reenactment include avoidance of the consequences of relinquishing the victim role. The fear of confronting racism head-on, the threat of discovering one's true abilities in a free but competitive society, the scorn of other minorities who choose to forsake their freedom—these and many other avoided consequences are the real benefits of remaining in the racial victim role.

Third, unresolved memories of victimization result in the denial of personal responsibility. Steele (1990), who focuses specifically on African Americans, offers this insight:

But most of all they reinforce the collectivism of inversion by always showing black problems as resulting from an oppression that can only be resisted by collective action. And here is where the distinction between societal change and racial development is lost, where the individual is subsumed by the collective. . . . The price blacks pay for inversion, for placing too much of the blame for our problems on society, is helplessness before those problems. (p. 163)

Counselors must intervene skillfully to help minority clients resolve issues of racial victimization. Such interventions should flow logically from the dynamics of the clients' problems. One therapeutic strategy is to challenge the minority client's distortions of reality directly. For example:

Counselor: I've noticed that every time you bring up a new problem— whether it's your academic studies, your part-time job in the

> bookstore, or intramural basketball—you end up saying that your failures are due to the racist system. I do not want to make light of your feelings or the real injustices that exist on campus, but is it possible that your constant focus on racism actually distracts from some deep feelings you have about being an ethnic minority?

By confronting the client in this way, the counselor tries to ascertain how much the client exaggerates racism as a problem. The counselor wants to find out whether the client has a legitimate complaint or unresolved racial conflicts manifested in blaming the system. In using this strategy, the counselor must be sensitive to the client's experience of racism and its meanings for the client.

With some minority clients, the problem is more complex, involving a confluence of the clients' reactions to real racism and their unresolved feelings about racial victimization. The clinical picture is complicated by a mixture of a healthy reaction to racism and a skillful use of attributions of racism as a defense mechanism. The therapist must balance support for that portion of the client's experience that truly results from racial victimization with confrontation of the portion that results from unresolved memory. Here is an example of a counselor's attempt to sort out the nuances of racial meaning for one client:

Counselor: As I listen to you, I'm wondering if there might be two problems. One is that there are some instances in which you really do get the brunt of other people's racial insensitivity. Some of your experiences don't seem like they would happen except for the fact that you are African American. The other problem is that you tend to see many of your difficulties through the eyes of memory. What I mean is that because you really have been hurt, you may think racism is always the source of your problems. Is it possible that both of these are true?

Another therapeutic strategy a counselor might use is to challenge the minority client's racial victim role directly. The counselor must show the client that the victim role is self-fulfilling. As long as the client clings to secondary gains, he or she will do nothing to relinquish the racial victim role. Such a client may inadvertently provoke defensive responses from people the client fears as being racist. To initiate a challenge to the client's victim role, the counselor might say something like the following:

Counselor: There is a certain amount of comfort in being a victim. It connects you to all other members of your race who are victims. And I know that is important. But what are the risks for you choosing not to be a victim anymore? It might test your real ability to succeed in college without blaming every problem on racism.

Yet another strategy is to encourage the client to accept individual responsibility. Once disarmed of defensiveness and the racial victim role, minority clients are free to take full advantage of their opportunities and move beyond helplessness. Counselors should do everything possible to equip these clients with problem-solving skills. Here is an example of a counselor's challenge:

Counselor: No one said it is going to be easy. Of course, you may encounter some racism on campus, and, of course, you are going to have to work hard. But let's try to examine your strengths and weaknesses, and let's see how you can make the best use of the resources on campus. You are the only one who can pursue your own goals.

Bicultural Competence

Most members of minority groups in the United States are continually faced with the conflicting values and demands of two worlds: their own communities and the dominant White society. Their interactions are not limited to people of their own races or cultures. Many of their activities, such as work, schooling, recreation, and personal business, take them outside their minority communities and require numerous transactions across cultures. Therefore, an important outcome goal for minority clients is to learn to function effectively in both the majority society and their own minority communities. As Phinney, Lochner, and Murphy (1990) explain, to function well in U.S. society, minorities must assert their own ethnic values and traditions without rejecting those of the majority. They must revitalize and strengthen aspects of their own cultures that have been devalued by the majority. The ongoing challenge of negotiating two worlds can be illustrated as follows:

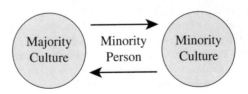

Minorities pay handsome psychological dues in attempting to balance two worlds. The experience can lead to considerable stress, tension, and frustration. These reactions can be especially severe among minority students who attend predominantly White schools (Mabry, 1988; Rousseve, 1987) and among immigrant families in which traditional parents clash with acculturating adolescents (Arax, 1987; Szapocznik & Kurtines, 1980). Phinney et al. (1990) describe several strategies that minorities use to cope with life in two worlds:

- *Alienation/marginalization:* "Individuals accept the negative self-image presented by society, become alienated from their own culture, and do not adopt the majority culture" (p. 57).
- *Assimilation:* "Individuals attempt to become part of the dominant culture and do not maintain their ties with their ethnic culture" (p. 59).
- *Withdrawal or separation:* "Individuals emphasize their ethnic culture and withdraw from contact with the dominant group" (p. 60).

Each of these responses has negative mental health implications.

Phinney et al. (1990) also describe a healthier response, biculturalism: "Individuals retain their ethnic culture and adapt to the dominant culture by learning the necessary skills" (p. 61). De Anda (1984) defines bicultural competence as the ability to understand and step in and out of two different cultural environments. The individual achieves such competence by adjusting to the norms of each culture as a means of attaining his or her objectives. W. E. B. Du Bois (1903/1969) explains this manner of adjustment among African Americans:

It is a peculiar sensation, this double consciousness, this sense of always looking at one's self through the eyes of others, of measuring one's soul by the tape of a world that looks on with amused contempt and pity. One ever feels two-ness—an American, a Negro; two souls, two thoughts, two unreconciled strivings; two warring ideals in one dark body, whose dogged strength alone keeps it from being torn asunder. (p. 45)

Beverly (1989) discusses the relevance of dual consciousness to clinical treatment:

One such technique is the use of dual consciousness, a concept that suggests that black clients must be able to navigate, orchestrate, and negotiate life in two worlds—one black and one white—and that success depends upon one's ability to function effectively in both. Black Americans have been forced to assess their social reality according to their primary point of reference—the black community and a broader reference—European-American culture. The two cultures rarely, if ever, merge; thus the competing and often contradictory imperatives of the two cultures create the

Table 8.1   Traditional Afrocentric and Eurocentric Values

Basic Values	Afrocentric	Eurocentric
Time	Present/here and now	Future
Worldviews	Systemic, holistic	Linear
	Spiritual	Materialistic
	Group/community	Individualistic
	Harmony	Master
Identity	Self and community	Self
Acquisition of knowledge	Gained through introspection and faith	Known by measuring
Transmission of knowledge	Oral expression	Ichnographic

SOURCE: Anderson, L. P. (1991). Acculturative stress: A theory of relevance to Black Americans. *Clinical Psychology Review, 11*(6), 685–702. Copyright © 1991. Reprinted with kind permission from Elsevier Science Ltd., The Boulevard, Langford Lane, Kidlington, OX5 1GB, UK.

need for dual consciousness. For the practitioner, dual consciousness means that all communications must be delivered and received at two levels—the inner reality of being black and the outer reality of living in a society in which being black interferes with opportunities for creative development, transcendence, and redemption. (p. 374)

To understand the challenge of bicultural competence more fully, it is useful to consider the inherent conflict between traditional Afrocentric values and Eurocentric values (see Table 8.1). Of course, not every African American is deeply Afrocentric, and not every White American is deeply Eurocentric. Nevertheless, most African Americans and other minorities regularly confront Eurocentric values. Whites do not face a similar need to negotiate minority cultures in order to survive.

Bicultural competence is necessary to the adjustment and survival of most minority group members in the United States. Although it often is stressful to negotiate life between two worlds, striking a successful balance has many benefits. In a study of Cuban immigrants, for example, Szapocznik, Scopetta, Arnalde, and Kurtines (1978) found that those who could negotiate both the Cuban community and the mainstream American culture had the best psychological adjustment. Biculturally competent children have been found to demonstrate greater role flexibility and creativity, have higher self-esteem, show greater understanding, and have higher achievement levels than others (Ho, 1992; Ramirez, 1983).

To focus on the topic of bicultural competence with a minority client, a counselor might begin this way:

Counselor: Your life takes on many dimensions, some of which are quite different from each other. You relate to your Latino family and friends in your community. You also work in a predominantly White office downtown. We need to explore how you can be successful in both places without sacrificing one for the other.

Obviously, minority clients vary considerably in their biculturality. Counselors should help each client determine what kind of change and how much change is needed in this area. Once clients realize the benefits of improved bicultural competence, they are likely to integrate it into their lives. LaFromboise, Coleman, and Gerton (1993) describe six skills of the biculturally competent person: (a) knowledge of cultural beliefs and values, (b) positive attitudes toward both majority and minority groups, (c) bicultural efficacy, (d) communication ability, (e) role repertoire, and (f) a sense of being grounded. Counselors who are attempting to facilitate bicultural competence among minority clients will find LaFromboise et al.'s discussion of these six skills invaluable.

Antiracism Assertion

Most minority group members encounter racism in one form or another at some time in their lives. Some deal with incidents of racism assertively, whereas others do not react overtly at all. Still others react with aggression. An important goal in counseling is to train minority clients in antiracism assertion. *Assertion* here refers to the use of behaviors that protect one's own rights without interfering with the rights of others. Three general classes of behavior fall under the rubric of assertion, or assertiveness: (a) refusals to acquiesce to the requests of others, (b) expressions of opinions and feelings, and (c) expressions of one's own requests (Christoff & Kelly, 1985).

Behaving assertively reduces an individual's anxiety. Assertive people express their feelings and thoughts honestly, make socially appropriate responses, and consider the feelings of others at the same time (Masters & Burish, 1987). Assertion is not the same thing as aggression, which is hostile and coercive and disregards the needs of others.

The following are just a few of the many kinds of situations that present minorities with opportunities to assert themselves against racism:

- When they are expected to play the role of the "model minority"
- When they must perform better than Whites to get recognition and rewards equal to those Whites receive
- When they hear others use racial slurs or make derogatory racial comments
- When they hear others imply that particular minority persons' accomplishments are due to their minority status rather than competence
- When they are excluded from the same access and opportunity that Whites enjoy

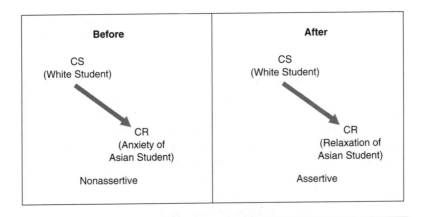

Figure 8.1   Assertiveness Training of an Asian Student

The basic mechanism of change in assertiveness is direct exposure to a threatening stimulus. However, because it is common for people to avoid threatening situations, the possibilities for this kind of change often are limited. Like other classical change procedures, the change to assertiveness rests on the premise that two incompatible responses cannot coexist simultaneously. A person cannot be both anxious and not anxious simultaneously. Thus to overcome their anxiety in racist situations, minority clients must assert themselves by facing racism, standing up for their rights, and refusing to be mistreated.

Consider an Asian American high school student who is teased about her slanted eyes by a White student. A nonassertive response on the part of the Asian student is to say nothing and subsequently avoid the White student as much as possible. The Asian student's anxiety is a conditioned response (CR) to the White student, who acts as a conditioned stimulus (CS). Because the White student is a previously neutral stimulus—one that does not naturally invoke anxiety—the Asian student can learn to overcome her anxiety about the White student. She can do so by asserting herself. She might say something like this: "Your comments are unkind and insensitive. I don't have to accept your ignorance. If this continues, I will report you to the principal." Behaving assertively tends to reduce anxiety because assertion and nonassertion are incompatible responses (see Figure 8.1).

Counselors can use a variety of techniques to facilitate their minority clients' antiracism assertion. They might begin by encouraging these clients to discuss the types of situations in which they have experienced racism and then model assertive responses to such situations. For example:

Counselor: Let me model for you what to say and then you can practice it on me. "I refuse to accept your disrespectful comments anymore. If you cannot appreciate differences in people, then you have a problem. If you don't stop it, I'll report you to the administration."

Next, counselors could employ the technique of behavioral rehearsal, in which clients have the opportunity to practice assertion in the safe context of the counseling setting. Behavioral rehearsal also allows counselors to provide clients with feedback on their assertive behaviors. The ultimate goal is to transfer the assertive behaviors that clients learn in counseling to actual situations in which they experience racism.

Chapter Summary

Counselors improve their clients' chances for success in counseling by setting realistic and attainable goals and collaborating with clients to achieve these goals. This chapter has examined culturally relevant process and outcome goals that are important to both the adjustment of minority clients and the success of therapy. Counselors who work with minority clients should add these goals to the other typical goals in counseling. Counselors, in collaboration with clients, should determine which goals are most appropriate in particular cases. Consistent with the idiographic perspective, the appropriateness of each outcome goal for the individual client is paramount.

9

Making Better Clinical Decisions

To improve the overall quality of their service delivery, counselors must improve their clinical decisions by reducing or eliminating judgmental and inferential errors. Sound clinical judgment and case conceptualization are the hallmarks of effective interventions. In fact, clinical decision making and interventions are inseparable processes. Effective interventions are impossible without sound clinical decisions, and sound decisions are useless if they are not put into practice. The prevalence of racism in counseling and therapy makes the need for sound clinical judgment all the more pronounced.

Counselors cannot improve the quality of their clinical decision making unless they take the responsibility of decision making seriously and employ well-founded decision-making guidelines. This chapter focuses on helping counselors improve their clinical decision-making abilities. The discussion is divided into two major sections, one addressing general decision-making strategies and the other concerned with personal debiasing strategies. Each section includes specific guidelines that counselors and therapists can follow to become more intentional and to expand the range of factors they consider in making clinical decisions.

General Decision-Making Strategies

Counselors can improve the quality of their decisions by employing four general strategies: broadening their views of assessment, particularizing their assessments, using multiple methods of data collection, and interpreting test scores cautiously.

Broadening Views of Assessment

Many counselors have narrow views of assessment, typically limited to psychological testing and diagnosis. Spengler (1992) recommends departing from such narrow views. He defines assessment as "all activities engaged in by the counselor in which the counselor forms an impression or a hypothesis about the client" (p. 4). Assessment is more than hanging a label on a client. It involves developing a comprehensive picture of the client as a unique person.

This broader view of assessment is consistent with the biopsychosocial model of mental health. Counselors must broaden their perspectives on assessment to include a variety of counselor decision-making activities and methods for gathering data about clients. The traditional image of the counselor who administers a test or battery of tests and then painstakingly tries to find the most suitable diagnosis will fall short of this broad perspective if the counselor's efforts lack multiple methods of assessment and cultural considerations. Counselors should be open to exploring any information that will help them better understand their clients and select appropriate treatment strategies.

Particularizing Assessments

When it comes to assessing clients, many clinicians have a tendency to make sweeping generalizations. As Kadushin (1963) notes, intake workers are prone to writing general diagnostic reports. These descriptions often fail to differentiate one patient from another. Along similar lines, Jones and Thorne (1987) assert that subjective experience often is de-emphasized in multicultural assessment. Malgady, Rogler, and Costantino (1987) comment on this problem in the mental health evaluation of Hispanics: "Without an individualized approach to culturally sensitive assessment and diagnosis, the unsuspecting clinician can easily be led down the proverbial well-intentioned pavement of the path to hell—cultural sensitivity is not stereo-typy" (p. 233).

It is essential that clinicians conduct thoughtful and accurate assessment of each individual client. Competent clinicians are not simply concerned about normative data or well-worn clinical clichés. It is too easy, for example, to describe an Asian client as "restrained" or a Hispanic male as "macho." It also is easy to say that a minority client "has blunted affect," "is disoriented to time, person, and place," or "shows inappropriate behavior," or that the "data contraindicate severe psychopathology." Although such statements may be accurate in some cases, they are too nondescript to be useful for meaningful treatment planning with most clients. Clinicians should be interested in the "rediscovery of the subject" in multicultural assessment (Jones & Thorne, 1987).

Contextualizing Assessments

Although assessment focuses on gaining an idiographic understanding of the client, clinicians must remember that behavior always exists in some context. The contextual view purports that behavior can be understood only within its context. Szapocznik and Kurtines (1993) have extended the concept of contextualism based on their work with Hispanic youth and families. Their model embraces the notion of embeddedness; that is, the individual is seen as embedded within the context of the family, which is embedded within the context of the culture. Moreover, cultural contexts are diverse and complex, requiring individuals to develop bicultural competence. Szapocznik and Kurtines's model provides an excellent way for counselors to understand the complexity of the cultural demands that minority clients face.

Using Multiple Methods of Data Collection

Because clinical assessment is fraught with pitfalls, clinicians should use a variety of assessment methods. In this way, the advantages of one method can compensate for the disadvantages of others. Of course, counselors must exercise some discretion in choosing among available assessment procedures.

In his extensive discussion of multicultural assessment, Dana (1993) divides assessment methods into two categories: those that concentrate intensively on the individual and those that compare examinees to others. Among the former kinds of methods are (a) behavior observations; (b) life histories, case studies, and interviews; (c) accounts; (d) life events; (e) picture-story techniques and tests; (f) inkblot techniques and tests; and (g) miscellaneous methods such as word associations, sentence completions, and drawings. Methods that compare examinees to others include (a) broad-spectrum and single-construct psychopathology measures, (b) personality measures, and (c) major tests of intelligence and cognitive functions. Dana provides examples of the various methods with specific application to minority populations.

A detailed discussion of assessment procedures is beyond the scope of this book, but I do want to make several brief suggestions here regarding multicultural assessment. First, clinicians should become familiar with the strengths and weaknesses of various assessment methods so they can make informed decisions about which methods to use. Second, clinicians should be committed to integrating the data from various sources of information to create a carefully constructed picture of each client. Third, clinicians should remember that each assessment method can provide only a limited amount of information; no single procedure is adequate for obtaining a comprehensive idiographic perspective on any given client. (For more thorough discussions of assessment procedures in general, see Dana, 1993; Jones & Thorne, 1987; Westermeyer, 1987.)

Interpreting Test Scores Cautiously

Test scores indicate *how well* individuals perform at the time of testing, but they do not indicate *why* they perform as they do (Anastasi, 1992). Consequently, test scores yield imprecise information about examinees. The imprecision increases when the examinees are members of ethnic and racial minority groups. For example, the average performance scores of minorities on intellectual abilities tests can differ by as much as a standard deviation below those of Whites (Helms, 1992).

There is always a danger that counselors will misinterpret test scores, and counselors must recognize the bias against minorities that is inherent in many psychological test instruments. The question then is, How should counselors interpret test data without biasing their interpretations against minorities?

Counselors first must understand several concepts related to testing and measurement. Every test designed to measure an attribute or trait comprises three elements:

X = the score on the attribute or trait obtained by the examinee

T = the "true" or actual amount of the attribute or trait possessed by the examinee

E = the amount of random error involved in the testing

As Kaplan and Saccuzzo (1993) explain, classical test theory assumes that every examinee has a true score that he or she would obtain if there were no errors in measurement. Because tests are imperfect, however, the examinee's observed score may differ from his or her true ability or characteristic. This difference between true score and observed score results from measurement error. Therefore, an examinee's obtained score (X) can be considered a combination of "truth" (T) and error (E). The more reliable a test, the more the obtained score reflects truth. The less reliable a test, the more the obtained score reflects error. The following equation depicts the relationship among the three elements:

$$X = T + E$$

Many counselors mistakenly use tests as though the tests were free of error, and this mistake leads to misinterpretation. Counselors often interpret test scores as though they perfectly represent the actual amounts of particular attributes possessed by examinees. They mistakenly base their conclusion on the following implicit formula:

$$X = T$$

To understand more clearly why X does *not* equal T, consider this illustration. Suppose a young man weighs himself on a scale. He is completely disrobed except for a pair of cowboy boots and shorts. He is not wearing his contact lenses, so his visual acuity is off. In addition, a spring in the scale's inner mechanism has lost some of its tension. The young man reads his weight on the scale and concludes that he weighs 173 pounds. However, this is a misinterpretation. His real weight is 165 pounds. The young man has not accounted for the extra weight of his cowboy boots or other possible sources of error, such as his visual deficiency and the reduced tension in the scale's spring.

Paper-and-pencil tests are subject to more sources of error than is a mechanical scale. By definition, an error is any trait or condition that is irrelevant to the purpose of testing and produces inconsistencies in measurement. A number of scholars have addressed the special sources of error that exist when examinees are ethnic minorities (Dana, 1993; Helms, 1992; Reynolds & Brown, 1984; Samuda, 1975). After counselors have accepted the imprecision of test scores, they are ready to interpret test results with appropriate caution. They should apply such caution to every general decision-making strategy they use.

Case Example

Jon Hawkeye is a 13-year-old Navajo. He travels to and from school 45 minutes each day because he lives on a remote part of the reservation. He has been learning to speak English for the past 5 years in school, but he speaks his tribal language when he returns home.

Jon's school district administers a testing program to place students in "appropriate" learning environments. One day, Jon took the WISC first thing in the morning, just after he arrived at school. He was sleepy when he took the test because he must wake up every morning at 6:00 to get ready in time to walk half a mile to catch the school bus. He was unfamiliar with some of the words on the test because he never hears them spoken in his area of the reservation. Also, he was frustrated by the objective approach to testing. He is used to an oral tradition that conveys information through storytelling.

Jon scored 88 on the test; an average score is considered to fall between 90 and 109. School counselors who look only at Jon's test score might conclude that he is low average or borderline in intelligence, whereas counselors who consider the potential sources of error in testing might arrive at a different interpretation. Given the bias inherent in testing and Jon's circumstances, it is possible that Jon is average or above average in intelligence. Counselors should familiarize themselves with testing concepts such as standard error of measurement and standard error of estimate so they can make well-informed interpretations of test scores.

Personal Debiasing Strategies

Counselors can reduce their chances of making judgmental and inferential errors by using four debiasing strategies: investigating alternative explanations for client behavior, considering probability and base-rate data, using both confirmatory and disconfirmatory hypothesis-testing strategies, and delaying decision making.

Investigating Alternative Explanations for Client Behavior

Counselors often get stuck on particular explanations for various client behaviors and fail to consider alternative explanations. They should realize, however, that they can improve their chances of arriving at correct explanations for behavior by examining more of the possible influences on their clients.

For example, Gold and Pearsall (1983) show the importance of ruling out hypothyroidism as a factor in depression, given that hypothyroidism has been found to be etiologically significant in approximately 15% of cases of major depression. The latest edition of the *Diagnostic and Statistical Manual of Mental Disorders* (*DSM-IV-TR*) requires clinicians to rule out organic factors before making a diagnosis of major depression (American Psychiatric Association, 2000). Counselors who do not rule out organic reasons for behaviors risk misdiagnosing their clients. Spengler, Strohmer, Dorau, and Gard (1994) observe that counseling and clinical psychologists rarely test a thyroid hypothesis in cases involving depression. They tend to overlook the condition even when there are clear symptoms suggesting hypothyroidism.

Counselors often overlook alternative explanations for the behavior of minority clients, even though such clients' experiences as victims of racism can influence their behavior significantly. When working with minority clients, counselors routinely should investigate a host of possible etiological factors. Racism, dietary deficiencies, socioeconomic conditions, health care, educational conditions, vocational and career opportunities, and social support are some of the areas counselors should investigate.

Research has shown that African American children are more likely than children in any other group to be mislabeled as learning disabled or emotionally handicapped (Committee for Economic Development, 1987; Reed, 1988; Rivers, Henderson, Jones, Ladner, & Williams, 1975). Thus school systems are more likely to place African American children inappropriately in special education or nonacademic tracks than they are to misplace White children in such tracks. Professionals should know, however, that the majority of cases of mental retardation fall within the mild range and can be attributed to environmental factors. As Goldstein, Baker, and Jamison (1986) report, such factors include impoverished living conditions, poor health care, and lack of cognitive stimulation. Professionals who rely primarily on heredity-based explanations of intellectual development not only overlook important etiological factors but also fail to provide the most appropriate educational and psychological interventions.

Considering Probability and Base-Rate Data

The base rate of a given characteristic or feature is the proportion of individuals from an identified population who share that characteristic or feature. Unless counselors are aware of the base-rate data for the characteristics they want to measure in their clients, they may make inappropriate decisions. If counselors are familiar with the relevant base-rate data, however, they can integrate this information into their decision making. Consider these base rates, which are derived from epidemiological research: 1 out of 4 women and 1 out of 8 to 10 men were sexually abused during childhood (Finkelhor, 1984).

Base rates increase in certain diagnostic disorders. For example, Bemporad, Smith, Hanson, and Cicchetti (1982) report that the rate of childhood trauma may rise as high as 85% in individuals diagnosed with borderline personality disorder. According to Schonbachler and Spengler (1992), either clinicians are unaware of these higher base rates of childhood trauma or they eclipse the presence of sexual trauma with the more salient borderline profile.

To avoid misdiagnosing minority clients, counselors must consider base-rate data. For example, stress is regarded as a causal factor in the declining health and emotional well-being of many African Americans. According to Kessler (1979) and Mueller, Edwards, and Yarvis (1977), African Americans experience undesirable events more often than do Whites. In addition, African Americans have been found to require more adjustment than Whites to life-changing events such as employment, family, and economic problems, as well as the death of a friend (Komoroff, Masuda, & Holmes, 1968; Wyatt, 1977).

African Americans in general, and African American males in particular, have the highest reported incidence of severe forms of psychopathology and personality disorders in the United States (U.S. Department of Health and Human Services, 1986). Professionals who diagnose psychopathology among African Americans undoubtedly fail to factor in the high levels of stress in this population compared with other groups. Furthermore, many are unfamiliar with the added burden of acculturative stress evoked by the confrontation between Afrocentric values and Eurocentric values (Anderson, 1991). (To review the contrast between Afrocentric and Eurocentric values, see Table 8.1 in Chapter 8.) This observation is not to suggest that psychopathology does not exist among African Americans—of course it does. These findings suggest, however, that African Americans' higher probability of being misdiagnosed as psychopathological than members of other groups is in part related to their higher stress levels.

Using Confirmatory and
Disconfirmatory Hypothesis-Testing Strategies

Counselors need to maximize their likelihood of making true positive and true negative decisions and, at the same time, minimize their chances of making false positive and false negative decisions. To accomplish this task, counselors must employ both confirmatory and disconfirmatory hypothesis-testing strategies.

Confirmatory strategies are aimed at confirming or validating an initial hypothesis. If a counselor believes an adolescent client has a conduct disorder, for example, the counselor might place the adolescent in a situation with social rules to test the hypothesis. The counselor might give the client assignments to complete between counseling sessions, help the client's family structure rules for the client's conduct at home, and consult with the client's teachers on their expectations. If the adolescent responds to these interventions with noncompliance and rebelliousness, this behavior may confirm the hypothesis.

Disconfirmatory strategies, in contrast, are strategies aimed at disconfirming or invalidating an initial hypothesis. As Faust (1986) has observed:

> Clinicians would often do much better if they tried actively to disconfirm hypotheses rather than to support them. If one can find strong evidence that one's hypothesis is wrong, which may not be found unless one looks for it, one has a better chance of uncovering the right conclusion. (p. 427)

Consider the same adolescent hypothesized to have a conduct disorder. To attempt to disconfirm this hypothesis, the counselor might apply the diagnostic criteria for conduct disorders in the *DSM-IV-TR*. The counselor could investigate whether the client has shown a repetitive and persistent pattern of aggressive conduct or violating the rights of others, or whether the client's behaviors include a major violation of age-appropriate societal norms or rules (American Psychiatric Association, 2000). Specific *DSM-IV-TR* criteria for a diagnosis of a conduct disorder include the presence of at least three of the following: aggression toward people and animals, destruction of property, deceitfulness or theft, and serious violations of rules. If this adolescent client's behavior fails to meet one or more of these exclusionary criteria, the counselor has a strong basis for concluding that the conduct disorder hypothesis is disconfirmed.

Morrow and Deidan (1992) agree that counselors should ask both confirming and disconfirming questions of their hypotheses and diagnoses. They also suggest that counselors can further clarify their assumptions and biases by remaining open to information that seems to contradict their initial impressions, by generating reasons why their hypotheses may be wrong, and by writing down their impressions to make them explicit.

Competent counselors try to disconfirm their hypotheses as well as to confirm them. They recognize the complex nature of clinical decisions. They also recognize that taking a balanced approach to decision making minimizes their chances of making false positive and false negative decisions.

Delaying Decision Making

Counselors are continually engaged in complex decision-making processes. As they form the decisions that affect clients' lives, they must maintain decision uncertainty. That is, they need to allow themselves a period of uncertainty before they finalize their decisions.

Counselors should follow a series of steps in reaching their decisions. First, they should form tentative hypotheses. This is a natural step—everyone forms initial hypotheses, or first impressions, as they enter new situations. Counselors should begin to formulate hypotheses early in the counseling process with new clients. They should recognize, however, that hypotheses are just that—guesses based on perceptions and preliminary statements, not facts. Problems arise when counselors relate to clients as though their initial hypotheses about the clients are completely accurate. Sometimes these hypotheses are accurate, but often they are not. Counselors should remember that their hypotheses about clients are only speculative until they can gather more information to test them.

Second, counselors should take their time in making appropriate decisions, delaying arriving at any final judgments about clients until after they have gathered all the necessary information. Although decision making in counseling is unavoidable, counselors should minimize premature decision making. They should deliberately postpone finalizing important decisions until they have gathered as much information as they need. For example, a counselor might wait until the third counseling session to make a diagnosis.

Finally, counselors should be careful not to invest too much confidence in any given decision. They should realize that clinical data may be interpreted in more than one way. As Faust (1986) notes, few predictive judgments justify extreme confidence. For example, two different counselors can interpret the same clinical data on a minority client in completely different ways, with one concluding that the client is clinically paranoid and the other concluding that the client, as a victim of racism, is skillfully using racial issues as a defense mechanism. A more accurate interpretation of these same data might be that the client's pathology and racial victimization are mutually reinforcing. Only a competent counselor who forms tentative hypotheses, delays decision making until all the evidence is in, and allows for the possibility that his or her decisions may not always be accurate will arrive eventually at this conclusion.

Chapter Summary

Counselors must make numerous decisions. This chapter has described some general and personal debiasing strategies that counselors can employ to improve their decision making. Counselors should broaden their views of assessment, particularize their assessments, contextualize their assessments, use multiple methods of data collection, and interpret test scores cautiously. Counselors can reduce the effects of their personal biases on their decision making by investigating alternative explanations for client behavior, taking probability and base-rate data into consideration, using confirmatory and disconfirmatory hypothesis-testing strategies, and delaying decision making. By following these guidelines, counselors can make fewer judgmental errors about minority clients and improve their decisions about treatment planning.

10

Managing Resistance

An Asian American couple who had serious marital problems once came to me for counseling. The wife was a second-generation Chinese American, whereas the husband had a mixed European and Chinese heritage. During our sessions, the husband made it extremely difficult for us to work together, compounding an already tense situation. He was loud, sarcastic, and intimidating. When questioned about his role in the couple's marital problems, he shifted the blame to his wife. He accused her of holding on to traditional Chinese values, tried to cut her off when she expressed her feelings, and made excuses for his own shortcomings.

The husband in this case was a resistant client—that is, a client who interfered with progress in counseling. Client resistance very well could be the most challenging aspect of counseling. As Cavanagh (1982) notes, it is also quite common:

> Only the most naive counselor would think that being in counseling is an obvious sign that a person is dedicated to change. In reality, most people in counseling have ambivalent feelings toward change, and some people have a vested interest in not changing. Because resistance in counseling is common, it is important for counselors and people in counseling to understand the causes and signs of resistance. This knowledge paves the way for appropriate responses. (p. 240)

Managing minority clients' resistance is a special challenge for counselors, particularly when they and their clients are not of the same race; in these cases, counselors must work through the special dynamics related to racial issues in addition to the usual dynamics of resistance. Successful resistance management depends primarily on the counselor's ability to

(a) conceptualize resistance and (b) employ resistance management strategies skillfully. In this chapter, I first define resistance and then present a typology for classifying client behavior as resistant or nonresistant. Finally, I offer some specific strategies that counselors can use to manage client resistance.

Understanding Resistance

Helping clients to change poses an inherent dilemma for most counselors: They must determine whether or not their clients' reactions in counseling serve the clients' best interests. Not all of a client's change-opposing behavior is resistance, and not all of a client's change-promoting behavior is therapeutic. As a counseling psychologist, I define resistance based on my extensive experience in counseling clients of many backgrounds: *Resistance is countertherapeutic behavior. Resistant behavior is directed toward one goal: the indiscriminate avoidance of the painful requirements of change.* I discuss briefly below six principles that can be gleaned from this definition.

Principle 1: Resistance is reflected in behavior. Like racism, resistance is human motor activity. It can be observed, repeated, and measured. Resistance is not an attitude or a psychological state of the client, although resistant attitudes and psychological states are powerful motivators of client behavior. Although a counselor might infer from a client's behavior that the client is resistant in attitude, only the client's behavior is actual resistance. Therefore, strategies for managing resistance must aim at behavior first and attitudes second.

Principle 2: Resistance is countertherapeutic. In one way or another, resistance interferes with counseling. Resistance may slow down counseling, undermine the process, cause premature termination, or set the client up for self-defeat. Whatever form resistance takes, the client always loses. The ultimate effects of resistance depend on the degree and type of resistance and how the counselor manages the resistance.

Principle 3: Resistance is goal directed. Resistance is the client's attempt to avoid the painful requirements of change. Counseling can be traumatic, much like radical surgery. The client's avoidance of pain may be explained in terms of costs and benefits. The client may feel that changing is more costly than not changing; that is, the client may feel that the pain of changing outweighs the pain of remaining in an unhealthy state. Change can be very scary because of the uncertainty it inevitably creates.

Principle 4: Resistance typically involves indiscriminate avoidance of pain. In many cases, clients do not evaluate the merits of different kinds of pain.

They avoid any type of pain, whether it is the necessary pain related to therapy or unnecessary pain without therapeutic value. They may feel the pain of change so intensely that their first and only reaction is to avoid it. But their avoidance comes at a high price: forfeiture of personal growth, healing, and the possibility of having a more fulfilling life.

Principle 5: Resistance can take a variety of forms. Any countertherapeutic behavior, regardless of the shape it takes, is resistance. Different clients may use different types of resistance, and one client may employ several types of resistance. Cavanagh (1982) identifies a number of resistant behaviors, including canceling appointments, showing up late, evading questions, focusing attention on the counselor, controlling the content of the conversations, and placing the counselor in a dilemma.

Principle 6: Resistance may or may not be observed, depending on whether the behavior occurs in public or private. When resistance is private, the counselor is unlikely to know it exists unless he or she is astute enough to discern its effects. Even perceptive counselors find it hard to detect private resistance, as in the case of a client who withholds important information that could affect diagnosis and treatment planning. Counselors must acknowledge that unobserved resistance, like observed resistance, interferes with counseling.

Client Responses in Counseling

In managing resistance, counselors must classify client behavior as either resistance or nonresistance. The typology presented in Figure 10.1 is designed to aid counselors with this classification. The typology has two dimensions: client behaviors in counseling and effects of client behaviors. Each of these dimensions is further divided into two categories. Client behaviors in counseling are either change opposing or change promoting. When clients oppose change, they cling to their old patterns of behavior. When clients promote change, they seek to adopt new patterns of behavior. The effects of client behaviors in counseling are either therapeutic or countertherapeutic. Therapeutic effects on clients enhance their personal functioning; clients begin to face their problems and relate more realistically to the outside world. Nontherapeutic effects on clients hinder their personal functioning; in extreme cases, they lead to serious psychopathology.

The combination of the two categories of client responses and the two effects of client responses yield four possible client response modes: (a) change-opposing behavior contributing to countertherapeutic effects (antagonism), (b) change-promoting behavior contributing to countertherapeutic effects (acquiescence), (c) change-opposing behavior contributing to therapeutic effects (protest), and (d) change-promoting behavior contributing

Manage Resistance

Client Behaviors

		Change Opposing	Change Promoting
	Countertherapeutic	Antagonism (Resistance)	Acquiescence (Resistance)
Effects of Client Behaviors	Therapeutic	Protest (Nonresistance)	Compliance (Nonresistance)

Figure 10.1   Typology for Classifying Client Behavior as Resistant and Nonresistant

to therapeutic effects (compliance). Each of these client response modes occupies a quadrant of the typology. Client behavior in counseling is either therapeutic or countertherapeutic, meaning that it is nonresistance or resistance. Two quadrants of the typology, antagonism and acquiescence, represent resistance. The other two quadrants—protest and compliance—represent nonresistance.

Most counselors think of resistance as behavior found in the first quadrant, antagonism. Antagonistic clients directly oppose counselors' efforts to promote change. They often arrive at premature conclusions about the benefits of counseling, and many of them pay little attention to the merits of counselors' treatment recommendations. Most resistance probably falls into this category. Examples of antagonism are attacking the counselor, rationalizing the problem, pressing for quick and easy solutions, and dropping out of counseling prematurely.

Acquiescence, however, is also a type of resistance. On the surface, acquiescent clients may seem to go along with the counseling, accepting counselors' treatment recommendations uncritically. In actuality, they are uncommitted to change. For example, when asked, an acquiescent client is likely to offer no feedback on the counselor's interpretation of the presenting problem; such a client might say, "I do not question your interpretation. I trust your professional opinion." In reality, the client may have his or her own opinion but is quietly resisting change by refusing to collaborate with the counselor.

Many counselors overlook acquiescence as a form of resistance. Perhaps the word *resistance,* which connotes direct force in common usage, prevents some counselors from understanding relatively passive client responses as resistance. Nevertheless, acquiescence can be as countertherapeutic as more active forms of resistance.

Protest, which occupies the lower left-hand quadrant of the typology, is change-opposing behavior that is therapeutic. At first glance, protest may appear to be similar to antagonism, but there is a major difference between these classes of client behavior: Unlike antagonism, protest involves the client's critical evaluation of the counselor's treatment recommendations. A protesting client is a client who has made a basic commitment to therapeutic change.

Sometimes clients cooperate with counselors in a therapeutic way. This type of client behavior is compliance. Compliant clients participate actively in counseling. They are dedicated to personal change and growth. Although change may be painful, they do not allow the pain to prevent them from complying with their counselors' recommendations.

Although the overt behaviors of the acquiescent client appear to be similar to those of the compliant client, they are actually different in nature. Acquiescent clients are passive, uncritically accepting counselors' proposals for change despite remaining uncommitted to actual change. Compliant clients, on the other hand, participate actively in counseling, own their problems, and accept responsibility for changing. Compliance includes such behaviors as asking clarifying questions, offering the counselor additional insights, following through on homework assignments between sessions, and showing up for appointments punctually and regularly.

Strategies for Managing Resistance

How should counselors handle resistance? They could try to ignore it, but competent mental health professionals know that resistance will not go away automatically. Ironically, unchallenged resistance is self-perpetuating: The behavior is negatively reinforced by its avoidance of the painful demands inherent in change. Counselors can manage resistance, however, by channeling it so it becomes an asset rather than a liability. Below, I discuss six strategies that counselors can use to manage client resistance: avoiding defensive reactions; classifying the client's behavior; confronting the client's contradictions, discrepancies, and inconsistencies; exposing the client's secondary gains; reframing the client's definition of control; and confronting normative resistance.

Avoiding Defensive Reactions

Counselors sometimes may be frightened or intimidated by resistant clients. Several years ago, I supervised a psychology intern who had a very angry client. During one session, the client jumped out of his chair and pounded on the office walls and door. The intern was frightened by the client's behavior, although he was not immediately aware of how deeply the experience affected him. As I listened to tapes of the intern's subsequent sessions with the same client, I noticed that he had changed his counseling style and had become rather passive. He allowed the client to ramble on at length and avoided probing for insights or making other therapeutic demands. When I told the intern what I had observed and asked him about it, he began to realize how much he feared the client.

Counselors who react defensively to resistant clients are often unaware of their defensiveness and their attempts to reduce their own emotional pain. On the contrary, they expend considerable effort unconsciously avoiding their uncomfortable feelings. Because of the unrealistic nature of their responses, defensive counselors cannot help their clients. If anything, their reactions tend to intensify their clients' resistance.

Counselor defensiveness with resistant minority clients can take many forms, including the following:

- The counselor talks excessively about racial issues.
- The counselor avoids discussion of racial issues.
- The counselor's treatment expectations for the client are unnecessarily low.
- The counselor's treatment expectations for the client are unnecessarily high.
- The counselor inappropriately uses expressions and idioms associated with the client's minority group to gain acceptance.
- The counselor emphasizes his or her friendships with other members of the client's race.
- The counselor makes claims of impartiality concerning minorities.
- The counselor overemphasizes his or her support for minority causes.
- The counselor fails to examine his or her reactions to client resistance.
- The counselor fails to channel client resistance so it becomes an asset rather than a liability.

Counselors can overcome defensiveness toward resistant minority clients by anticipating that resistance will occur. Resistance comes in many shapes and forms, and counselors should consider resistance the norm rather than the exception in counseling. Then counselors should alert themselves to their uncomfortable feelings. They should try to differentiate between feelings triggered by the client and those emanating from other sources. Finally, counselors should identify any racial content associated with their feelings. One of the most accurate indicators of racial defensiveness is when counselors try to convince themselves that they are not prejudiced.

Classifying the Client's Behavior

Counselors should classify clients' behavior as either resistance or non-resistance. Successful resistance management depends on the counselor's ability to assess the client's behavior thoroughly and match it to one of the four quadrants of the client behavior typology presented above. In classifying the behavior of a client, a counselor can make one of four possible decisions: He or she can correctly identify behavior as resistance, correctly identify behavior as nonresistance, incorrectly identify behavior as resistance, or incorrectly identify behavior as nonresistance.

One common counselor mistake is classifying acquiescent behavior as compliance. Another is classifying protest as antagonism. Counselors must be careful to avoid these types of errors in judgment. Nonresistant behaviors are a sign of a cooperative counseling relationship, and resistance management is unnecessary with clients who exhibit these behaviors.

If counselors initially identify client behavior as acquiescence or compliance, they must rule out the possibility that they have mistaken one behavior for the other. They should note that compliance involves the client's critical examination of interventions, whereas acquiescence involves passivity and uncritical acceptance of the counselor's suggestions. Counselors should be aware that acquiescence can take the form of lack of feedback, constructive criticism, or suggestions from the client. If a counselor has reexamined a client's apparently cooperative behavior and is still unsure how to classify it, he or she should ask the client directly for feedback on the subject. If the client does not provide any feedback, the counselor may be reasonably sure that the client is acquiescing.

If counselors initially classify client behavior as antagonistic, they must rule out the possibility that the behavior is actually protest. Because the surface behaviors of protest and antagonism may be similar, counselors must distinguish between them by thoroughly examining their own interventions for flaws. Of course, a counselor cannot always be certain that selected interventions are perfectly suited for a particular client. However, the counselor can attempt to ascertain whether client opposition stems from the use of inappropriate interventions or from resistance. To do so, the counselor should ask him- or herself these questions: Do the interventions meet the needs of the client? Do I put too much stock in my preferred theoretical orientation? Does my theoretical orientation have implicit cultural bias? Are my expectations of minority clients realistic? Do I expect the client to change too quickly? By answering these questions, the counselor should be able to determine the meaning of the client's seemingly change-opposing behavior.

If the counselor is satisfied that he or she has classified the client's behavior appropriately and counseling continues to be problematic, the counselor may be facing private antagonism. Such behavior cannot be observed, and the counselor may have no direct evidence of its existence except for the client's lack of progress. In such a case, the counselor should pay particular attention to the client's homework assignments between sessions and work on strengthening the therapeutic alliance.

Confronting the Client's
Contradictions, Discrepancies, and Inconsistencies

Resistant clients send contradictory messages that tend to confuse counselors, who must interpret what clients are actually communicating. For instance, a client may claim that he or she wants to benefit from counseling and yet try to keep the conversation during sessions at a surface level. Against this apparent contradiction, the counselor must somehow determine if the client really is interested in changing.

Interactional counseling is helpful in explaining discrepant behaviors. As Watzlawick, Beavin, and Jackson (1967) explain, communication occurs on two levels: the content level and the relationship level. The content level of communication contains the factual or semantic meaning of a message. The relationship level contains a message about the content message, and it always accompanies the content message. According to Haley (1963), the relationship message classifies and qualifies the content message. It is metacommunication, or communication about communication.

Consider the client who delivers the following content message:

Content message   I'm used to dealing with White people. I talk to
(compliance implied): them at work and school. So it doesn't bother me
                          that you are a White counselor.

Then suppose the client contradicts this content message by sending a different relationship message. When the counselor inquires about intimate details of the client's anxieties, the client consistently skirts the issues and metacommunicates to the counselor:

Relationship   Don't expect me to spill my guts to you. You're
message (resistance): just one more White person who doesn't under-
                          stand the African American experience.

Many counselors do not perceive the incongruence between their clients' content messages and relationship messages. These counselors are, in effect, oblivious to resistance. Before they can effectively confront resistance, they need to listen attentively to their clients' content messages, ferret out the relationship messages, and attempt to determine the degree of congruence between them. A perceptive counselor notices when a resistant client camouflages relationship messages with content messages. The counselor first presses the client to acknowledge that he or she is sending two different messages and then attempts to help the client recognize the inconsistency between the two messages. Finally, the counselor challenges the client to become congruent in communicating subsequent content and relationship messages. The counselor might confront such a client in the following manner:

Counselor: On the one hand, you have strongly emphasized your positive relationships with White people outside of counseling. You imply by your comments that race does not make a difference when it comes to being open with people. However, your behavior seems to tell a different story. Every time I encourage you to talk openly about your struggles, you skirt the issues. I'm wondering if the fact that you are so closed really means you don't trust White people and don't care to talk intimately with a White counselor.

Exposing the Client's Secondary Gains

Some clients are skillful at manipulating counselors, and although such behavior is countertherapeutic, these clients benefit from their actions. Consider the minority client who exploits his or her White counselor's desire for the client's approval by playing games and putting the counselor on the defensive. Given that minorities are victims of racism, it is easy to understand how a minority client might find it exhilarating to exploit the power differential in the counseling relationship. The client's aim in such gaming is to gain a psychological one-up position—a tremendous benefit to a minority client who is usually in a one-down position.

Many counselors are oblivious to this kind of gaming. Others sense that their clients are manipulating them but do not know what to do about it. To counteract this resistance, counselors' best approach is to be alert to signs of manipulation and then directly expose manipulation when they find it. One White teacher told me how she handled a couple of young African American female students who were attempting to manipulate her. When she realized what was happening, she said to the students, "You're playing a game with me." The girls laughed, indicating that they knew the teacher had caught on to them. Once such gaming is exposed, clients find it difficult to continue using this manipulative strategy.

Exposing the client's secondary gains is not the only responsibility the counselor has under such circumstances. In addition to exposing the client's gaming, the counselor should take the lead in discussing the gaming's purpose for the client. Minority clients must come to terms with their need to play these games in the first place. Consider this counselor intervention:

Counselor: You seemed to take great delight in using rap rhetoric, which you knew I didn't understand. It was really important to you that I did not know where you were coming from. I think this is one of the reasons we are not making much progress now. What do you get out of playing games with me? Why do you feel so good when you are trying to fool me? We need to talk about this.

Reframing the Client's Definition of Control

Many clients are afraid of counseling. They may fear the pain of growth that goes with starting new behaviors and stopping old behaviors, or they may be afraid of disclosing intimate details of their lives to other persons. To deal with such insecurities, they often try to control their counselors and the counseling situation. Counselors can disarm this type of resistance by giving clients a new definition of control.

First, counselors should empathize with their clients' fears. In this way, counselors can help clients accept their feelings as legitimate. The last thing counselors should do is overlook, minimize, or invalidate their clients' feelings. Competent counselors know that clients typically act out their unacknowledged fears in the form of self-defeating behaviors. When a client is fearful, a counselor might use a general empathic intervention such as the following:

Counselor: It's not uncommon for people to have apprehensions about changing their lives. It can be really scary.

When working with a fearful minority client, a counselor might employ a more specific kind of empathic intervention. For example:

Counselor: Your reluctance to talk to a White counselor is perfectly understandable. You don't want to put yourself in another position to discuss your feelings with one more White person who thinks he understands when he really doesn't.

Second, counselors should help resistant clients understand that their resistance is a form of control, and they should explain how clients' fear-motivated actions are countertherapeutic. A counselor might point out the short-term benefits the client receives from using these control strategies, but he or she also should explain how these strategies are costly to the client. The counselor can use this discussion to suggest constructive strategies to the client. The following illustrates a helpful intervention:

Counselor: There are real benefits for you in trying to put me on the defensive. You might succeed in getting me to back off, and if you do, you might not have to look at yourself. But this could be costly to you. You may pass up an opportunity to learn how to handle your problems. Let me suggest that you give up trying to control our conversation and put that same energy into speaking up for yourself when people try to take advantage of you.

Third, counselors should encourage clients to talk openly about their fears and insecurities. A counselor can help a client understand that feelings, even so-called negative ones, serve a useful purpose. The counselor can then lead the client to connect his or her feelings with personal problem-solving strategies, as in this example:

Counselor: Tell me about your experiences of being misunderstood by White people. I want to hear your side of the story. I also want to be the type of person who helps you put your feelings into perspective and find workable solutions to your problems.

Confronting Normative Resistance

With a minority client, some resistance may reflect the norms of the client's minority culture rather than individual idiosyncrasies. The counselor should attempt to trace the resistance back to the client's cultural values. When resistance is culture-based, anyone from the client's culture likely would show the same type of resistance. Many Asian clients, for instance, avoid discussing family problems with counselors because of the cultural value of saving face. They do not want to bring shame on themselves or their families by admitting they have psychological problems. Counselors who ignore such cultural norms probably create more problems than they solve.

To confront normative resistance, counselors should begin by recognizing the anxiety-reducing function of cultural norms. A counselor can learn what cultural values are important to the client by observing and listening to the client's reactions to proposals for change. Although counselors should avoid imposing their own cultural values on their clients, they may need to challenge normative resistance when it is obviously countertherapeutic. In so doing, counselors must also show support and respect for minority clients' cultural traditions. A counselor might use an intervention such as the following to confront a client's normative resistance.

Counselor: Like many people from your culture, you do not want to bring shame on your family. That is a long-standing tradition and one that is important to you. I want you, however, to reevaluate your unwillingness to talk about family matters. You have a lot of feelings bottled up inside you, and you continue to feel very depressed. This is one time I think you should consider how your tradition is hurting you rather than helping you.

Chapter Summary

Unmanaged resistance in multicultural counseling can lead to unintentional racism on the part of counselors. Many counselors who are skilled in diagnosis and intervention planning are equally unskilled in handling resistance, especially with minority clients. This chapter has defined resistance, presented a typology for classifying client behaviors as resistance or non-resistance, and described six strategies that counselors can use to manage resistance. Counselors who adopt these strategies should find themselves better able to facilitate therapeutic change with minority clients, some of whom do not prioritize constructive change.

11

Terminating Effectively

Every counseling relationship must come to an end. How the relationship ends—like every other phase of counseling—is critical to the success of treatment. As Hackney and Cormier (2001) note, termination is not just a significant moment in the counseling relationship; it is an essential part of the therapeutic process. Ideally, the conclusion of counseling should be timely, occurring only after the client has achieved the chosen outcome goals. Goal achievement is not the ultimate test of termination's effectiveness, however; the real test lies in the client's ability to maintain therapeutic gains long after counseling ends.

Effective termination of counseling contributes to the client's personal growth and development. Ineffective termination, in contrast, can jeopardize the gains made in counseling, even when the counseling relationship has been successful. Because minority clients often have poor outcomes, express dissatisfaction with counseling, and drop out of counseling prematurely, counselors who work with such clients must be skilled in effective termination.

Effective termination does not happen automatically; the counselor must have a plan of action. Teyber (2000) explains clearly why a conscientious plan of termination is necessary:

> Termination is an important and distinct phase of therapy that needs to be negotiated thoughtfully. Ending the therapeutic relationship will almost always be of great significance to clients—for some, this may be the first positive ending of a relationship they have ever experienced. The way in which this separation experience is resolved is so important that it often influences how well clients will be able to resolve future losses and endings in their lives. It also helps determine whether clients leave therapy with a greater sense of self-efficacy and the ability to successfully manage their own lives more independently. Most beginning therapists greatly

underestimate how powerful an experience termination is for clients. It holds the potential either to undo or to confirm and extend the changes that have come about in therapy. Therefore, therapists must be prepared to utilize the further potential for change that becomes available as therapists and clients prepare to end their relationship. (p. 296)

This chapter examines termination in counseling. As Gladding (1996) observes, termination is a multidimensional process, and the discussion below addresses the various dimensions involved in the termination of counseling with minority clients. Counselors can counteract unintentional racism by using the termination-related procedures described in this chapter.

Reducing the Chances of Premature Termination

In a meta-analysis of 125 studies of psychotherapy dropout, Wierzbicki and Pekarik (1993) found that dropout is significantly related to racial minority status. Specifically, minority clients show higher rates of premature termination than do nonminority clients. Although it is impossible to know all of the factors contributing to this outcome, two factors related to process goals are probably influential.

First, many counselors fail to establish strong therapeutic alliances with minority clients. The consequences of this failure cannot be overemphasized. Some counselors do not realize the depth of the anxiety and intimidation that minority clients feel. Add counselor insensitivity to the equation, and client dropout seems inevitable. The case of Nor Shala described in Chapter 8 clearly illustrates this point.

One of my own counseling cases that turned out to be a failure provides another example of the result of the lack of a therapeutic alliance. A young African American woman was referred to me for counseling. In every sense of the word, the client was clinically paranoid. She felt extremely vulnerable and did not allow people to get to know her. Almost from the outset, I began to confront her strongly because I wanted to break through her defenses. By taking this approach, however, I violated one of my own therapeutic principles: The counselor must establish a therapeutic alliance before confronting the client. Indeed, I was acting out of frustration and impatience, which proved to be a fatal mistake. The more I pressed the client to open up, the more she withdrew. After three sessions, she terminated. Not only did we not make any progress, but it also is possible that I discouraged her from ever seeing another counselor.

Second, many counselors fail to clarify the nature of counseling sufficiently for their minority clients. Minority clients are often unfamiliar with how counseling works, or they may have different expectations about the process than counselors have. For instance, Dauphinais, Dauphinais, and Rowe (1981) have reported that counselors who are committed to client-centered or nondirective methods are ineffective with Native American adolescents. The adolescents do not understand the counselors' good intentions; rather, they think the counselors are being evasive. The counselors in turn probably assume that the adolescents are being resistant. This example demonstrates why counselors must minimize any confusion their minority clients may have about counseling. It also illustrates the importance of counselors' employing culturally responsive counseling styles and generally communicating clearly with minority clients.

Concluding Each Session Effectively

One way counselors can help prevent premature dropout is to conclude each counseling session effectively. Effective conclusions include summarizing the major themes and accomplishments of counseling up to that point, reinforcing clients for their accomplishments and therapeutic work, and encouraging clients to return for the next session. Counselors should remind themselves consistently that minority clients face ongoing challenges outside of counseling in addition to the pain involved in dealing with personal issues in the counseling setting—it is easy to see how these clients might get discouraged and drop out. Effective session termination can counteract such discouragement.

Research indicates that counselors can help end sessions effectively by clearly defining each session's time limits, by avoiding the introduction of new topics near the end of sessions, and by "building bridges" between sessions. I discuss each of these strategies briefly below.

Clearly defining time limits (Hackney & Cormier, 1994; Pietrofesa, Hoffman, & Splete, 1984). As Scissons (1993) notes, the conclusion of a counseling session never should be a surprise to the client. He suggests that the counselor might say something like the following at the beginning of the session: "Cornelius, we will have one hour together this morning. Let's start by . . . " (p. 178). Counselors should understand that establishing time parameters is especially important in their work with minority clients, whose expectations and cultural values may clash with those of nonminority counselors. Unless counselors clarify session time limits, minority clients may be surprised when counselors end their sessions.

Avoiding the introduction of new topics near the end of a session (Benjamin, 1981; Scissons, 1993). Introducing a new topic near the end of a session can interfere with the effective conclusion of the session. If a client introduces new material as the session is ending, the counselor should show empathic understanding but try to postpone discussion of the topic to the next session. Scissons (1993) gives a useful example:

Counselor: Maxine, I sense that the matter of your relationship with your father is an important one. I doubt that we will be able to deal with it adequately today because we have only about five minutes left. Perhaps next week we should devote as much time as we need to talk about your relationship with your father. In the meantime, why don't you think about what you will want to talk about next week. (pp. 178–179)

Because many minority clients mistrust the counseling process, counselors must be especially careful about how they handle any information these clients introduce late in a session. Counselors cannot afford to turn off minority clients, so they must show that they take the clients' concerns seriously. At the same time, they must be professional and keep their appointments on schedule.

Building bridges between sessions. A common flaw in counseling is the lack of connectedness and continuity between sessions. To overcome this problem, counselors should take a few minutes at the end of each session to (a) summarize the progress made thus far, (b) outline future directions, and (c) assign homework for clients to complete between sessions. Homework assignments are useful because they allow clients to test out their accomplishments and implement lifestyle changes. They also serve as links to subsequent sessions, during which counselors review their clients' progress. Scissons (1993) gives an example of a transitioning intervention:

Counselor: Jardine, there are several things you can do during the week we are apart that will help us in our time together next week. Perhaps the most helpful thing would be . . . (p. 179)

Recycling or Referring When Appropriate

Sometimes counseling reaches an impasse that has nothing to do with client resistance. Factors that may contribute to such an impasse include issues related to the particular counselor and the counseling setting. Among these are the following:

- Inadequate problem definition
- Inappropriate or poorly implemented interventions
- Miscommunication of expectations between counselor and client

- Judgmental and inferential errors
- Incompatibility of counselor and client
- Counselor's misunderstanding of cultural dynamics

When an impasse occurs, the counselor must change his or her strategy. Two alternative strategies the counselor might consider are recycling and referral.

Recycling involves reexamining all phases of the therapeutic process (Baruth & Huber, 1985). After counseling with a given client has lasted for a number of sessions, the counselor should reflect on what has been accomplished. The counselor should evaluate the strengths and weaknesses of the counseling process and try to determine where improvements are needed. Because counseling is a human endeavor, some well-intentioned efforts of counselors may not succeed. Recycling offers counselors opportunities to review, reevaluate, revise, and reinvest in their counseling efforts.

As I have noted in Chapter 4, many counselors assume the role of expert. Reflecting their orientation toward the medical model of mental health, counselors who view themselves as experts are prone to attribute therapeutic failure to their clients rather than to themselves. When counseling reaches an impasse and recycling has not helped the counselor identify the cause, the counselor should look honestly at his or her own contribution to the problem. Counselors should have the courage and humility to acknowledge their limitations. If they determine that they cannot help particular clients, they should refer those clients to other professionals.

As Okun (2002) explains, a referral involves the counselor's arranging other assistance for a client when the initial counseling situation is not helpful. Counselors who cannot relate to minority clients or who are incompetent to treat them should refer those clients to counselors who can provide the help they need. Several scholars have argued that it is unethical for counselors to attempt to treat minority clients without appropriate training (e.g., Fields, 1979; Korman, 1974); I would go further and assert that it constitutes a violation of minority clients' civil rights (Ridley, 1985a).

Regarding the timing of referral, Gladding (1996) notes:

> If a counselor suspects an impasse with a certain client, he or she should refer that client as soon as possible. On the other hand, if the counselor has worked with the client for a while, he or she should be sensitive about giving the client enough time to get used to the idea of working with someone else. (p. 178)

Counselors should become familiar with local mental health resources so they can match clients who need referrals with the best possible counseling situations (Baruth & Huber, 1985). To make referrals that serve minority clients well, counselors must be aware of the professionals in their areas who are multiculturally competent.

Evaluating Counseling Outcomes

The only way to tell whether counseling is successful is by evaluating outcomes. Counselors cannot be certain if they are benefiting minority clients unless they track clients' progress toward their counseling goals. Baruth and Huber (1985) suggest that counselors use the five measures described below to determine clients' progress in reaching therapeutic goals.

Verbal self-reports. As Baruth and Huber (1985) note, the easiest and most convenient type of evaluation is based on the client's verbal self-reports, which are direct sources of data. Self-reports tend to have low reliability, however, because many clients give socially desirable responses. Cormier and Cormier (1991) suggest that counselors use self-reports in conjunction with other outcome measures that produce more concrete and quantifiable data.

Frequency counts. This type of measurement reflects how often a specific aspect of client functioning occurs. The functioning may be an emotional state, thought, or behavior. For example, a counselor might count the number of anxiety attacks, self-denigrating thoughts, or inappropriate behaviors a client exhibits within a particular time frame.

Duration counts. This type of measurement reflects the duration of a client response or collection of responses. Baruth and Huber (1985) give the examples of the amount of time spent speaking, length of depressive thoughts, and length of anxiety attacks.

Frequency counts and duration counts may be obtained in two ways: through continuous recording or through time sampling. In continuous recording, the client responses of interest are recorded each time they occur. In time sampling, the client tracks selected responses during specific time intervals. Time sampling measurements are not as precise as continuous recording measurements, but they are more practical.

Rating scales. Rating scales assess the intensity or degree of specific responses. Baruth and Huber (1985) give the example of anxiety, which can be measured using a rating scale of 1 (*calm*) to 5 (*panic-stricken*). Cronbach (1970) specifies several criteria that a rating scale must meet in order to be useful: It must have well-defined responses, a description for each point on the scale, and at least four but no more than seven gradations.

Checklists. Counselors can use checklists to determine the presence or absence of particular responses in clients. Checklists involve a type of judgment different from that used in rating scales, which assess degree or intensity.

Baruth and Huber (1985) suggest that counselors use checklists to observe and record the behaviors of assertive clients.

Recommending Alternative Modalities

In addition to providing individual counseling and therapy, counselors may recommend other treatment modalities. Tharp (1991) lists a number of modalities that have been used with culturally diverse clients, including group therapy, problem-solving and social-skills training, family therapy, home-based treatment, network treatment, and community interventions. To varying degrees, each of these modalities includes family and community members and settings.

Counselors can employ alternative modalities with minority clients in several ways. For some clients, counselors may decide that one of these interventions should replace individual therapy as the treatment of choice. For other clients, counselors may recommend that one or more of these modalities be used to complement individual therapy. For example, a counselor may see a Native American client in weekly sessions at the same time the counselor is using network treatment to solve shared problems among the client's clan members. (Certainly, when mixing modalities in this way, counselors must be especially careful to use discretion and show sensitivity to ethical issues such as confidentiality.) For still other clients, counselors may recommend alternative modalities once individual therapy has ended. After a client has gained some insight into his or her personal issues, family therapy or home-based treatment may be a logical sequel to individual therapy.

Following Up When Counseling Is Over

It may be helpful to minority clients for counselors to show continued interest in them after termination by occasionally checking in with them and asking about their progress. According to Okun (2002), many counselors do not follow up with clients after termination. They probably believe their responsibilities to clients are over once counseling has ended formally.

It is understandable why counselors do not follow up. Most have busy schedules; they carry heavy caseloads and must make certain numbers of billable hours. In some cases, service agencies restrict the numbers of hours that counselors may spend with clients by requiring time-limited therapy. Despite these pressures, counselors should make time for client follow-up. As Young (1992) notes, follow-up contacts offer clients opportunities to return to therapy if necessary. Even if clients do not need to return, they benefit from the encouragement such contacts provide. In minority communities, where many are suspicious of mental health agencies, counselors can help improve the image of mental health care by following up on clients.

During the final counseling session, the counselor should reassure the client that he or she can return. By leaving the door open in this way, the counselor encourages the client to feel free to deal with old problems that flare up or new problems that develop. Later, the counselor might follow up with the client by doing one or more of the following:

- Writing the client a personalized letter or telephoning to show interest in the client's progress
- Sending the client relevant self-help materials
- Inviting the client to attend relevant workshops or seminars
- Informing the client of new treatment services that might be beneficial

Preventing Relapse

Changing problem behavior is one accomplishment; maintaining constructive change is another. The real test of termination's effectiveness lies in whether or not therapeutic gains last long after counseling is over. Competent counselors attempt to help their minority clients avoid the relapse of problem behaviors.

More than 20 years ago, Marlatt (1982) developed a model of the relapse process that scholars have used to understand relapse as it relates to addictive disorders such as alcoholism, smoking, and obesity. As Watson and Tharp (1997) note, however, Marlatt's model also may be applied to any self-change effort in which there is danger of an individual's falling back into problem behaviors. This includes problems related to such wide-ranging issues as gambling, exercising, studying, depression, unwanted sexual behavior, and procrastination.

Counselors can help minority clients prevent relapse by working with them to identify high-risk situations, develop coping skills for dealing with these situations, learn how to prevent lapses from becoming relapses, and develop social support.

Identifying high-risk situations. High-risk situations are situations in which a client's problem behavior is most likely to occur. The factors that constitute high-risk situations vary from person to person—that is, what may be a high-risk situation for one client may pose little or no risk for another. Counselors can help clients map out the relationships between their problem behaviors and the contexts in which those behaviors tend to occur. Counselors also can help clients identify situations in which their problem behaviors are less likely to occur. When clients are aware of their own high-risk situations, they can avoid those situations more easily, maximize the time they spend in low-risk situations, and minimize their chances of relapse.

Developing coping skills for dealing with high-risk situations. Because high-risk situations are not always avoidable (Watson & Tharp, 1997), clients must learn how to handle risky situations successfully when they arise. Marlatt and Gordon (1985) suggest that counselors should teach clients the following steps for dealing with high-risk situations:

- List the details of the problem.
- Think of as many solutions to the problem as possible.
- Select the solutions you will use.
- Check to ensure that you actually implement the solutions.

Preventing lapses from becoming relapses. A lapse is a single reemergence of a previous problem behavior. It may or may not lead to a state of relapse (Brownell, Marlatt, Lichtenstein, & Wilson, 1986). A lapse does not mean the client is a total failure, and counselors must make sure their clients understand that. Counselors should help clients view any lapses they have as opportunities to learn from their mistakes and make steady improvement.

As Watson and Tharp (1997) note, clients must have plans in place to deal with lapses constructively before they can become relapses. Such a plan should include self-monitoring of the problem behavior, a self-contract that specifies what the client is to do in the event of a lapse, and a reminder card that puts the lapse into proper perspective and encourages the client to continue maintaining the positive changes achieved in therapy.

Developing social support. Social support is one of the most important factors associated with successful relapse prevention. Before therapy terminates, counselors should assist minority clients in developing and cultivating social support networks. Counselors can accomplish this task in a variety of ways; for example, they might train clients' family members and friends in how to play supportive roles, or they might help clients get involved in community services and support groups. Counselors also can work with clients to develop the support available from churches in their communities or from other natural support systems. Some of the alternative treatment modalities that Tharp (1991) describes also may be useful for developing social support.

Chapter Summary

Termination of counseling is inevitable. As this chapter has emphasized, competent counselors use this culminating phase of counseling to advance the goals set for clients. Counselors can aid their clients at this stage of the process by reducing the chances of premature termination, concluding each session effectively, recycling or referring when appropriate, evaluating counseling outcomes, recommending alternative modalities, following up when counseling is over, and teaching their clients relapse prevention techniques. By employing these termination-related procedures, counselors can help minority clients maximize the gains made during the course of counseling.

Part III

Examining and
Overcoming the Unintentional
Racism of the Mental Health System

12

--

Racist Practices of Institutions

In the first two sections of this book, I have focused primarily on the unintentionally racist behavior of individual practitioners. As the preceding chapters have shown, mental health practitioners, in their one-on-one counseling with clients, are responsible for many of the race-related disparities in service provision found in the mental health care system in the United States. But is the problem of unintentional racism in mental health care totally attributable to what happens between counselors and minority clients during their 50-minute sessions? The answer to that question is a resounding no. In this and the next two chapters, we turn our attention to the problem of institutional racism. This examination reveals that the American mental health care system, a vast network of powerful machinery, contributes immeasurably to the patterns of behavior that systematically deny ethnic minority consumers access to high-quality treatment. It is no exaggeration to say that, in regard to mental health care services, institutional racism is just as problematic as individual racism, if not more so.

To understand the concept of institutional racism and how it differs from individual racism, it is useful to understand the concept of organizational behavior. Organizational behavior encompasses the collective attitudes and behaviors of individuals and groups as members of organizations, which are human systems designed for specific purposes (Johns, 1992). Scholars who study organizational behavior aim to predict and explain the behavior that occurs in organizations in order to understand how that behavior is created and controlled. Institutional racism can be framed as an issue of organizational behavior because it involves the collective responses of stakeholders in the mental health care system. In keeping with this book's theme, the discussion in this chapter demonstrates that although many of the policies and practices of mental health institutions are well intended, their consequences ultimately are detrimental to minority clients.

Without a doubt, institutional racism is pervasive and deeply woven into the fabric of the U.S. mental health care system (Wade, 1993). Virtually no aspect or subsystem of mental health care is untouched by its tentacles. In fact, given its foundation in psychiatry, the mental health care system actually is conducive to covert racism (Fernando, 1988; Wade, 1993). Several factors contribute to this conduciveness, including the dominance of Western cultural values in psychiatric theory and practice, the system's tendency to disregard or depreciate the cross-cultural content of assessment and diagnosis, and the system's susceptibility to the racism of the larger society (issues discussed in some detail in Chapters 1, 3, and 4).

Indeed, the pattern of institutional inequity warrants an explanation, but getting the correct explanation hinges on asking the right question. Generally, the wrong question for a mental health professional to ask about any given setting in which he or she practices, teaches, or conducts research is, Is this a racist institution? It is often hard to uncover an accurate answer to that question, given the subtlety of most unintentional racism. A more useful question to ask is, How does this institution unintentionally perpetuate racism? In seeking an answer to this question, many mental health practitioners may be surprised to discover that despite their sincerity, they are stakeholders in organizations that perpetuate many of the very outcomes they seek to avoid.

This chapter is organized into three main sections. In the first two sections, I discuss consequences and causes of unintentional institutional racism. In the third section, I describe several categories of unintentional institutional racism, discuss some specific types of institutional practices, and provide illustrative case vignettes.

Consequences of Unintentional Institutional Racism

In Chapter 2, I set forth 15 propositions that support the definition of racism applied throughout this book. One of these propositions states that the criteria for determining racism lie in the consequences of behavior, not the causes. Racism is not determined by the causes of behavior because good intentions often lead to bad interventions. Of course, some mental health professionals do harbor prejudices and biased attitudes against people of other races. In this day and age, however, it is difficult for such professionals to behave in overtly racist ways without being held accountable.

The consequences of institutional racism can be explained from the perspective of their temporality or from the perspective of their blatancy. From a temporal perspective, such consequences are either proximal or distal.

Proximal consequences are those that have immediate influences; that is, soon after the racist behavior occurs, minority consumers are adversely affected. Closing a mental health facility, for example, immediately affects the availability and accessibility of services to residents in that facility's local area. *Distal consequences,* in contrast, are delayed. Considerable time may elapse between the occurrence of the behavior and its adverse effects. Some distal consequences are so far removed in time from the behaviors that caused them that many professionals do not connect the two. Often, only observers with keen insight and a fundamental understanding of institutional racism can connect the racist behaviors of institutions with their distal consequences. A doctoral program in counseling psychology may provide inadequate multicultural training, for example, and years after they receive their training, graduates of the program may continue to counsel ethnic minority clients incompetently; for instance, they may fail to manage cultural transference or to integrate culture-related data into their assessments. It is likely that many of the adverse outcomes affecting minority mental health clients are distally connected to counselors' inadequate multicultural training.

From the perspective of blatancy, the consequences of institutional racism may be apparent or unapparent. *Apparent consequences* are those that are easily recognized as resulting from racism. For example, Lewis, Shanok, Cohen, Kligfeld, and Frisone (1980) have reported on the obvious discrepancy in treatment between African American adolescents and White adolescents who exhibit similar psychopathology and violent behaviors: African American youth are overwhelmingly sent to correctional facilities, whereas their White counterparts are referred primarily to mental hospitals. *Unapparent consequences* are those that are not easily recognized. Such consequences may surface when stereotypical characterizations of ethnic minorities in the social science literature contribute to clinicians' misjudgment of minority consumers. Clinicians may have such stereotypes so deeply etched in their minds that they escape the clinicians' awareness, and, consequently, clinicians cannot separate their biases from the reality of their clients' psychological presentation.

Combining the two perspectives on the consequences of institutional racism, we can conceptualize a four-quadrant typology for understanding the effects of institutional racism on minority consumers (see Figure 12.1). In quadrant 1, the consequence is proximal and apparent; in quadrant 2, the consequence is proximal and unapparent; in quadrant 3, the consequence is distal and apparent; and in quadrant 4, the consequence is distal and unapparent.

To determine the magnitude of institutional racism, mental health professionals must notice the various consequences and combinations of consequences of racism. If the criteria for determining whether or not behavior

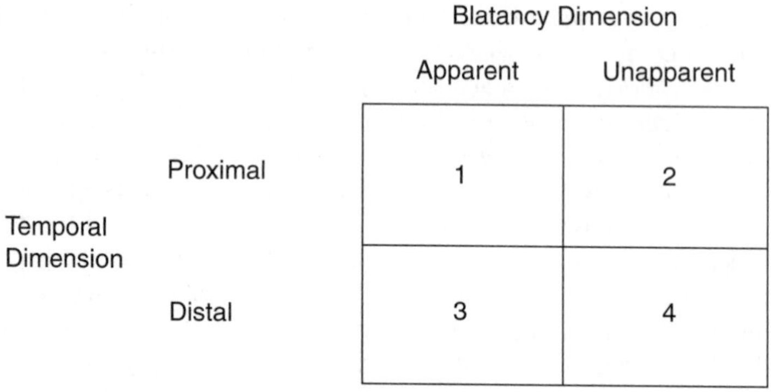

Blatancy Dimension

	Apparent	Unapparent
Proximal	1	2
Distal	3	4

Temporal
Dimension

Figure 12.1   Interactions of the Consequences of Institutional Racism

is racist lie in the consequences of the behavior, then professionals must broaden their view of the possible consequences of racism. Otherwise, they are likely to underestimate the magnitude of institutional racism in the mental health care system and, by default, fail to intervene adequately to correct the problem. Such an oversight, as innocently as it might occur, is yet another example of institutional racism because it perpetuates inequitable outcomes.

The consequences of institutional racism that are the easiest to remedy are those that are proximal and apparent (quadrant 1). Although confronting apparent racist behavior may be difficult, identifying the behavior is easy. When the consequence is proximal and unapparent (quadrant 2), the hard part is identifying an adverse consequence. When the consequence is distal and apparent (quadrant 3), the primary challenge lies in connecting the behavior and the consequence. The most difficult consequences to remedy are those that are distal and unapparent (quadrant 4). It is difficult not only to identify but also to establish the connection between the behavior and the consequences.

Overcoming unintentional racism in mental health institutions is almost impossible unless mental health professionals understand the nature of racism's real consequences and establish connections between racist behaviors and these consequences. Indeed, the insidious way in which the behavior-consequences relationship of unintentional racism is embedded in the fabric of the larger mental health care system is undoubtedly the reason many antiracism interventions are ineffective: They overlook this relationship. Professionals at all levels in the system keep failing to make the connection between behaviors and consequences, and their failure becomes a truly systemic problem that has consequences for all stakeholders.

Establishing the connection between behaviors and their consequences requires a great deal of insight, however; professionals must be astute observers, vigilant analysts of organizational behavior, and nondefensive, open-minded critics. Given that this new way of conceptualizing racism contradicts some of professionals' long-held perceptions and deeply entrenched views of the problem, it is not surprising that many practitioners resist it.

Causes of Unintentional Institutional Racism

The logical question to ask about institutional racism is, Why? Why do intelligent, socially informed, and well-meaning professionals perpetuate racism? To answer this question, we must examine the mind-set of the unintentional racist. Individuals' mind-sets fuel their behaviors, and institutions, where groups of people with similar mind-sets tend to gather, are the stages for the drama of collective behaviors.

The Mind-Set of the Unintentional Racist

Unintentional racists perpetuate racism not because they are prejudiced but because they deny that they are racists. Denial—the refusal to recognize the reality of external threats—is the essence of the unintentional racist's mind-set. For an unintentional racist, admitting to racism is a threat to the individual's conception of him- or herself as a nonracist person. Fostered by three prominent factors—miseducation, dysconsciousness, and group-think—the mind-set powerfully influences the unintentional racist's behavior. These factors interact to reinforce each other and enable the unintentional racist to justify his or her inadequate response to racial inequity (see Figure 12.2).

Miseducation. Miseducation is not the lack of education. Many unintentional racists are highly educated. Miseducation is a mentality that harbors incorrect information—in the case of unintentional racists, misinformation about race and race relations abounds. Ingrained in unintentional racists is a belief in an oversimplified cause-effect relationship: Prejudice is the cause, and racial inequality is the effect. This proposition is reinforced subtly by the popular media and individuals' everyday interactions and explicitly by the academic mental health literature. Mental health professionals are especially susceptible to this ideology because they are trained to be empathic, and anything that hints at mistreatment or injustice is an affront to their professional self-image. It is often difficult for them to accept that, despite their good intentions, they can victimize their clients; after all, in their minds, any

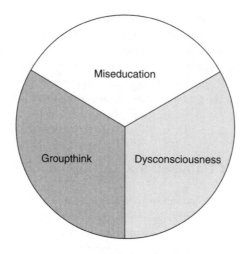

Figure 12.2   Mind-Set of the Unintentional Racist

perpetuation of racial inequality on their part must indicate that they are prejudiced. However, as Whaley (1998b) notes, "the research supports the notion of aversive racism, that racial bias influences 'well-intentioned' white mental health professionals' judgments about blacks and leads to subsequent racial discrimination with severe consequences" (p. 52).

In all fairness, mental health professionals are not the only people who are miseducated. Professionals in every field tend to oversimplify racism, overlooking its potential to surface on an institutional level as well as on an individual level, covertly as well as overtly, and unintentionally as well as intentionally. Furthermore, such oversimplification is not just a problem among Whites. As Woodson (1969) pointed out many years ago, minorities also are prone to miseducation about race.

Dysconsciousness. Professionals react in a variety of ways when confronted about their miseducation. One common reaction is to adopt an uncritical stance toward racial inequity. King (1991) has coined the term *dysconsciousness* to describe the psychology of Whites who take for granted their privileged position in society. She defines dysconsciousness as an uncritical mind-set (i.e., a set of perceptions, attitudes, assumptions, and beliefs) that leads an individual to justify racial inequity without questioning the beliefs under which it exists. King describes the phenomenon this way:

> Dysconscious racism is a form of racism that tacitly accepts dominant White norms and privileges. It is not the *absence* of consciousness (that is, not unconsciousness) but an *impaired* consciousness or distorted way of

thinking about race as compared to, for example, critical consciousness. Uncritical ways of thinking about racial inequity accept certain culturally sanctioned assumptions, myths, and beliefs that justify the social and economic advantages White people have as a result of subordinating diverse others (Wellman, 1977). Any serious challenge to the status quo that calls this racial privilege into question inevitably challenges the self-identity of White people who have internalized these ideological justifications. (p. 137)

According to King, the essential feature of dysconscious racism—the tacit and uncritical acceptance of the status quo—rests on two dominant beliefs: that racism is solely a historical consequence of slavery and that racism is a consequence of prejudice and discrimination. Both beliefs are the products of miseducation. King further observes that both beliefs defend White privilege, and, citing Wellman (1977), she notes that they constitute a "consistent theme in racist thinking" (p. 139). King concludes that few Whites attribute racial inequity to the structural framework of American society—a social order where racial victimization is normative. This conclusion clearly fits with the present proposition regarding institutional racism.

Groupthink. Groupthink extends uncritical thinking beyond the individual to the group as a whole. It is a state that maintains harmony among members of the group at the expense of wise decision making. Janis (1989) describes the mantra of this unspoken heuristic: "Preserve group harmony by going along uncritically with whatever consensus seems to be energizing" (p. 57). In this state, group members diligently work to retain a positive view of the group's current state of functioning (Turner, Pratkanis, Probasco, & Leve, 1992), but they sacrifice their ability to make realistic assessments.

Groupthink is supported by group members' collective perception of threat or danger, especially as threat or danger appears increasingly imminent. The characteristics of groupthink include the illusion of invulnerability, self-censorship, the illusion of unanimity, direct pressure on dissenters, collective rationalization, belief in the inherent morality of the group's views, stereotyped views of out-groups, and the emergence of self-appointed "mind guards" (Baron, Kerr, & Miller, 1993; Janis, 1982, 1989). Among unintentional racists in the field of mental health care, groupthink surfaces as the collective view that group members are not prejudiced, and therefore their institutions are not racist.

Collective Reinforcement of Racism

Miseducation, dysconsciousness, and groupthink interact dynamically to reinforce unintentional racism in mental health professionals. In their conscious minds, unintentional racists advocate equality and social justice.

Because of their miseducation, however, they have erroneous views about the major causes of racism. In their unconscious minds, they defend themselves against psychological pain, especially pain resulting from any challenge to their fundamental beliefs about race. Yet they have no intentions of harming minorities. They simply feel threatened, and that feeling leads them to prioritize the avoidance of their own psychic pain over the critical examination of alternative explanations of racism. The response is dysconscious. An additional layer of reinforcement occurs through groupthink, which moves uncritical thinking beyond individuals to the group. The erroneous beliefs and uncritical reflection inherent in groupthink tragically lead mental health practitioners to collective inaction and, as Thomas (1973) ruefully notes, the system-maintenance role that perpetuates the racist status quo.

Categories of Unintentional Institutional Racism

The unintentional institutional racism that permeates the American mental health care system is perpetuated by behaviors that can be divided into three distinct categories: no initiatives, misguided initiatives, and mismanaged initiatives. All of these categories are behavioral in nature and fit the definition of racism as the systematic denial of access and opportunities to members of minority groups coupled with the perpetuation of access and opportunities for members of the majority group. I discuss each of these categories below.

No Initiatives

The most overlooked and undocumented form of institutional racism is inaction—the failure to undertake any antiracist initiatives. Most people are prone to think of racism only as direct action; they do not consider that individuals' and institutions' failure to act also may constitute racism. Complacence in the face of racism—whatever its cause—has adverse consequences just as direct, overt racism does. The collective inaction of members of an institution can perpetuate racial inequities even though such consequences often paradoxically oppose the good intentions of individual members. A quotation usually attributed to Edmund Burke punctuates this point: "The only thing necessary for the triumph of evil is for good men to do nothing."[1]

Arredondo and Rice (2004) note that mental health practitioners tend to shirk responsibility for the institutional racism that exists in their field. Indeed, practitioners often conform to the status quo even when the organizations to which they belong strive to make positive changes in the realm of diversity. In a poignant criticism, Arredondo and Rice state:

Though the attribution for racism is made to the institution, it is important to note that organizations exist because of the presence of people. Thus, to separate clinicians from responsibility for institutional racism is erroneous. Helping professionals too often externalize responsibility by invoking institutional racism as the culprit for the lack of cultural competency, rather than admit to their own passivity when faced with social injustices and opportunities to change inequities in the system. (p. 87)

The behavior of inaction, like the behavior-consequences relationship, is insidious—perhaps more so than any other form of unintentional institutional racism. It is difficult, and sometimes almost impossible, to hold professionals accountable for what they fail to do. When professionals take action, their behavior at least is identifiable, even if it has unintentional consequences. The difficulty of addressing an institution's failure to act is exacerbated when the members of that institution present a compelling rationale for their inaction, such as the rationale described above that typically lies in the mind-set of the unintentional racist.

Case vignette. Very few minority students are enrolled in a top-ranked doctoral program in clinical psychology at a prestigious university. This pattern has persisted in the program for many years, and there are no indications of change on the horizon. The members of the clinical psychology faculty, many of whom are prominent researchers in the field, consistently resort to tired arguments: "We cannot find qualified minority applicants"; "We cannot lower our standards"; "Admitting minority students who have lower test scores than nonminority candidates is reverse discrimination." The program consequently continues to employ traditional admissions standards. Notably, research has shown that test scores have poor predictive validity concerning later student success and that universities make a higher proportion of false negative decisions regarding minority students than they do regarding White students.[2] The posture of this program's faculty members is paradoxical and inherently racist. These eminent scientist-practitioners, who extol the virtues of science, are uncritical of the unscientific nature of their admissions process. As a result, they systematically deny admission to applicants from underrepresented groups, even though the data indicate that some of these students, if given the opportunity, would perform successfully in the program.

Misguided Initiatives

A number of institutional behaviors and practices fall into the category of misguided initiatives. Few of them are generally recognized as racism, although they consistently fail to overcome the racial inequities in the mental health care system. They fail because they are flawed, and they are flawed because they do not tackle the structural and systematic patterns that underlie racism. These initiatives are marked by five salient characteristics:

- *Sincerity of the promulgators:* Many people who promulgate unintentional racism in the mental health system believe their behaviors are appropriate and beneficial for minority consumers. They deserve credit for their good intentions, but their intentions are much of the problem—good intentions can mask unintentional racism. Attempts to get such individuals to see beyond their intentions and recognize the adverse consequences of their initiatives often are met with resistance, indifference, or disbelief. At the core of these responses is the promulgators' fear of a threat to their socially liberal self-image.

- *Oversimplification of racism:* As noted in Chapter 3, racism involves multilevel patterns of behavior. Racism can be individual or institutional, and, within each of these categories, it can be overt or covert. Moreover, covert racism can be intentional or unintentional. Misguided initiatives that perpetuate institutional racism fail to account for this complexity; they attempt to achieve outcomes through shortcuts instead of appropriately elaborate and in-depth interventions. Institutions need to initiate interventions that jar people from their comfort zones.

- *Focus on surface-level symptoms:* Misguided initiatives focus on symptoms rather than on the underlying dynamics and organizational behaviors that perpetuate racial disparities. This practice is similar to treating hay fever with facial tissues rather than antihistamines: The tissues might seem to make things better, but only antihistamines will really eliminate the problem. Change agents must understand the dynamics at work under the surface of the organization if they are to overcome the disparities in the mental health system.

- *Illusion of progress:* On the surface, misguided initiatives appear to combat racism. This appearance can generate excitement, especially during the early stages of implementation, among both professionals who carry out the initiatives and consumers who benefit from them. But in the final analysis, these initiatives are little more than hoaxes, deceiving both professionals and consumers. Because these initiatives focus only on surface-level symptoms, they cannot effect real change, and early enthusiasm easily turns into disenchantment.

- *Maintenance of the power differential:* The real but unacknowledged and often unintentional function of misguided initiatives is to maintain the status quo by further solidifying the dominance of the majority group and the subordination of minority groups. Anyone who examines such initiatives in retrospect is bound to discover that the same inequitable outcomes that were present before the initiatives were undertaken remain in place afterward.

Overall, misguided initiatives are deceptive; their true function and their inability to stop real racism are masked. Although professionals expend a great deal of effort on such initiatives and may really believe they are working on something constructive, these initiatives are in fact counterproductive. In addition, the continual implementation of misguided initiatives has a compounding effect. Each one taken alone can have serious repercussions, but collectively, the repercussions escalate exponentially. Below, I discuss six different kinds of misguided initiatives.

Special Programs

The mental health establishment in the United States, supported by government agencies and special interest groups, often develops special programs that are intended to address the unmet mental health needs of particular populations. Common programs of this type include counseling for unwed teenage mothers, job training for unemployed people, and educational programs for high school dropouts. These special programs, which are especially prevalent in minority communities, are wide-ranging and target a variety of human needs.

The most important fact about special programs is that they are not really special. The word *special* denotes a quality of being distinguished, extraordinary, and exceptional in importance. In reality, the only thing special about these programs is their name. Special programs rest on a foundation that leads to eventual failure and obsolescence. It is worth noting that the only mental health programs that are ever called special are those that are not institutionalized. The implicit contract between an institution and a special program includes no long-term commitments, and special programs typically are funded with "soft money." Block grants are an example of this type of funding. The continued existence of any given special program is literally at the mercy of funding sources that may withdraw support and have no further obligations to the program's stakeholders. During financial or other crises, special programs typically are the first to be eliminated. Knowles and Prewitt (1969) comment on this phenomenon in their informative edited volume *Institutional Racism in America:*

> Countless programs go on the rocks simply because of poor judgment which grows out of misinformation and inexperience in the field of social action. Social reform at the present time is not a profession, not a science, but a hodge-podge of amateurs spurred on by a number of different ideologies and rationales that are only tenuously related to each other. There is little wonder that many failures are the result of sheer incompetence. (p. 116)

The rationales that accompany the elimination of special programs often are phrased in the grandest of terms: "Economic exigencies have forced us to reconsider our priorities"; "The program is no longer the best use of tax dollars"; "A significant investment already has been made in the community." When special programs are initiated, they are lauded as constructive responses to local mental health problems, but little is said about the setbacks the elimination of such programs represent, especially for communities that need truly constructive mental health programs. Special programs exist in all corners of the country, but they are especially prevalent in minority and socioeconomically disadvantaged communities. When these programs are eliminated, it is a setback for society in general because the racism inherent in eliminating mental health programs in minority and poor communities reverberates widely. The time, effort, and money devoted to special programs could be more constructively applied to the development of effective and institutionalized structures.

Case vignette. A special program devoted to alcohol and drug rehabilitation was established in an inner-city community. The program, which was funded by a block grant, was more successful than many others of its kind because it involved community leaders, emphasized prevention as well as rehabilitation, and included an organized network of churches, schools, community centers, and businesses. During the program's fifth year of operation, the program director learned that the block grant would not be renewed. The official word was that the state had to shift the money to other priorities. After community leaders mounted an assertive appeal to the state, the program received an additional year of funding, but then it was forced to shut down. Overnight, all of the gains the program had made were lost, and local consumers who needed treatment were left without any viable alternatives. The impact of the loss of the program was immediate and apparent.

False Generosity

Not every offer of help is followed with real help. Compare what a donor might sacrifice when making a real contribution with what a donor might gain in making a false contribution. As Frederick Douglass (1857/1950) once said, "Power concedes nothing without a demand" (p. 437). That is, it is not in the oppressor's self-interest to give anything of real value to the oppressed.

Whenever a bureaucracy makes an apparently generous offer of help to a minority community, the members of that community should be wary.[3] The offer may not really be so generous, and the bureaucracy may derive a secondary gain or hidden benefit from making it. At the same time, the minorities who are supposed to benefit actually may incur hidden losses. In his classic work *Pedagogy of the Oppressed,* Freire (2000) coins the phrase *false generosity,* describing it this way:

> Any attempt to "soften" the power of the oppressor in deference to the weakness of the oppressed almost always manifests itself in the form of false generosity; indeed, the attempt never goes beyond this. In order to have the continued opportunity to express their "generosity," the oppressors must perpetuate injustice as well. An unjust social order is the permanent fount of this "generosity," which is nourished by death, despair, and poverty. (p. 44)

In the mental health system, so-called generous contributions to minority communities may be inherently racist. Such contributions may appear to serve the interests of minority communities and may be cloaked in enticing rhetoric, but in reality they may do minority communities a gross disservice.

Case vignette. The state's Mental Health and Human Services Administration has come under fire for the significant underrepresentation of minorities among administration employees, especially at senior levels. In response to the criticism, the administration, which has the responsibility for policy setting, funding, and monitoring of mental health programs and initiatives around the state, creates a new position, assistant deputy for minority affairs. The person hired to fill the position is a Mexican American woman who has a Ph.D. in clinical/community psychology from a renowned university.

The hiring sends a message throughout the state: Minorities are now welcomed into the establishment, and reform in the mental health system is on the way. However, this message is misleading, given the reality that the new assistant deputy holds a staff position, not a line position. She reports to the deputy director, who is the administration's chief executive officer. On the organizational chart, the assistant deputy position appears near the top, but there is no real authority invested in the position. The deputy assistant travels around the state and evaluates programs in various minority communities. She reports her findings to the director. Although the position has a high profile, the assistant deputy is excluded from important decision making and policy reform. After a year of service, she resigns out of frustration. Her frustration comes from two sources: First, she has little real input into policy setting, and the decision makers do not seem to understand the perspectives of the minority communities; and second, because minority professionals in the field had high hopes for meaningful reform, some have begun to criticize her, claiming that she has been incompetent and has sold out to the establishment. Her resignation symbolizes a lack of progress and "business as usual."

Divide and Oppress

One tactic used in military warfare is to create confusion and disarray among the enemy. If one can induce conflict somehow within enemy ranks, one can weaken the enemy's fighting position and strengthen one's own. Less effort is needed to defeat the enemy because, in a real sense, the enemy defeats itself.

Freire (2000) describes a similar concept, *divide and rule,* and its use against impoverished people in his homeland of Brazil. Here the oppressor maintains a dominant position by creating division and disunity among the subgroups of the oppressed. Freire regards this type of action as essential to the interest of the oppressor, who uses a variety of repressive methods to achieve this end. In his discussion, Freire labels the dominant group the *oppressor minority* and the subordinate group the *majority;* thus he does not use the terms *majority* and *minority* in the racial/ethnic sense used throughout this text. A lengthy quote from Freire captures the essence of the divide-and-rule tactic:

> This is another fundamental dimension of the theory of oppressive action which is as old as oppression itself. As the oppressor minority subordinates and dominates the majority, it must divide it and keep it divided in order to remain in power. The minority cannot permit itself the luxury of tolerating the unification of the people, which would undoubtedly signify a serious threat to their own hegemony. Accordingly, the oppressors halt by any method (including violence) any action which in even incipient fashion could awaken the oppressed to the need for unity. Concepts such as unity, organization, and struggle are immediately labeled as dangerous. In fact, of course, these concepts *are* dangerous—to the oppressors—for their realization is necessary to actions of liberation.
>
> It is in the interest of the oppressor to weaken the oppressed still further, to isolate them, to create and deepen rifts among them. This is done by varied means, from the repressive methods of the government bureaucracy to the forms of cultural action with which they manipulate the people by giving them the impression that they are being helped.
>
> One of the characteristics of oppressive cultural action which is almost never perceived by the dedicated but naïve professionals who are involved is the emphasis on a *focalized* view of problems rather than on seeing them as dimensions of a *totality*. In "community development" projects the more a region or area is broken down into "local communities," without the study of these communities both as totalities in themselves and as parts of another totality (the area, region, and so forth)—which in its turn is part of a still larger totality (the nation, as part of the continental totality)—the more alienation is intensified. And the more alienated people are, the easier it is to divide them and keep them divided. These focalized forms of action, by intensifying the focalized way of life of the oppressed (especially in rural areas), hamper the oppressed from perceiving reality critically and keep them isolated from the problems of oppressed men in other areas. (pp. 141–142)

In the human services, a similar dynamic occurs with respect to the treatment of minority consumers. The major difference is that the repressive strategies in these settings are carried out by well-intentioned but misguided bureaucrats. Unsuspecting consumers from minority groups place their faith in the goodwill of bureaucrats and later find themselves in a weakened position concerning their mental health needs. When minority consumers trust bureaucrats to take care of their needs, consumers' input into decisions is automatically reduced. This reduction leads to programs that inadequately address the issues of minority communities.

Case vignette. The leaders of several minority communities in cities around the state complain in the news media about the inadequacy of mental health services in their areas. Presented with compelling data on this issue, state government officials and senior administrators in the state's mental health establishment are forced to agree. The state officials decide to build a comprehensive mental health center on the south side of the state's largest city, where the city's minority residents are concentrated. The center is built, and it is hailed at its opening ceremony as a sign of great progress. State, county, and city officials are on hand to laud this achievement, and the event receives major coverage in the news media.

On the surface, the building of the center appears to be a solution to a number of problems in the minority community. Below the surface, however, a different picture emerges. The appropriation of funds for the endeavor is grossly inequitable. The $3.5 million project represents only 7% of the local mental health budget, even though the combined minority groups represent 29% of the local population. Although minorities can use other services in the county, these services are inaccessible to many local residents, who are socioeconomically disadvantaged. For all intents and purposes, a de facto funding inequity exists: Minority consumers are underfunded disproportionately in comparison with their numbers in the general population (see Figure 12.3).

In addition, many minority residents mistakenly see the center as a blanket solution for all the needs of the city's various minority groups. Strong voices among these groups have ideas about service delivery that differ from those of the establishment. Moreover, conflict ensues among minority group leaders over who ultimately will manage the facility. The African Americans argue that because they are the largest minority group, the center's CEO should be African American. The Hispanics argue that because they are the fastest-growing group, the center's leadership should be bilingual. The Native Americas argue that, as the original Americans, they should play an important role in managing the center. The conflict escalates, and the tensions that surround it have several adverse consequences for the center. Service delivery is poor, and several minority psychologists resign, seeking higher salaries and more stable work environments elsewhere. Attention is deflected from the real problem—inadequate funding. As the news media hear of the conflict, members of the establishment blame the victims, stating, "The local leadership in the community is unable to manage the center's generous resources." A reasonable case could be made, however, that with input from minority community members from the outset and an equitable foundation, these outcomes could have been averted.

Scientific Racism

The goal of science is to predict, control, and interpret natural phenomena and events (Holland & Skinner, 1961). In essence, science seeks to understand

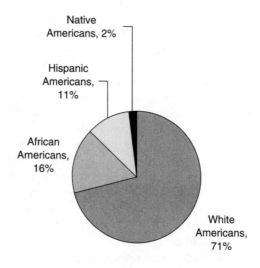

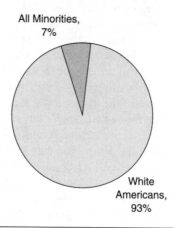

Figure 12.3   Strategy to Divide and Oppress

and explain the physical and social world in which we live. Science is supposed to be a value-free enterprise, but the applications of scientific methods and scientific discoveries clearly may represent any number of value orientations. Scientific discoveries may be used to promote human welfare, as when medicines are developed to fight diseases, but people are also sometimes abused and exploited by scientists. An example of such abuse is the infamous Tuskegee Syphilis Study, in which scientists from the U.S. Public Health Service deliberately did not treat African American males who had syphilis in order to study the progress and long-term effects of the disease (Jones, 1981; Williams, 1974).

The racism inherent in the Tuskegee study was clearly apparent and intentional, but a subtler type of racism pervades the social sciences today. Thomas and Sillen (1972) refer to it as "scientific racism"—a practice that perpetuates a biased view of African Americans and other ethnic minority groups. Scientific racism interferes with the discovery of knowledge that can inform the psychotherapeutic treatment of minorities. It entails a persistent, flawed approach to social science research.

Sue (1999) asks the question, "Is science biased against ethnic minority research?" (p. 1070). Answering this question in the affirmative, he posits three problems specific to psychological science that contribute to this bias: a relative lack of research on ethnic minority populations, a relative lack of high-quality research among the work on ethnic minorities that is published, and inadequate funding for ethnic minority research.Other researchers have corroborated Sue's assertions (Graham, 1992; Hall, 1997; Jones, LaVeist, & Lillie-Blanton, 1991; Loo, Fong, & Iwamasa, 1988; Miranda, Nakamura, & Bernal, 2003; Padilla & Lindholm, 1995; Ponterotto, 1988). Furthermore, other scholars have identified additional problems contributing to bias: treating culture as a nuisance variable (Shweder, 1990), referencing Whites as the standard of normality (Steinberg & Fletcher, 1998), using race as a proxy or substitute variable (Steinberg & Fletcher, 1998), using minority samples to study pathology but not normal development (MacPhee, Kreutzer, & Fritz, 1994), and using samples of convenience (Quintana, Troyano, & Taylor, 2001).

Sue's (1999) explanation of these problems fits perfectly with this chapter's description of institutional racism in its covert, unintentional manifestation:

> The reasons for these problems are subtle and systematic. Science and scientific methods are not the culprit. Rather, the culprit is how science has been practiced—an effect caused by the selective enforcement of the principles of science. This selective enforcement of the principles of science emphasizes internal validity over external validity, which discourages the growth and development of ethnic minority research. (p. 1070)

Therefore, the apparent consequence of scientific racism is "the disparity in research sophistication and publication rates" (p. 1071). In addition, I would argue that this type of racism has distal and unapparent consequences, and these consequences have far-reaching implications, as the disparity in research hinders the advancement of knowledge and ultimately the field's ability to develop best practices for ethnic minority consumers. Given the importance placed on the scientist-practitioner model, the field is severely handicapped in the amount of good science available to put into practice. As Sue (1999) bemoans, most of the controversies that Thomas and Sillen (1972) wrote about more than 30 years ago continue today as contentious themes in American psychology.

Case vignette. The National Institute of Mental Health funded a major investigation of the cognitive behavioral treatment of depression. The study included a treatment group and a control wait-list group. The researchers used a manualized protocol and employed a well-researched inventory of depression that had been shown to have good reliability and validity. The researchers used some behavioral outcome measures as well. Participants were drawn from treatment facilities that had low numbers of minority clients. In addition, the researchers did not identify the races of participants in reporting the sample's demographic characteristics. Furthermore, they made no attempt to investigate culture's role in the participants' psychological presentations or to examine how practitioners might use information about clients' cultures to facilitate therapeutic change. Like many studies, the research produced findings that lack external validity. The findings shed no light on how the interventions of interest might apply to minority populations.

Medicalization of Racism

In recent years there has been renewed interest in defining racism as a disease or clinical disorder, even among mental health professionals (Dobbins & Skillings, 2000; Poussaint, 1999; Skillings & Dobbins, 1991; Wilkins, 1992). This causal view contrasts with the behavioral definition of racism used in this book. As Wellman (2000) notes, a number of practical problems are associated with the medicalization of racism. Most notable among these is that medicalization perpetuates rather than solves the problem of racism:

> The disease model is a symptom—and a perpetuation—of the problem; it is not a solution for racism. Medicalizing issues of power, domination, and control, treating them as diseases, leaves the organization of racial advantage in America virtually untouched. (p. 30)

Wellman goes on:

> First of all, when a problem is defined as being medical, it is removed from the public realm; it is no longer within the purview or the power of ordinary people. It is put on a plane where only professionals—in this instance, medical or mental health practitioners—can analyze and discuss it. Since the language of expertise is not generally accessible to lay people, the possibility for public debate is diminished.

Secondly, medicalizing racism individualizes troubles shared by all Americans. Causes as well as solutions to a complex problem are located in the individual, seen as problems someone "has," rather than as being rooted in the social system. The goal, then, is to "cure" the affected individual, not the socially constructed hierarchy.

Thirdly, by individualizing racism, the process of medicalization depoliticizes what is essentially a public issue. Beliefs that exclude certain groups from America's social resources are treated as personal problems rather than political constructions.

Finally, defining racism as illness absolves the citizenry of responsibility for its behavior. By divorcing accountability from social action, and locating the causes of behavior in the psyche or biophysiology, we exempt Americans from their basic political obligations. Used like the insanity defense, this medical rationale could serve to absolve white Americans from responsibility for the organization of racial advantage and their relationship to the arrangement. This is troublesome not because white Americans should be made to feel guilty, but rather because racial division and racism are human constructions. And since they are socially constructed, they can only be deconstructed and reconstructed by human beings deciding, self-consciously, to reorganize their priorities and rearrange their hierarchies. (pp. 30–31)

Mental health professionals are the most venerable perpetuators of the medicalization of racism. They are the only group of professionals who are socially and legally sanctioned to diagnose and treat mental disorders. By medicalizing racism, they both divert attention from institutional practices and absolve themselves of the responsibility of correcting inherently racist psychological practices.

Case vignette. All professional staff at a county mental health agency were required to attend a workshop devoted to cultural sensitivity training. The administration wanted the professionals to check themselves for prejudice, bias, and cultural insensitivity and to examine how their attitudes might influence their work with clients. Psychologists, psychiatrists, social workers, mental health counselors, occupational therapists, and administrators participated in the training. The focus was on helping the professionals "get in touch" with their feelings and attitudes. The workshop had a significant experiential component, challenging the participants to identify their reactions in simulation exercises that involved sensitive racial encounters. Although there were some mixed reactions to the training, most of the professionals reported in their evaluations that the training had met its objectives. However, the training never addressed the structural and organizational patterns of the mental health care system. Although many of the professionals left the workshop with new insights into their own cultural biases, most of them could not identify the unintentional patterns that cause disparities in their agency.

Inadequate Performance Appraisal

In an organization, each individual member's performance contributes to the organization's overall performance (Murphy & Cleveland, 1995). If the collective performance of individuals in an organization indicates competence, then the organization will perform well. If the collective performance of individuals indicates incompetence, then the organization will perform poorly. Certainly, there may be a range of competence levels reflected in the performance of individual employees across an organization. As in any kind of organization, the competence of individual counselors and therapists in a mental health care agency contributes to the overall quality of service that agency provides. Therefore, it is in such an agency's best interest to ensure the competence of its staff.

The most important method of ensuring employee competence is through performance appraisal, or the systematic description of individual employees' job-relevant strengths and weaknesses (Cascio & Aguinis, 2005). The process of performance appraisal consists of two elements: observation, which includes the detection, perception, and recall of job-related behavior; and judgment, which entails the categorization, integration, and evaluation of the observed behaviors (Thornton & Zorich, 1980).

Both observation and judgment are subject to bias (Cascio & Aguinis, 2005), and therein lies one source of unintentional racism in the mental health system. All of the major mental health–related professional associations in the United States uphold competence as an ethical standard in their codes of ethics (e.g., American Association for Marriage and Family Therapy, 2001; American Counseling Association, 1995; American Psychological Association, 2002; National Association of Social Workers, 1996). They also stress the importance of mental health professionals' competence in working with diverse clientele, yet their codes of ethics provide no clear, conceptually sound definitions of competence. This problem is exacerbated by the professional literature on multicultural counseling competence, which has emerged as an important and widely discussed topic in the field (Ridley & Kleiner, 2003). Despite the development of models of multicultural counseling competence in recent years (e.g., Mollen, Ridley, & Hill, 2003), no widely accepted definition of multicultural counseling competence exists (Constantine & Ladany, 2000; Holcomb-McCoy, 2000). Thus there are no uniform performance indicators available for measuring mental health practitioners' ability to provide high-quality service to minorities.

The purpose of establishing standards of professional conduct, such as competence, is to make it possible to hold practitioners accountable for their actions (Cottone & Tarvydas, 1998). In the absence of a sound definition of multicultural counseling competence, the appraisal of professionals' performance in this area is subject to logical errors and to errors in ratings concerning leniency, severity, central tendency, halo effect, and proximity (Cascio & Aguinis, 2005). The net effect is the mental health system's lack of a sound basis for distinguishing competence from incompetence in multicultural counseling. This problem extends across the entire mental health field and is shared by all mental health professionals and institutions.

There are numerous explanations for this debacle. In fairness, however, it should be noted that mental health scholars and practitioners have displayed increasing appreciation of the importance of multicultural competence over the past two decades. But this increased attention has not yet resolved the problem of inadequate performance appraisal concerning multicultural competence—a systemic problem that is enacted at the agency level.

According to Cascio and Aguinis (2005), performance appraisal serves six main purposes. I list these purposes below, along with the potential adverse consequences that inadequate appraisal of multicultural competence can have for mental health agencies:

- *Personnel decisions:* Promotion, training, transfer, discipline, and salary decisions hinge on performance appraisal. In the absence of clear criteria for multicultural counseling competence, incompetent professionals may be rewarded and competent professionals punished.
- *Personnel research:* In the absence of clear criteria for multicultural counseling competence, it is impossible to investigate the relationship between multicultural competence and therapeutic outcomes.
- *Prediction:* In the absence of clear criteria for multicultural counseling competence, it is impossible to make valid promotional decisions.
- *Training:* In the absence of clear criteria for multicultural counseling competence, it is impossible to establish objectives for professional training programs and measure the results of training.
- *Feedback:* In the absence of clear criteria for multicultural counseling competence, it is impossible to identify the strengths and weaknesses of counselors and therapists or to provide them with good coaching.
- *Organizational diagnosis and development:* In the absence of clear criteria for multicultural counseling competence, it is difficult to establish any connection between individual performance and organizational performance or to set goals to improve the organization.

Every area of organizational functioning in the mental health system is touched by the problem of inadequate performance appraisal regarding multicultural competence, making adverse effects on minority consumers almost inevitable. Service delivery to minorities never will be equitable until the mental health field demonstrates definitively that the rhetoric of multicultural counseling competence has been translated into actual practice.

Case vignette. A mental health consortium is well-known for the emphasis on multicultural training in its predoctoral internship program. Located in a major metropolitan area on the East Coast, the consortium has three training sites where interns do their rotations. Minorities compose 35% of the consortium's staff; they include African American, Hispanic, and Asian American psychologists. A psychologist who is a native of India provides an additional cultural perspective. A major theme in the consortium's training is multicultural counseling competence, and much attention is devoted to the demographics of the training sites' client populations.

One White intern sought out the consortium's internship program because she has a strong social justice orientation and wants to spend her career working in inner-city neighborhoods. During her first rotation, her supervisor was a bilingual Latino clinical psychologist. During her second rotation, her supervisor was an African American counseling psychologist. Both supervisors stressed the importance of accounting for the client's culture during assessment and treatment planning. When the intern requested more guidance in how to do this, the first supervisor told her that she needed to realize that Hispanics have a more collectivist orientation than do many White people. The second supervisor recommended some readings for the intern that discussed the cultural values of various minority populations. During the intern's yearlong training, she learned a great deal about her training site's local population, and her supervisors noted her good therapeutic alliances with her clients. However, she finished the internship very frustrated, knowing that she did not have the confidence to put the cultural knowledge she had gained into beneficial practice. Although her supervisors were themselves members of minority groups, they had been unable to provide her with any clear criteria for developing multicultural counseling competence.

Mismanaged Initiatives

Some initiatives that fail to overcome institutional racism are philosophically and structurally sound. They rest on solid scientific principles, and they match well with the profiles of the intended consumers. These initiatives fail not because they are misguided, but because they are mismanaged. A variety of poor managerial behaviors may be involved:

- Inadequate top-down commitment and support
- Failure to establish leadership credibility
- Failure to inspire collaboration
- Failure to delegate effectively
- Failure to hold people accountable
- Failure to establish measurable goals
- Failure to confront resistance

Case vignette. A major university's counseling and psychological services center initiated an outreach program to promote better relations on campus among students from various racial and cultural groups. The initiative came about after several racist incidents had occurred in some of the university's residence halls. The only African American psychologist on the center's staff headed the program. Although the initiative originally was intended to involve collaboration among all of the center's psychologists, the responsibility for managing the program fell almost exclusively on the African American psychologist. She was more than willing to accept the challenge of leading the program, but the center's other psychologists showed a lot of passive resistance and contributed little in the way of ideas or programming. The center's director recognized that their behavior reflected their own fears and discomfort over the issue of race, but she never confronted them about their resistance or held them accountable. As a result of the limited support the outreach program received, it never met expectations or achieved its goals. Another unfortunate consequence of the initiative's failure was that some faculty and students came to see the African American psychologist as inept—another example of blaming the victim.

Chapter Summary

Unintentional racism is endemic and ubiquitous in the American mental health care system. It extends beyond the routines of individual practitioners to the very fabric of the system itself, including policies and institutional practices. As this chapter has shown, the collective behaviors of the system's stakeholders are implicated in institutional racism. To overcome unintentional institutional racism, mental health professionals must first accept the nature of its consequences. Then they must identify specific institutional practices that are racist, many of which are seldom recognized or acknowledged as such. Finally, they must target particular interventions to the macrosystem of the mental health establishment as well as to the various microsystems it comprises.

In the final chapters of this volume, I propose some specific macrosystem and microsystem interventions. The discussions in Chapters 13 and 14 clarify the complexity of institutional racism. The possibility for real change lies in mental health professionals' ability to grasp this complexity. Stakeholders in the mental health system will find new ideas in my proposed interventions as well as new principles and actions they can apply to combat an old problem.

Notes

1. Extensive searches by many scholars have failed to find this quotation in any of Burke's writings. Emily Morison Beck, in her preface to the 15th edition of *Bartlett's Familiar Quotations* (1980, p. ix), suggests that the quotation may be a "twentieth-century paraphrase" of the following from Burke's *Thoughts on the Cause of the Present Discontents* (April 23, 1770): "When bad men combine, the

good must associate; else they will fall one by one, an unpitied sacrifice in a contemptible struggle."

2. Atkinson, Brown, and Casas (1996) note that ethnic minority applicants to graduate training programs often are deselected because of low scores on the Graduate Record Examination. However, research seriously calls this practice into question. The relationship between aptitude test scores and performance in graduate training programs is generally weak (Dollinger, 1989; House & Johnson, 1993; Marston, 1971).

3. I do not advocate paranoia, just healthy wariness. Furthermore, I would advise minorities to be wary of majority-dominated bureaucracies rather than majority members in general. After all, many members of the majority population have legitimately helped further the causes of minority populations, through participation in the civil rights movement, the women's movement, and numerous other constructive initiatives. Of course, many of these people operated outside of any bureaucracy.

13

Macrosystem Interventions

Organizational patterns of behavior in treatment settings are not the only sources of institutional racism in the U.S. mental health care system. We certainly cannot discount the institutional racism that emanates from clinics, community mental health centers, hospitals, student counseling services, and private practices. However, we must recognize that a huge amount of the racism that occurs in treatment settings stems from structural problems in American society in general, from policies set at higher levels by governments and professional organizations, and from the training mental health professionals receive in educational institutions. Therefore, to overcome racism in mental health services, professionals must target these wide-ranging forces that reach down from higher tiers and ultimately influence practices at the local level.

Macrosystem interventions are interventions that aim to make changes that will radiate throughout a given system—in this case, the vast network of mental health institutions, including licensing boards, government regulatory agencies, funding agencies, professional associations, training institutions and programs, managed care organizations, third-party organizations, and service centers. All of these institutions, whether or not they deliver services directly, have a stake in the success of mental health services delivery; thus they are the targets of macrosystem interventions.

The main purpose of the macrosystem interventions discussed in this chapter is to *define* the nature and scope of high-quality mental health care. Such a definition clarifies how minority clients should be treated and, by implication, clarifies how they should *not* be treated. Each of the three macrosystem interventions discussed below—practice-based minority research, mental health care reform, and multicultural training—plays a unique and important role in defining what constitutes high-quality mental health care for minority consumers.

Practice-Based Minority Research

The best way to improve practice in any profession is to solidify the knowledge base on which that practice is built. Practice that is rooted in evidence provided by research contrasts starkly with uninformed practice, which is at best an exercise in guessing and at worst an exercise in futility. An increase in research-based knowledge elevates practitioners' overall competence within a profession, thereby benefiting the consumers of that profession's services. Of course, whatever the level of knowledge in a profession, some individual practitioners will perform incompetently for a variety of reasons; they may be poorly trained, they may fail to keep up with the most recent research in their field, or they may be unable to master their field's knowledge base. In general, however, as the storehouse of knowledge in a field grows and expands, so does the quality of the field's professional services. As Seligman (1996) notes, science is an ally of practice.

The work of Ignaz Semmelweiss (discussed briefly in Chapter 2) shows the importance of applying new knowledge to professional practice. Semmelweiss's discovery of the cause of many fatalities in new mothers revolutionized the delivery practices of obstetricians and significantly decreased the rates of mortality associated with childbirth. The key was obstetricians' application of the new knowledge that Semmelweiss discovered.

The U.S. mental health care system needs an infusion of new knowledge that will lead to improved service delivery to ethnic minority clients. Unless researchers provide useful knowledge about the experiences of minorities in the mental health care system, the system will continue to treat minority clients unfairly. Practice-based research that examines the experiences of minority clients is unquestionably the intervention most likely to gather the knowledge required to alter professional practice and counter the institutional racism of the mental health system.

A Proposed Research Agenda

Mental health professionals, especially those in applied psychology, are already committed to knowledge-based practice. They endorse the scientist-practitioner model, which aims to put scientific knowledge into practice and practice into science (Baker & Benjamin, 2000; Belar, 2000; Peterson, 2000). The model envisions this cycle of activities as ongoing because so much scientific knowledge remains untapped. But what type of knowledge is needed to improve delivery of mental health services to minority consumers?

Professionals in the field struggle with this question. Unresolved issues hinder the establishment of a unified agenda and a more fruitful yield of knowledge, despite great strides in multicultural scholarship as well as the view among many scholars that multiculturalism represents the "fourth force" in psychology (Pedersen, 1990b, 1999). Currently, the support for treatments often recommended to minority clients is more speculative than empirical in nature (Doyle, 1998; Hall, 2001). Below, I discuss three unanswered questions that are prominent in the search for a research agenda concerning multicultural counseling.

Is competence in multicultural counseling inclusive or exclusive? There is a sharp division in the literature over the nature of multicultural counseling competence. Some scholars advance the idea of inclusiveness, suggesting that multiculturally competent practitioners can treat clients of any cultural background. Constantine and Ladany (2000), for example, include groups united by gender, social class, and sexual orientation along with racial and ethnic groups under the rubric of cultural groups that multiculturally competent practitioners can counsel. Essentially, they define the concept of multicultural counseling competence as broadly as possible, implying that every client has cultural peculiarities. Their underlying assumption is that counselors who can process culture in counseling are equipped to counsel minority clients.

Other scholars advance the idea of exclusiveness by using the term *multicultural counseling competence* to refer to the facilitation of change with specific populations. A popular version of this perspective particularizes multicultural counseling competence to competence in counseling racial and ethnic minority populations (Abe-Kim & Takeuchi, 1996). Success in counseling African Americans, Latinos/Hispanics, Asian Americans, and Native Americans is often noted as evidence of multicultural counseling competence (Castro, 1998).Sue (1998) strikes at the heart of the debate by asking a series of questions:

> If a person is culturally effective with one group, is that person a culturally competent therapist? Or does culturally competent mean that one is effective with more than one culturally distinct group? If one of the characteristics of cultural competency is knowing the cultures of groups, and if it is impossible to really know the cultures of all groups in society, can one ever be truly culturally competent? (p. 445)

These questions can be answered only through the application of a deliberate research agenda. As Turner and Kramer (1995) observe, "A focused research agenda is desperately needed to understand and respond appropriately to the mental health needs of ethnic minorities" (p. 23). This research agenda must include investigations of a variety of psychological problems as well as a variety of treatment modalities in which all participants, both practitioners and clients, are culturally diverse. The purpose of such research is to determine how multicultural counseling competence manifests itself in real-world clinical practice.

Do multiculturally competent counselors use culture-specific or culture-generalized interventions? A debate exists in the literature about the types of interventions that are appropriate to competent multicultural counseling. On one side, scholars argue that multiculturally competent counselors may use culture-universal interventions because, in the hands of competent counselors, all interventions are equally effective across various groups (Roark, 1974). This position assumes that competent practitioners do not need specialized systematic knowledge or skills to tailor interventions to each client's unique needs (Larson, 1982).

On the other side of the debate, scholars argue that multicultural counseling competence requires culture-specific interventions. These scholars assert that equal treatment in counseling is inherently discriminatory (D. W. Sue, 1977) and disregards individual and cultural differences among clients (Smith, 1981). They maintain that differential treatment does not imply discriminatory treatment. Do scholars who take this position argue that the culturally inclusive model of multicultural competence is discriminatory? If the model means treating clients *identically,* discrimination probably occurs. If the model means treating clients *equitably,* discrimination is probably less of an issue.

Overall, in considering the use of culture-specific or culture-generalized interventions, is one position right and the other wrong? Or is there a middle ground? The current base of knowledge does not provide answers to these questions. However, when equal access and equal opportunity are priorities, there is a need for differential interventions that are nondiscriminatory (D. W. Sue, 1977). The ultimate answers to these questions probably will reveal that both culture-universal and culture-specific interventions are necessary to treatments tailored to the uniqueness of each client.

Are the major theories of counseling and psychotherapy relevant to people of color? Most major theories of counseling and psychotherapy are Eurocentric. They were developed by White males, and they promote values—such as individualism and independence—that are characteristic of White, Western culture (Romano & Kachgal, 2004). The formidable question pertains to relevance: Are these theories relevant to clients from cultures that promote different values, such as collectivism and interdependence? There is a paucity of research comparing the effectiveness of theories across cultures; therefore, there is little evidence to support the claim that theories' Eurocentric bias adversely affects minorities. At the same time, however, there is little evidence to contradict the claim. These concerns are subject to empirical investigation.

As important as it is to answer the three questions discussed above, I would argue that these questions are secondary; they should not be the central focus of minority research. Rather, the research agenda should focus on a more fundamental question: *How can practitioners incorporate cultural considerations beneficially into counseling and therapy to facilitate therapeutic change in minority clients?* This question is fundamental because (a) nothing is more important in counseling and therapy than helping the client change, and (b) clarification of the roles that race and culture play in facilitating therapeutic changes is urgently needed. By driving the research agenda with this question, researchers may discover how to use culture to activate the mechanisms of therapeutic change. In doing so, they are likely to answer the secondary questions. However, the ultimate benefit will arise in the practice arena, where minority clients will receive better treatment and equitable service delivery. This outcome supports the proposition that good research is the most important macrosystem strategy for overcoming institutional racism in the mental health system.

Characteristics of the Research Agenda

How can mental health professionals advance the research agenda? Asking this question presupposes that the agenda can indeed advance and that it is possible to answer the fundamental questions of minority research. Mental health professionals must establish an agenda for minority research that is programmatic, theory driven, and culturally valid, and that is based on explicated presuppositions, operationalized constructs, and accumulated knowledge.

Programmatic research. The fundamental question of the research agenda demands an elaborate answer, for therapeutic change is complex. Consider that the beneficial incorporation of racial and cultural considerations should occur at all stages of therapy: in the formation of the therapeutic alliance, in assessment and diagnosis, in the planning of treatment, in the management of the therapeutic process, and in the evaluation of treatment outcomes. Then consider the many questions that may arise about therapeutic change: What is therapeutic change? How do people change? How do racial and cultural characteristics factor into the equation? Do people of different backgrounds change in different ways? These questions cannot be answered through single-study, uncoordinated efforts.

To make progress on the research agenda, mental health professionals must display several characteristics. First, they must act purposefully. Because therapeutic change is an intricate process, one thing is certain: Discoveries about the relationship between race/ethnicity and therapeutic change will not be accidental. Second, advancing the agenda requires commitment. As Sue (2003) reflects soberly on his experience as a leading minority researcher, "Becoming involved in ethnic research has taught us that such research is very difficult to conduct, and many researchers have not been exposed or trained to deal with these difficulties" (p. 203). Third, making progress on the agenda requires planning. Not only must researchers address their research questions, but, as Sue points out, they also must anticipate a series of investigations occurring over a lengthy time period. Fourth, moving the agenda forward requires funding. Major funding agencies such as the National Institutes of Health's Office of Research on Minority Health must support the agenda if it is to be successful.

Theory-driven research. By definition, a theory is "a set of interrelated ideas, constructs, and principles proposed to explain certain observations of reality" (Hjelle & Ziegler, 1992, p. 7). One of a theory's purposes is to drive research. In fact, theory bridges research and practice. Mental health practitioners make observations as they conduct counseling and therapy and then theorize about what has transpired in practice. Researchers, in turn, employ the scientific method to test the theories that practitioners develop. They use the theories to generate hypotheses, which they then test; the results of their hypothesis testing confirm the theories or inform any necessary elaboration or revision of the theories. Then the cycle starts over, as practitioners implement the researchers' findings, again observe during counseling and therapy, and theorize once more about what has transpired. Through repeated cycles, the field moves closer to an understanding of the complexity of the counseling and psychotherapy process.

In the proposed research agenda, the observations in greatest need of explanation are those related to therapeutic change and those related to the process of using racial and cultural considerations to facilitate change. Unfortunately, little of the scholarship devoted to multicultural counseling has included theory-driven research. Ponterotto and his colleagues have criticized researchers consistently for failing to use conceptual/theoretical frameworks to guide their investigations of multicultural counseling (see, e.g., Ponterotto & Casas, 1991; Ponterotto, Costa, & Werner-Lin, 2002; Ponterotto, Fuertes, & Chen, 2000). Although contemporary theories of counseling and psychotherapy are inadequate to describe or explain the richness and complexity of culturally diverse populations (Sue, Ivey, & Pedersen, 1996), researchers in the field of minority mental health no longer can afford to conduct research that is not theory driven.

Several scholars have recognized the need for theory-driven research to advance the knowledge base regarding multicultural counseling (Atkinson, Morten, & Sue, 1998a; Betancourt & López, 1993; Miranda, Nakamura, & Bernal, 2003). Miranda et al. (2003) arrived at this conclusion after conducting a review and finding few studies that provide "information on outcomes of mental health care for ethnic minorities" (p. 467). Unless scholars commit to developing theories of multicultural counseling and psychotherapy such as the theory proposed by Sue et al. (1996), progress on the proposed research agenda will be meager.

Culturally valid research. Scientific findings are externally valid only to the degree that they represent the populations to which they are generalized. Sue (1999, 2003) argues that social science research has emphasized internal validity at the expense of external validity. Historically, minorities have been either excluded from major investigations or unaccounted for in the reporting or interpretation of the data. Therefore, Sue (2003) cautions,

> Because much of the psychological research is not based on ethnic minority populations, it is actually unclear whether a particular theory or principle is applicable, whether an intervention has the same phenomenological meaning for different cultural groups, or whether measures or questionnaires are valid for these populations. (p. 205)

To rectify this problem, according to Sue (1999), researchers must attend to external validity and specify the populations to which their findings are to be generalized. Other scholars go a step farther. In reconceptualizing Leong and Brown's (1995) notion of *cultural validity,* Quintana, Troyano, and Taylor (2001) propose this definition:

> the authentic *representation* of the cultural nature of the research in terms of how constructs are operationalized, participants are recruited, hypotheses are formulated, study procedures are adapted, responses are analyzed, and results are interpreted for a particular cultural group as the *usefulness* of the research for its instructional utility in yielding practice as well as theoretical implications about the cultural group, and its service utility in "giving back" to the community in important ways. (p. 617)

In essence, these authors assert that research must be conducted in ways that optimally benefit the cultural populations to which the findings will be applied. They further discuss threats to cultural validity and propose strategies to address those threats. In general, Quintana et al. provide a helpful discussion about the problem of generalizing findings to minority groups.

Explicated presuppositions. The identification and critique of underlying principles and presuppositions are integral to good theory building. For theories to be cogent and internally consistent, researchers must make their presuppositions explicit and subject them to rigorous criticism. For example, here are two opposing presuppositions that may serve as starting points for research concerning a theory of therapeutic change that embraces racial and cultural considerations: (a) All people change through an identical process, regardless of their racial and cultural backgrounds; and (b) People change through different processes, depending on their racial and cultural backgrounds. These presuppositions, which are anchored in different theories of therapeutic change, are typically implicit in the thinking of the theories' proponents. Unless scientist-practitioners first identify and then test the presuppositions that underlie theories, they likely will behave in therapy as though the presuppositions are valid. It should be apparent that the two presuppositions used as examples here lead to different treatment modalities, given that the former argues for culture-generalized interventions and the latter argues for culture-specific interventions. Scientific evidence supporting either of these presuppositions over the other would have serious implications for practice.

Operationalized constructs. The operationalization of major constructs is another aspect of theory explication. To arrive at meaningful findings that allow for clear interpretation, researchers must carefully define the constructs under investigation. Most social science research on minority issues has fallen short of this requirement. Scholars have noted conceptual difficulties in the operationalization of key variables such as race (Miranda et al., 2003; Sue, 2003), culture (Betancourt & López, 1993; López, 2003), acculturation (Marín, Organista, & Chun, 2003), and cultural sensitivity (Ridley, Mendoza, Kanitz, Angermeier, & Zenk, 1994). As Sue (2003) notes, defining these variables is both important and difficult. For instance, race is more of a social construct than a biological one, and it is often used as a proxy variable (Walsh, Smith, Morales, & Sechrest, 2000). Many variables also are multiordinal; that is, they have different meanings at different levels of abstraction (Rychlak, 1981). Despite these difficulties, researchers in the field of minority mental health have no choice but to define constructs carefully if they hope to advance the research agenda.

Accumulated knowledge. As researchers develop new knowledge about the effects of race and culture on therapeutic change, that knowledge should be integrated into a theory of therapeutic change. The theory necessarily will evolve and undergo revision as the knowledge base increases. The revision of any theory entails several crucial steps. First, researchers continually and diligently search for any information that is relevant to the theory (sometimes such information is found in the literatures of other disciplines). Second, researchers make informed interpretations of their research findings, weighing the findings in light of previous research and the best theories available about the phenomenon under investigation. Third, researchers add the information they have gathered to the storehouse of existing knowledge and attempt to explain how it sheds new light on the theory. Fourth, practitioners put the revised theory into practice, starting the cycle of investigation over again as researchers examine the results of that practice.

Recommendations

Carrying out the practice-based minority research agenda is a major undertaking. The following six recommendations are intended to help researchers accomplish this feat.

Use a wide range of research methodologies. Social science research investigates phenomena that often are difficult to measure, and each method of measurement has strengths and weaknesses. For example, in experimental designs, rigorous control over internal validity may compromise external validity, and vice versa. As Gelso (1979) notes in introducing the "bubble hypothesis," all research studies have weaknesses, and it is difficult for researchers to smooth out the various methodological "bubbles" that can arise in the design of a study.

Researchers can compensate for the limitations of individual research methods by employing a variety of approaches. Because the research agenda is programmatic, researchers have ample opportunity to conduct different types of studies—all in the interest of accumulating knowledge about the central research question. The selection of methodology should hinge first on the study's particular problem statement and then on the method's ability to test the hypotheses under investigation. Researchers should not select methods based solely on their own preferences. Instead, they should ask themselves, Which research design has the most integrity for testing the hypotheses? Certainly, they also must think about costs, ethics, and procedural matters, but, as a matter of practice, researchers should consider a wide range of methodologies. Sue (1999, in press) recommends that, in addition to traditional experimental methods, researchers use qualitative strategies such as ethnography, case study, phenomenological research, participative inquiry, and focus groups. The most important rules to follow are these: Research questions should dictate methodology, and personal biases should not restrict the choice of research methods.

Engage minority communities in research. To make a practice-based minority research agenda work, researchers need the cooperation of the members of minority communities. Cauce, Ryan, and Grove (1998) suggest some effective strategies for recruiting minority participants, noting that many minorities are likely to view researchers with suspicion, at least initially: Researchers might offer incentives to potential participants, solicit support from community leaders, and make personal contact with potential participants; in addition, they should take care not to stigmatize participants. Quintana et al. (2001) advise researchers to consult with members of the minority community before starting their studies and to build rapport with participants throughout the research process, as such efforts have been found to reduce dropout. These scholars also suggest that researchers find ways to give something back to the communities they study instead of just benefiting themselves. In one study, Quintana (1994) demonstrated to Latino parents the benefit to their children (who were research participants) of having Latino graduate students available to serve as positive role models. On a similar theme, Miranda et al. (2003) assert that researchers should make research a two-way learning process.

In 1996, the *Journal of Consulting and Clinical Psychology* published a special section titled "Recruiting and Retaining Minorities in Psychotherapy" that included articles offering advice and suggestions for researchers. In their contribution to the special section, Norton and Manson (1996) advise scholars conducting research with American Indians and Alaska Natives to do the following: Define the population, gain participation of the tribes and approval of the institutional review board, identify potential benefits to the community, and evaluate the scientific merits of the research. Thompson, Neighbors, Munday, and Jackson (1996) make these suggestions to researchers working with African American study participants: Form academic-public liaisons, recruit and select interviewers who are familiar with the research population, train interviewers appropriately, and demonstrate cultural sensitivity. Miranda, Azocar, Organista, Muñoz, and Lieberman (1996) make these suggestions to researchers studying Latinos: Include bilingual and bicultural members on the research team, recruit participants in settings other than mental health facilities, overcome barriers such as child-care needs and lack of transportation, and form respectful, warm, and personal relationships with participants.

Consider culture in all aspects and phases of research. Research cannot have cultural validity unless cultural considerations are integral to the entire research endeavor. As Sue, Kurasaki, and Srinivasan (1999) note, researchers must account for culture in all of the seven critical phases of the research process: while planning the research, defining the variables, selecting valid instruments, sampling participants, gaining participants' cooperation, designing the study, and interpreting the findings. (A detailed discussion of the intricate work of making research culturally valid is beyond the scope of this chapter; for excellent information on this topic, see Burlew, 2003; Ponterotto & Casas, 1991; Quintana et al., 2001; Rogler, 1989; Sue et al., 1999; Walsh et al., 2000.)

Conduct effectiveness studies on specific populations using empirically supported treatments. Effectiveness studies of counseling and psychotherapy are conducted in tightly controlled clinical settings (Seligman, 1995). Such studies are designed to address the problem of inappropriate generalization of research findings. Of course, as Miranda et al. (2003) note, the presumption underlying this strategy is that the "critical ingredients" of change are universal and work similarly for most human beings. These authors point out that this strategy is inappropriate for efficacy investigations, presumably because the results of those investigations lack generalizability (efficacy studies of counseling and psychotherapy are tightly controlled clinical trials; see Seligman, 1995). Investigations of treatment in the real world can provide knowledge about whether the investigated interventions are effective across different populations (Miranda et al., 2003).

Conduct efficacy studies on specific populations. By conducting efficacy studies, researchers may discover whether there are culture-specific ingredients of therapeutic change. Such studies aim to determine what works best in a given population. The presupposition is that each population is unique and responds uniquely to interventions. Therefore, researchers cannot make a priori assumptions about the mechanisms of change, nor can they hypothesize culture-specific mechanisms based on a theoretical framework.

Create practice research networks. One promising way for mental health professionals to implement the scientist-practitioner model is through the creation of practice research networks (Barlow, 1996). Researchers can use such networks to evaluate psychological interventions across a broad range of treatment settings. They can gather aggregate data on therapeutic processes and outcomes, which allows them to analyze data in large data sets. With these data sets, researchers can investigate within-group and between-group differences. This strategy can solve the problem of sample sizes that are too small to allow the generalization of findings to minority populations. The strategy also permits the study of practice in the real world.

Mental Health Care Reform

Mental health care reform is another macrosystem intervention aimed at combating the mental health system's institutional racism. Research has firmly established the need for policies that promote better mental health service delivery for racial/ethnic minorities (Casas, Pavelski, Furlong, & Zanglis, 2001; LaFromboise, 1988; Sue, 1992; Vernez, 1991). Current U.S. mental health care policies, which directly influence the types of services provided, have evolved over centuries (Goodwin, 1997). Layers of deeply entrenched policies tied to political and economic exigencies pose an awesome challenge to even the most assertive advocates of reform. Moreover, arguments for reform often strike at the core of values and ideologies that are deeply held by various constituencies. These factors are difficult to overcome, but if mental health professionals do not challenge the status quo, the perpetuation of racism in the system is guaranteed.

Philosophical Foundation of Reform

Five themes are critical to the reform of mental health care policies as they relate to services for minority consumers: equitable service delivery, data-driven policy making, proper targeting of resources, flexibility, and partnerships. These themes collectively should constitute the philosophical foundation of reform.

Equitable service delivery. Achieving equitable outcomes across all client populations is the most important goal of mental health care reform. No client, regardless of race, culture, ethnicity, or socioeconomic status, should receive inferior treatment or experience negative outcomes as a result of treatment. Every consumer should benefit from high-quality service and should experience positive treatment outcomes. To achieve these expectations, the entire mental health system must coordinate its resources and efforts. In addition, the system must make a critical departure from harmful past practices and misconceptions. The mental health establishment must accept the reality that many of the system's inequities stem from well-meaning practice, not intentional bigotry.

Data-driven policy making. Policy concerning the treatment of ethnic minority consumers of mental health services, like all mental health policy, should be anchored in sound psychological evidence. Although there are ongoing tensions over the science-policy alliance (Phillips, 2000), the value of this alliance cannot be overstated. As Garland and Zigler (1993) note, "Data provide a much firmer foundation for social policy than do good intentions" (p. 179). The American Psychological Association's Task Force on Education, Training, and Service in Psychology (1982) affirms the association's commitment to using psychological knowledge in the formulation of policy to serve the public interest.

A research project conducted in Seattle provides an example of research findings' usefulness in shaping mental health policy (S. Sue, 1977, 1992). When the study uncovered inequities in the delivery of mental health services to ethnic minority clients, the state of Washington initiated culturally responsive programs in its mental health centers. In a 10-year follow-up study, O'Sullivan, Peterson, Cox, and Kirkeby (1989) found that the dropout rates for ethnic minority clients had improved to the point that they resembled the rates for Whites.

Proper targeting of resources. Communities vary greatly in the resources they can devote to mental health services. Those with high proportions of socioeconomically disadvantaged and minority residents have fewer financial resources than do other communities. Mental health care reform efforts should strive to provide resources to communities that need the most and to ensure that enough resources are provided to make a difference. This principle is similar to the one that underlies Title I legislation aimed at improving funding for schools (Tirozzi & Uro, 1997). Resources should be targeted so as to achieve equity in funding and improve the quality of services. The provision of resources never should amount to an act of false generosity. It should not lead to problems in the form of special programs, divide-and-oppress tactics, or mismanaged initiatives (see Chapter 12).

Flexibility. Because needs for mental health care services, social programs, and educational services vary greatly across communities, reform efforts cannot take a one-size-fits-all approach to mental health care service delivery. Even when effectiveness research establishes a particular treatment as having universal application, that treatment still should be culturally contextualized for a given community. For example, suppose that cognitive therapy is demonstrated to have cross-cultural application. The implementation of this treatment in a Hmong refugee community should involve the use of different cultural symbols and idioms than those used among Navajo living on a reservation. Particularly in public mental health care service delivery, local communities should have the freedom and support to design and implement services that are tailored to local needs.

Partnerships. No single entity can implement the large-scale reforms that are necessary to overcome institutional racism in the mental health system. The collective and collaborative efforts of a broad range of constituents and stakeholders hold the greatest promise for positive change. Mental health professionals must take the lead in establishing linkages among families, schools, social and human services agencies, and other natural support systems.

A Blueprint for Reform

Having established a philosophical foundation for reform of the mental health care system, I present below a blueprint intended to guide actual reform. Reform efforts must consider three major dimensions of reform: areas of reform, issues of care, and levels of policy making. Advocates of reform must recognize these dimensions and understand the interactions among them. Figure 13.1 presents a conceptualization of these dimensions.

Areas of reform. The U.S. mental health care system requires changes in three critical areas: social policy, policy management, and funding of mental health services. Tropman's (1995) definition of policy is useful here: "Policy is an idea, which is a guide to action, is written, and has the approval of legitimate authority" (p. 288). As Tropman elaborates, the area of social policy focuses on the advancement of laws, rules, and guidelines that are

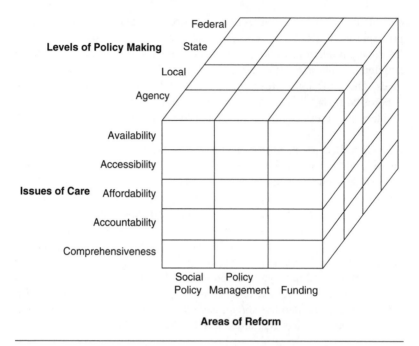

Figure 13.1   Blueprint for Mental Health Care Reform

humane, just, and inclusive. The area of policy management involves the critical skills that individuals need to translate laws, rules, and guidelines into action. The area of funding entails the procurement and allocation of financial resources for mental health service delivery. Clearly, sound social policies, competent policy management, and adequate funding are needed to overcome the many documented disparities infesting the mental health system. Reforms must occur in all three areas if the system's racism is to be eliminated.

Issues of care. Issues of care are the issues involved in the actual delivery of mental health care services. Five issues are particularly important:

- *Availability:* No one can benefit from services that do not exist. Sometimes adequate mental health services are not available to minority communities, even though these communities may be the ones most in need of services. Unless minority consumers have the opportunity to receive services, the overall quality of mental health in their communities cannot improve.
- *Accessibility:* Services that are available but not accessible to those who need them are pointless. Minority populations must be able to access the mental health services that are available to other consumers. Treatment facilities must be established in locations that are convenient for minority clients to visit, or transportation to and from such facilities must be affordable.

As De La Cancela, Chin, and Jenkins (1998) state, "A policy perspective on health system reform relevant to communities of color requires universal access regardless of residency, employment, citizenship status, or pre-existing conditions" (p. 38).

- *Affordability:* Even if services are available and accessible, poor and minority consumers will remain underserved if treatment costs more than they can afford to pay. As De La Cancela et al. (1998) observe:

> Ideally, systems of care for communities of color would ensure universal access, comprehensive services, universal coverage, and cultural competence. They would include explicitly defined benefits and coverage which are relevant to that community for primary, acute, chronic, developmental, and long-term care; they would not discriminate among segments of the communities through deductibles or coinsurance for legal immigrants, undocumented individuals, part-time, seasonal, and temporary workers or their dependents. Coverage would also be portable. (p. 32)

- *Accountability:* Even when mental health care is available, accessible, and affordable, it is of little consequence if the provided services are ineffective and fail to help minority consumers reach their treatment goals. There is a need for effective (including cost-effective) interventions within the context of practitioners' multicultural counseling competence. To ensure that minority clients receive high-quality care, the mental health care system must hold professionals accountable for their activities with these clients. Professionals at all levels should receive research-informed appraisals of their performance, constructive feedback, and, when necessary, correction. As Barlow (1996) notes, when professionals are held accountable, the quality of care increases and the costs of care are reduced.

- *Comprehensiveness:* High-quality mental health care may be available, accessible, and affordable, and the providers may be held accountable, but treatment options are limited for many minority clients. Treatment centers and service agencies must provide high-quality, comprehensive care that spans the full range of services for major disorders and psychological conditions (e.g., anxiety disorders, organic mental disorders, substance abuse disorders, personality disorders, affective disorders, schizophrenic disorders, and adjustment disorders). High-quality care also should be available for clients of all ages and levels of development, such as children, adolescents, adults, older adults, and families. Finally, high-quality care should be available to clients of all races, ethnicities, and cultures. Unless mental health practitioners offer comprehensive care, some consumers will not receive the type of treatment they need.

Levels of policy making. Mental health care policies are created by government bodies at three levels: federal, state, and local. To initiate reform in mental health care policies, professionals in the field must lobby the bodies that make policy. To lobby effectively, professionals need documentation of problem areas in the system and information on how specific policies at the various levels of government bear on the problem areas. Thus mental health professionals must take a systematic view of reform. If they fail to examine the effects of policies at each level of government, their reform efforts will be hindered.

Policy making also occurs at the micro level, in individual mental health care agencies. An agency must conform to the policies set by the federal government and by the governments of the agency's state and the locality of operation. In addition, each agency must set its own policies because organizational challenges and service obligations vary widely across agencies. Mental health professionals should examine the policies of individual agencies as well as those set on higher levels to ensure that agency policies do not cause deleterious consequences for minority clients.

Recommendations

The following six recommendations are intended to help professionals negotiate the arduous challenge of advocating mental health reform.

Frame issues in a user-friendly way for policy makers. Even conclusive and compelling data do not guarantee that policy makers will formulate policies that make the best use of the evidence. Policy makers often undermine their own ability to make good policy decisions by exercising limited thinking. It is common practice for policy makers to demand that researchers provide one "best answer," for example, even though the data may be inconclusive (Kiesler, 1980; MacRae, 1976; Weiss, 1978).

Because policy makers tend to oversimplify complex issues, advocates of reform must focus policy makers' attention on the real meanings of the social science data they receive from researchers (Weiss, 1978). Rappaport (1981) suggests that advocates can accomplish this goal through a two-step process. First, they should articulate paradoxical definitions of the social problems under discussion. For example, they might argue that culturally responsive interventions help overcome race-related disparities in the mental health system while simultaneously empowering minority consumers to confront the racism they encounter in the larger society; thus minority consumers can be both beneficiaries of and contributors to the solutions to racism. Second, advocates should support multiple and divergent, rather than singular, solutions for service delivery. For example, they might propose that to overcome race-related disparities in the mental health system, policies should require minimal standards of multicultural competence, regular evaluations of service centers, and programmatic research on interventions for minority populations.

Engage minority communities in advocacy for reform. The minority communities affected by many mental health care policies typically are excluded from the process of advocacy and policy formulation even though they have the greatest stake in the success of the services resulting from the policies. Phillips (2000) points out the discrepancy, found in many policies regarding human services delivery, between the empowerment orientation, which views the consumers as competent individuals, and the deficit orientation, which views the consumers as victims. By engaging minority communities in advocacy, mental health professionals can help empower these communities and draw on the communities' expertise to contextualize research findings, which can aid in reform efforts. Also, when minority communities are engaged in advocacy, policy makers are better able to hear the "voices" of the minority populations at hand. The best way for professionals to engage minority communities in advocacy is to invite minority leaders to participate, educate them on the merits of research, and collaborate with them.

Reinitiate reform efforts as scientific knowledge accumulates. Mental health care policy in the United States has a history of radical shifts, but these shifts have not always been beneficial (Goodwin, 1997). In a disheartening analysis of deinstitutionalization, Goodwin (1997) concludes that "rather than being a policy intended to address first and foremost the interest of people with mental problems, it addresses first the needs of government and the requirements of the economic and social system more generally" (p. 113). The problem of the switch from policies favoring institutionalization to policies favoring community-based services for ethnic minorities has been exacerbated, in part, by policy makers' failure to consider the importance of race and culture in the establishment of these services (Goodwin, 1997; Wade, 1993). It is ironic that in an era of deinstitutionalization there has been a rise in the disproportionate overrepresentation of minority consumers in custodial institutions and among involuntary commitments (Snowden & Cheung, 1990; Townsend, 1995).

This situation exposes the flaw in policy making that fails to consider relevant and sound data. Not only should reform be data driven, but the data should be revisited periodically. As knowledge about treating minority mental health care consumers accumulates, advocates should reinitiate reform efforts. As Phillips (2000) explains, policy is temporal because it evolves over time, and it is organizational because it involves a multitude of decision points. Therefore, policy making is not a discrete decision but a cumulative product (Hayes, 1982). Because science is the best vehicle for arriving at sound policy making, it is logical that the accumulation of data necessitates cumulative policy making.

Be true to your position as either a social scientist or a policy advocate. With or without the direct input of social scientists, for better or for worse, psychological evidence has been used in the formulation of social policy. Currently, there is some controversy among social scientists concerning their proper involvement in policy making (Phillips, 2000), but my purpose here is not to attempt to resolve those issues. Rather, given mental health professionals' involvement in advocacy, I argue that they must be true to their respective roles as scientists and as advocates of reform. As scientists, they have a responsibility to discover the nature of naturally occurring events. They should not attempt to use their position as scientists to push any particular mental health agenda, even if the agenda is based on good intentions. As advocates of mental health reform, they have a responsibility to present clear and unbiased interpretations of research findings and explain the implications of those findings for service delivery. They should avoid using mental health advocacy to advance their research agenda. Certainly, social scientists may benefit from maintaining fidelity to their different roles, but the benefits should not be their motivation. They should be motivated to behave as responsible and ethical scientists and advocates.

Confront the values that underlie the opposition's policies. All policies are predicated on sets of underlying values. Values are the criteria that social systems use in determining objectives as well as the methods for attaining those objectives. One of the most difficult aspects of advocating reform lies in the resistance that advocates encounter from individuals who oppose new policies. Their resistance typically is linked to unstated values, and, because these values are unstated, advocates of reform mistakenly aim their rebuttals directly at opposing policies rather than at the values underlying the policies. Aiming rebuttals directly at a policy is similar to treating the symptoms rather than the cause of a disease.

To counter opposition to reform, advocates first should listen carefully to the arguments for and against reform. A proposal for reform may be to deinstitutionalize patients and place them in the "least restricted environments," for example. "Liberal" residents of a middle-class community may support such a policy in principle but withdraw their support when they realize that, if it is enacted, minority clients will live in halfway houses in their neighborhoods. Their open opposition reveals the priority they place on maintaining their community in its present form rather than caring for disenfranchised persons. In such a case, advocates of the reform must identify the values that underlie opposition to the reform, expose them for what they are, clarify the contradiction between these values and the purported liberal stance of the opponents, and hold the opponents accountable for their position. Advocates should "attack" positions, not persons, on the basis of principles; the last thing they should do is attempt to counter resistance without first ascertaining the values that underlie the resistance.

Evaluate mental health policies after they have been enacted. Policies are not automatically effective just because they are enacted. Many ineffective policies have been implemented by policy makers who had good intentions.

The U.S. government's policy concerning the inclusion of ethnic minorities in research investigations is an example of one such flawed policy. The National Institutes of Health (NIH) Revitalization Act of 1993 (P.L. 103-43) states:

> It is the policy of NIH that women and members of minority groups and their subpopulations must be included in all NIH-supported biomedical and behavioral research projects involving human subjects, unless a clear and compelling rationale and justification establishes to the satisfaction of the relevant Institute/Center Director that inclusion is inappropriate with respect to the health of the subjects or the purpose of the research. Exclusion under other circumstances may be made by the Director, NIH, upon the recommendation of an Institute/Center Director based on a compelling rationale and justification. Cost is not an acceptable reason for exclusion except when the study would duplicate data from other sources. (NIH, 1994)

Unfortunately, this policy does not require researchers to include women and minority participants in their study samples in numbers sufficient to permit the investigation of group differences, except in Phase III clinical trials or larger effectiveness studies (Miranda et al., 2003). The unintentional consequence of the flaws in this policy is that scholars have obtained little evidence to demonstrate the effectiveness of psychological interventions with ethnic minorities (U.S. Department of Health and Human Services, 2001).

Moreover, the editorial policies of scientific journals discourage researchers—apparently in the interest of color blindness—from reporting on the race or ethnicity of research participants in their analyses unless they provide scientific justification for doing so (Miranda et al., 2003). It is ironic that researchers are required to include minorities as participants in clinical trials, but the outlets for reporting their findings discourage them from publishing information on the effects of psychological interventions on minority populations. Is this yet another example of the exploitation of the victims of scientific racism?

As this example illustrates, the enactment of well-intentioned policies does not necessarily overcome racism. Mental health professionals must routinely evaluate the policies of the mental health care system if race-related disparities within the system are to be eliminated. How can professionals evaluate these policies? If a policy pertains to research, professionals must review the body of research that is based on the policy and determine what knowledge has been discovered and what methodological limitations exist. The absence of new discoveries may point to methodological limitations. In the case of the NIH policy noted above, we can easily determine that nothing has been learned and that sample sizes of minority populations are too small for meaningful data analysis. If a policy pertains directly to practice, Mechanic (1999) suggests that professionals can evaluate it by (a) measuring consumers' subjective responses to the service provided, (b) measuring consumers' objective performance and quality of life, and (c) assessing the economic and administrative costs of the services.

Multicultural Training

Multicultural training, as an intervention to overcome racism in the mental health system, is a logical sequel to practice-based minority research and mental health care reform. Pedersen (2003) regards training as a primary prevention strategy in efforts to end racism in the mental health system. Why should training be considered an intervention? Training is a conduit through which mental health professionals can apply practice-based knowledge and improve the performance of practitioners. Beebe, Mottet, and Roach (2004) define training as "the process of developing skills in order to more effectively perform a specific job or task" (p. 5).

In recent years, researchers have devoted increasing attention to the topic of multicultural training for mental health professionals (Abreu, Chung, & Atkinson, 2000; Brown, Parham, & Yonker, 1996; Kiselica, 1998; Kiselica, Maben, & Locke, 1999; Neville et al., 1996; Pope-Davis & Coleman, 1997; Ridley, Mendoza, & Kanitz, 1994; Speight, Thomas, Kennel, & Anderson, 1995). Many scholars have noted that traditional training for counselors and therapists inadequately prepares them to practice in a pluralistic society. These scholars stress the need for multicultural training at all levels of preparation for professional practice, including graduate programs, postdoctoral programs, and continuing education. Their writings cover a variety of issues, such as training philosophy, learning objectives, instructional strategies, program designs, and evaluation. In the discussion below, I distill this body of knowledge into some salient principles and recommendations.

Multicultural Counseling Competence

Because training concerns the development of skills, training programs should determine the skills that mental health professionals need to treat minority clients successfully. The literature emphasizes the need for counselors and therapists to develop multicultural counseling competence, but there is no consensus on how this construct should be defined. For purposes of this discussion, I propose the following definition: *Multicultural counseling competence consists of a set of skills that enables the mental health professional to facilitate therapeutic change through the beneficial incorporation of cultural considerations in counseling.* This definition has several key components:

- *Set of skills:* Several different skills are the building blocks of multicultural counseling competence. As Beebe et al. (2004) put it, skills are abilities "to *do something* as opposed to knowing something" (p. 5). To be multiculturally competent in counseling, a practitioner must have the following skills: the ability to set culturally relevant goals, the ability to assess a client from the cilent's cultural perspective, the ability to be culturally self-aware, the ability to individualize the change process, the ability to communicate cross-culturally, the ability to demonstrate cultural empathy, the ability to solicit the client's cultural perspective on both the psychological presentation and the therapeutic process, the ability to confront culture-based resistance, and the ability to seek culture-related consultation. The practitioner also must be able to coordinate all these skills to achieve therapeutic change.

- *Facilitation of therapeutic change:* Multicultural counseling competence enables counselors to assist minority clients in making real, first-order changes in their lives. Therapeutic change includes cognitive, emotional, behavioral, interpersonal, and spiritual aspects of the client's personal experience. Therapeutic change is always specific to the individual client. Given that the holistic experience of each client is unique, each client has unique goals to reach in therapy. Nothing should take priority over therapeutic change, and every facet of counseling should contribute to facilitating therapeutic change.

- *Incorporation of culture:* All people are cultural beings, and culture is always implicit in counseling. Draguns (1976, 2002) describes culture as an inevitable but usually "silent" participant in counseling. However, multiculturally competent counselors make culture explicit in counseling, and they make it integral to both *process* and *content.* Regarding process, counselors attend to culture at each stage of counseling, from engagement to termination. They attend to relationship dynamics, seeking to overcome cultural barriers and using culture to facilitate therapeutic change. Regarding content, counselors attempt to understand how culture factors into the psychological presentation. They frame their assessments and diagnoses from a cultural perspective, seeking to understand their clients' idiographic experiences as clearly as possible. They also help clients set culturally relevant treatment goals.

Guiding Principles of Training

Mental health professionals' multicultural training should be based on clear guiding principles such as the four suggested below.

Training should be trainee centered. An important element of effective training is the maximization of the experience for every trainee. Trainees vary in a number of ways, including in their pretraining knowledge and skills and their learning styles. Furthermore, trainees, like clients, come from different cultures. The multicultural training curriculum and its methods of training should take into account the differences among trainees.

Training should be developmental. Given that it entails a complex set of skills, multicultural counseling competence is acquired over time. The skills should be taught in step-by-step fashion, with trainees learning simple skills before more complex skills (Beebe et al., 2004, p. 76). For example, the complex skill of cultural empathy (Ridley & Lingle, 1996; Ridley & Udipi, 2002) consists of two superordinate processes—cultural empathic understanding and cultural empathic responsiveness—as well as a number of subordinate processes. Before counselors and therapists can master cultural empathy, they must learn the microskills that support it, such as attending behavior, open-ended inquiry, reflection of feeling, and paraphrasing.

Training should be outcome oriented. Training must include clear objectives for trainees to strive for if their learning is to be evaluated. The objectives to be achieved in this case are the skills that constitute multicultural counseling competence. Each training objective should meet four criteria: It should be observable, measurable, attainable, and specific (Beebe et al., 2004). Without objectives, there is no basis for determining whether learning has occurred, and without criteria for the objectives, there is no basis for determining how well learning has occurred.

Training should be relevant to practice. Only a certain amount of the knowledge in the field of counseling can be subsumed under the domain of multicultural counseling competence. Even in the burgeoning specialty of multicultural psychology, only a certain amount of knowledge is relevant to multicultural counseling competence. Certainly, some of the knowledge in counseling generally and multiculturalism specifically is more relevant to multicultural counseling competence than other knowledge, and there is always an element of judgment regarding what knowledge pertains to multicultural counseling competence. Training programs should place high priority on providing training in the skills and knowledge judged to help trainees facilitate therapeutic change through the beneficial incorporation of cultural considerations in counseling. Training in skills and knowledge that fails to achieve this end is irrelevant to the development of multicultural counseling competence.

Recommendations

The following six recommendations are intended to aid mental health professionals who provide multicultural training to counselors and therapists.

Balance the use of didactic and experiential training methods. A variety of training methods are appropriate for use in multicultural training. Generally, these methods fall into two broad categories: didactic and experiential. Using didactic methods, trainers impart information to trainees. Using experiential methods, trainers focus on changing trainees' feelings and behaviors. The literature provides ample evidence of the importance of balancing these two approaches. Abreu et al. (2000) suggest that instructors providing multicultural training should begin with didactic, cognitive instruction and then switch to experiential methods. They assert that this sequence of instructional methods helps to minimize trainees' resistance to the training.

Design a systematic, organized training experience. Multicultural training programs must design their training experiences to fit the needs of the trainees, the context of the training, and the level of the training. In fact, the American Psychological Association (2003) encourages training programs to make multicultural training thematic to their program missions. Five particular program designs have been found to facilitate multicultural training: workshop design, separate course design, interdisciplinary design, area of concentration design, and integration design (Ridley, Mendoza, & Kanitz, 1994). Each design has its strengths and weaknesses. Programs must select the designs that most closely match their training philosophies and that will achieve their learning objectives. Vázquez (1997) provides a helpful systemic model for the inclusion of multiculturalism in graduate training programs.

Create a training environment that is conducive to learning. Optimal learning occurs in an environment that is marked by psychological safety and support. Trainees who feel threatened will not benefit fully from training. As I have noted previously, the topics of culture and race can be sensitive, and instructors should be prepared for the possibility that trainees will respond emotionally to these topics. Trainers should encourage trainees to explore the topics of culture and race without becoming unduly defensive or resistant. Kiselica (1998) identifies the following components as critical to an environment that is conducive to multicultural training: gentle confrontation with ongoing support, sharing of the joy that characterizes the learning of multiculturalism, and trainer self-disclosure. Tomlinson-Clarke and Wang (1999) note that trainers must intentionally create an accepting environment for multicultural training. Without acceptance, subtle and covert messages can incite defensiveness and resistance among trainees.

Preevaluate trainees' multicultural counseling competence. Training programs cannot evaluate improvements in the multicultural counseling competence of trainees without baseline data or adequate criteria regarding the skill set. Therefore, training programs should preevaluate trainees to gather pertinent information about variations in trainees' backgrounds, experiences, and developmental needs. Failure to preevaluate may result in erroneous conclusions about trainees' needs and interests or about their improvements in multicultural counseling competence as a result of training.

Evaluate learning outcomes. Evaluation of learning outcomes is essential to ensure that a program is providing high-quality training. The American Psychological Association's Task Force on Education, Training, and Service in Psychology (1982) has emphasized the need for evaluation of training outcomes, as the following statement illustrates:

> The best hope for the profession may be in its ability to demonstrate that it has a serious, systematic program for evaluation that will provide a regular, dependable flow of information by means of which to validate and improve its practices and requirements. (p. 2)

Evaluations of learning outcomes should be conducted periodically (Beebe et al., 2004). If trainees are not meeting their learning objectives, the training should be changed to accommodate the trainees' learning needs. If trainees are meeting their objectives, training may still be refined to improve the quality of the experience. Training programs can use a number of methods to evaluate learning outcomes, including objective instruments, qualitative methods, anecdotal reports, self-reports, and behavioral analyses.

Provide organizational leadership and support. Multicultural training is rarely successful without top-down leadership and institutional commitment (Ridley & Thompson, 1999; Sue & Sue, 2003). Top-down leadership in a multicultural training program yields several benefits: (a) Leaders model desirable behaviors and attitudinal expectations for others in the organization, (b) stakeholders are more likely to embrace the organization's commitment to multicultural training, and (c) leaders can hold others accountable for tangible evidence that they have embraced multicultural objectives (Ridley & Thompson, 1999; Sue et al., 1998).

Chapter Summary

Combating institutional racism in the mental health system must begin at the macrosystem level. Many of the disparities that occur at the local level of treatment centers are tied to policies and procedures that are enacted outside of these settings. This chapter has discussed three macrosystem interventions: practice-based minority research, mental health care reform, and multicultural training. Each of these has the potential to help make service delivery more responsive to minority consumers. Macrosystem interventions provide the foundation for microsystem interventions, or interventions on the level of individual treatment settings.

14

Microsystem Interventions

Microsystem interventions in the mental health care system are interventions intended to enhance service delivery within individual treatment settings, such as hospitals, community mental health centers, private practices, clinics, and counseling centers—anywhere professional counseling or psychotherapy takes place. All of these service settings can be subject to and benefit from macrosystem interventions, as they are part of the overall mental health care network.

The purpose of microsystem interventions is to *implement* particular mental health care delivery practices. In the struggle to eliminate racism in the mental health care system, macrosystem interventions are concerned with how minority clients *should be* treated, and microsystem interventions focus on how minority clients *actually are* treated. In this chapter, I discuss six microsystem interventions: an organizational core ideology that embraces diversity, integrated service networks, consultation, prevention and health promotion, action research, and affirmative action.

A Core Ideology That Embraces Diversity

The core ideology of an organization defines the organization's enduring character (Collins & Porras, 2002); it gives the organization a consistent identity that pervades organizational life. An effective organization has a well-established core ideology, and the ideology offers guidance and inspiration to members and constituents of the organization. As Collins and Porras (2002) note, the core ideology comprises a set of basic precepts that state for the organization's members and constituents, "This is who we are;

this is what we stand for; this is what we're about" (p. 54). In addition, an organization's core ideology does not change easily. Although an organization may change its strategic plans and organizational practices out of necessity, perhaps in response to changing external environments, its core ideology often remains fixed. As I have noted in an earlier work,

> A core ideology reflects on what an organization stands for and why it exists. A core ideology is not an organizational strategy. Strategies are subject to change, and they are negotiable. Core ideologies—based upon reasoned values and purpose—should not be subject to change, and as such, they are non-negotiable. Core ideologies are the foundations upon which organizations are built and the basis for developing organizational strategies. (Ridley & Goodwin, 2003, p. 48)

An organization's core ideology consists of two components: a core purpose and core values. An organization's core purpose is its reason for being (Collins & Porras, 2002). The organization pursues its core purpose but never fully reaches it; the core purpose continually stimulates change and progress in the organization. Warren (1995) points out that nothing revitalizes an organization faster than the rediscovery of its core purpose.

An organization's core values are its essential and enduring tenets (Collins & Porras, 2002). Visionary organizations typically have well-established core values, which essentially are small sets of three to five guiding principles. An organization's core values do not require external justification because they have intrinsic importance to the organization's major stakeholders. Regardless of the landscape of the external environment, an organization decides its core values for itself.

One way for mental health treatment settings to overcome institutional racism is by establishing organizational core ideologies that embrace diversity. Reynolds and Pope (2003) recommend that counseling centers identify diversity as central to their mission statements and explicitly include words such as *multicultural* and *diversity* in those statements. An organization can establish a diversity-inclusive core ideology by doing the following:

- Making explicit the role of diversity in the core ideology
- Communicating the core ideology often
- Communicating the core ideology through a variety of media and channels
- Publicizing testimonials that illustrate the core ideology in actual practice
- Rewarding organizational practices that reflect the core ideology

Table 14.1 displays some examples of organizational core purposes that embrace diversity. It is noteworthy that in each of these examples, diversity is relevant and essential to the core purpose. Although mental health care agencies do not need to make diversity their exclusive purpose, diversity

Table 14.1   Examples of Organizational Core Purposes That Embrace
                   Diversity

Organization	*Core Purpose*
Wayne County Department of Children's Services	To promote the welfare of children by incorporating cultural considerations in the prevention, investigation, and treatment of child abuse and neglect
Counseling Psychology Program, University of the East	To recruit, train, and graduate scientist-practitioners who are multiculturally competent
Midtown Behavioral Health Center	To deliver high-quality psychological services and achieve equitable treatment outcomes across the racial and cultural populations served

should be integral, as opposed to ancillary, to mental health care organizations' core purposes. In this way, diversity initiatives can be endemic to these organizations, and the organizations can embrace diversity without necessarily making it the only reason for their existence.

Integrated Service Networks

In most communities, a variety of specialty agencies and organizations provide mental health care services. Each agency has a unique mission and offers its own special type of service, but few organizations are equipped to treat clients holistically. For the treatment of minority clients, integrated service networks offer realistic alternatives to individual specialty agencies. In an integrated service network, specialty agencies and other mental health care organizations join a formal alliance to provide the most comprehensive treatment possible by coordinating and integrating their collective resources. Such networks are particularly valuable in communities that are economically challenged. As De La Cancela, Chin, and Jenkins (1998) note, integrated service networks coordinate clients' care and thus help to control the costs of mental health services. Five features characterize these networks: They involve multiple agencies, they include practitioners from multiple disciplines, they offer comprehensive care, they provide competent care, and they coordinate and integrate services to benefit clients.

Multiple agencies. Integrated service networks are composed of multiple mental health agencies and other organizations that participate in service

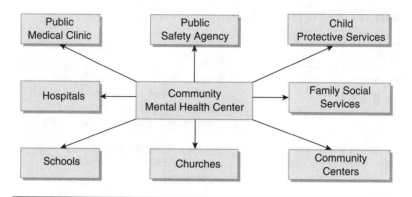

Figure 14.1   Model of an Integrated Service Network

delivery (see Figure 14.1). The number of agencies participating varies across networks, depending on factors such as the availability of resources and local politics. Networks might include hospitals, schools, public safety agencies, churches, family and social service agencies, mental health centers, and community and recreation centers. Each of the agencies involved in a network can be viewed as a subsystem of a larger delivery system.

Establishing an effective integrated service network is always a challenge; it requires significant time and effort from many individuals and organizations. Communities often support the creation of such networks because they offer a cost-effective way to deliver mental health services, but low costs are not their only advantage. Integrated service networks also provide returns to communities in the form of more productive citizens and reduction of the expenses associated with citizens who have untreated psychological problems.

Multiple disciplines. Integrated service networks include professionals from a variety of human service areas. Among the mental health disciplines, psychiatrists, psychologists, marriage and family therapists, and social workers may participate. Specialized professionals such as drug and addiction counselors also may play strategic roles. In addition, networks may include professionals from allied health fields, such as physicians and nurses, as well as legal aid advisers and career specialists. Some networks also may include spiritual advisers, such as members of the clergy, to address clients' problems from a religious perspective. The combined expertise of the many professionals involved in a service network allows the network to address a wide variety of problems and to treat clients holistically.

Comprehensive care. Effective integrated service networks provide services that meet the full range of human needs. Mental health care should be treated within the context of a client's total health and life care. The professionals involved in effective service networks recognize that an individual's mental health cannot be separated from his or her holistic life experiences. Therefore, to provide truly comprehensive care, service networks include agencies and organizations that focus on education, career, and family life guidance.

Competent care. Effective integrated service networks provide high-quality service delivery. The social workers, nurse practitioners, rehabilitation counselors, physical therapists, and other professionals who participate in such networks have state-of-the-art knowledge and skills in their fields. This expertise includes multicultural competence.

Competent mental health care also entails providing facilities and resources that allow for optimal service delivery. The most competent professionals in the world cannot fully demonstrate their competence if they lack adequate means for service delivery. Therefore, an effective integrated service network ensures that all professionals in the network have the proper equipment and supplies, that participating clinics have accessible and affordable professionals on staff, and that pupil personnel services in schools are appropriately connected to the network.

Coordination and integration of services. Given their multiagency and multidisciplinary nature, integrated service networks are complicated affiliations of organizations and people. Although all of a network's participating agencies and professionals may be competent in their own right, more is needed for the network to fulfill its mission. An effective service network requires managerial competence in the coordination and integration of the wide array of agencies, services, and professionals who participate in the network. When integrated service networks are managed successfully, with efficient coordination and seamless integration of services, ethnic minorities are more likely to view them as consumer-friendly and responsive to their needs.

Consultation

Sometimes organizations need help in deciphering their organizational dynamics and overcoming institutional racism. For instance, a mental health care agency might seek assistance in crafting a diversity-inclusive core ideology, training staff in multicultural counseling competence, or establishing best practices in minority recruitment, selection, and retention of clients from underrepresented populations. In short, organizations may benefit from consultation with experts in particular areas. Arredondo and Reinoso (2003) address the importance of multicultural consultation to mental health care agencies, discussing the competencies needed, the challenges that diversity consultants face, and the benefits of such consultation. Atkinson, Thompson,

Principles Roles	Collaboration	Problem Reframing	Open Systems Perspective	Accountability	Ethics
Advocate					
Expert					
Trainer/ Educator					
Investigator					
Process Specialist					

Figure 14.2   Roles and Principles of Consultation

and Grant (1993) note that consultants can help set up preventive programs "to ward off or at least minimize the problems that result from racism and discrimination" (p. 268).

Defining the concept of consultation is essential for appreciating how consultants can help mental health organizations overcome institutional racism. Dougherty (2000) gives this definition: "Consultation is a process in which a human service professional assists a consultee with a work-related (or caretaking-related) problem with a client system, with the goal of helping both the consultee and the client system in some specified way" (pp. 10–11). Embedded in this definition is the commonly accepted notion that consultation involves three parties: a consultant, a consultee, and a client system. Consultants provide direct services to consultees. Consultees, often the ones who request the services of consultants, provide direct services to client systems. Thus client systems benefit indirectly from the work of consultants, who essentially serve as intermediaries.

How might consultation help organizations to overcome institutional racism? To answer this question, two elements of consultation are particularly noteworthy: consultation roles and consultation principles. Figure 14.2 organizes these elements along two dimensions.

Consultation Roles

Consultants play a number of roles (Dougherty, 2000). The five consultation roles discussed below are especially relevant to consultation regarding issues of racism.

Advocate. In the role of advocate, a consultant attempts to persuade the consultee to behave in ways the consultant believes are desirable or appropriate. Sometimes consultant advocacy is regarded as "protecting the rights of those who are unable to help themselves, and seek due process, aid, and treatment for those persons" (Kurpius & Lewis, 1988, p. 1). Advocacy for social justice is the clearest demonstration of this role. Vera and Speight (2003) suggest that such advocacy is an indicator of multicultural competence, expands the scope of psychological practice beyond counseling and psychotherapy, and can benefit society in the long term by improving institutions. As advocates for social justice, consultants may encourage mental health agencies to confront racism and oppression in their local communities. Given that racism is a psychological stressor (Clark, Anderson, Clark, & Williams, 1999), and given that mental health agencies are responsible for trying to reduce psychological stressors, these agencies logically should strive to reduce racism.

Expert. In the role of expert, a consultant functions much like a technical adviser who provides knowledge, advice, or service to the consultee. Sometimes consultees seek consultants with particular expertise because the consultees recognize that they cannot solve problems without the consultants' specialized knowledge. For example, when the U.S. Department of Health and Human Services was formulating a supplement to its 1999 publication *Mental Health: A Report of the Surgeon General,* it consulted with a number of noted researchers. The supplement, titled *Mental Health: Culture, Race, and Ethnicity,* which was published in 2001, documents large and unfavorable disparities between members of minority groups and Whites in their access to and utilization of mental health services. The work of the consulted researchers is described in a recent special issue of the journal *Culture, Medicine, and Psychiatry* (see, e.g., López, 2003; Miranda, Nakamura, & Bernal, 2003; Richardson, Anderson, Flaherty, & Bell, 2003).

Trainer/educator. In the role of trainer/educator, a consultant attempts to change the consultee's professional functioning. As a trainer, the consultant creates conditions in which the consultee can acquire skills. As an educator, the consultant teaches the consultee a body of knowledge. Diversity consultants most often take the role of trainer/educator in helping consultees develop multicultural competence. In my own experience as a diversity consultant, I have found that the most difficult barrier to successful training is trainee resistance. However, effective training and education techniques can help consultants overcome such resistance (Ridley & Thompson, 1999). For example, diversity consultants should avoid taking an overly confrontational stance with trainees. Diversity consultants must empathize with consultees' fears and apprehensions, especially given the sensitive nature of the topic of race. They also must stay current with advances in knowledge, especially given the recent explosion of research on multicultural counseling.

Investigator. In the role of investigator, a consultant gathers information, analyzes it, and gives feedback to the consultee (Lippitt & Lippitt, 1986). In this role, the consultant must (a) find as much information relevant to the problem as possible, (b) analyze and interpret that information accurately, and (c) effectively communicate the information, along with his or her interpretation of it. In the mental health system, this is the role most urgently needed for consultants to play, because stakeholders must understand the dynamics of institutional racism in their organizations before they can overcome it. Institutional racism is often covert and thus hard to detect; most organizations therefore could benefit from consulting with experts who are not enmeshed in their organizational dynamics and who have a solid understanding of the behavioral model of racism.

Process specialist. In the role of process specialist, a consultant observes and facilitates the consultee's problem-solving process. As Schein (1988) explains, the process consultant enhances the consultee's understanding of regular problem solving. The goal of process consultation is to help the consultee become a better problem solver. Consultants who fill this role can have long-lasting effects on organizations. Organizations that work with such consultants to address institutional racism can become better equipped not only to overcome institutional racism but also to prevent it.

Consultation Principles

Consultation can be a complex and demanding process, and consultants must have strong cognitive and interpersonal skills. Because each consultation engagement is unique, effective consultants operate from a basis of sound principles as opposed to rigid rules. The five principles discussed below provide important guidelines for consultation.

Collaboration. For consultation to succeed, the consultant and consultee must establish a working alliance and recognize how both parties can contribute to the process. The consultant might share his or her expertise or knowledge of intervention strategies, and the consultee might provide background information on the organization and participate in implementing the intervention. Arredondo and Reinoso (2003), in discussing multicultural consultation, note that "collaboration is a skill embedded in the multicultural competencies" (p. 340). They suggest that consultants should view their client organizations as partners in planning interventions.

Problem reframing. Consultees' perspectives on their organizations' problems are colored by their experiences, backgrounds, and knowledge. Usually these perspectives are limited and, to some degree, inaccurate. For example, consultees commonly mistake symptoms for the underlying problems. A competent consultant consistently challenges and broadens the consultee's problem definition. Nowhere is problem reframing more necessary than in consultation with organizations that perpetuate unintentional racism. Competent consultants help these organizations reframe unintentional racism in terms of organizational behaviors rather than surface-level symptoms. They also assist individual stakeholders in examining themselves as unintentional racists even when the stakeholders are not prejudiced.

Open systems perspective. Although many consultants and stakeholders give lip service to open systems thinking, they often approach their work in a closed system manner. For instance, they may fail to appreciate fully how organizations are embedded in suprasystems or the connectedness between the parts of an organization. Consultants can facilitate long-lasting change only by attending to the cycle of input, throughput, and output inherent in open systems. This cycle demands that diversity consultants consider outside influences on organizations as well as internal entities that may seem removed but nevertheless contribute to race-related treatment disparities. Among the outside influences on mental health care organizations are policies that are set at higher levels in the mental health system. Internal influences may take the form of passively resistant organizational members, such as professionals who spout the virtues of diversity but sabotage diversity initiatives by withholding vital data concerning organizational practices.

Accountability. Consultants' work typically goes unmonitored by any professional organization, so consultants must hold themselves accountable for their performance by evaluating their own work. Unfortunately, diversity consultants easily can avoid being accountable for their performance, given that many of their clients are uninformed about the real issues involved in racism. Some consultees are intimidated by the prospect of confronting issues of race and dealing with an expert in this area. This dynamic creates a situation in which consultants may be virtually unchallenged about their consultation interventions. Therefore, it is of paramount importance that consultants adhere to the principle of accountability by monitoring their performance and seeking constructive feedback.

Ethics. Consultants sometimes encounter situations that raise ethical concerns and require sound judgment (Dougherty, 2000). Consultants are ultimately responsible for conducting themselves in an ethical manner.

Consultants who make good ethical decisions avoid compromising the integrity of their interventions. My colleagues and I have proposed a model of ethical decision making for multicultural practitioners that comprises a set of "thinking tools" (Ridley, Liddle, Hill, & Li, 2001). We argue that consultants should follow four important principles in making ethical decisions: (a) avoid oversimplifying the complexity inherent in ethical situations, (b) avoid applying ethical directives rigidly, (c) engage in critical reflection, and (d) solve problems creatively.

Consultation in Action

The five roles and five principles of consultation discussed above are useful for conceptualizing the overall process of consultation. For each consultation, the consultant should identify his or her most appropriate role: advocate, expert, trainer/educator, investigator, or process specialist. Depending on the role identified, the consultant should clarify what is expected of the consultee. If the consultant is assuming the role of process specialist, for instance, the consultee would be expected to develop the skill set needed for problem solving. If the consultant is functioning as an expert, the consultee would be expected to assume a passive role while the consultant does the primary problem solving.

Regardless of the consultant's role in a particular consultation, the consultant must adhere to the five principles discussed above. The consultant has no option but to collaborate, reframe problems, approach consultation from an open systems perspective, hold him- or herself accountable, and behave ethically. If the consultant fails to adhere to any of these principles, the consultation is jeopardized, even if the consultant is regarded as an expert.

Mental health agencies can benefit immensely from professional consultation. Because institutional racism is pervasive and few consultants are truly experts on racism, infinite opportunities currently exist for diversity consultants to provide their services (Arredondo & Reinoso, 2003). They should anticipate both fulfillment and challenge in accepting these opportunities.

Prevention and Health Promotion

Traditional counseling and psychotherapy, even when they are effective, have two major limitations (Romano & Hage, 2000; Rosenhan & Seligman, 1995). First, treatment typically occurs only after a client has experienced considerable personal difficulties. This timing is unfortunate because many of the clients' problems could have been prevented altogether (Hoffman & Driscoll, 2000). Second, the number of mental health professionals currently available to treat the psychological problems that exist in U.S. society is far smaller than the number needed. This problem is compounded by the lack of access to services among many of the people who are most in need of mental health services.

The racism that pervades the mental health system is another limitation of counseling and psychotherapy. Many minority consumers of mental health care services experience double jeopardy. As the victims of racism in society, they experience untold stress and psychological challenges. Research has shown that economic status and social class are primary determinants of how much stress, social injustice, and exploitation individuals experience, with the poor suffering more than others (Albee, 2000). Given that disproportionate numbers of socioeconomically disadvantaged Americans are members of minority groups, the mental health consequences of stress clearly are significant for minorities. In addition, as consumers of mental health care services, many minorities are victimized again by a system that fails to make services available, accessible, and affordable.

The prevention of mental health problems offers an attractive alternative to treatment, given the limitations of traditional counseling and psychotherapy noted above.

Defining Prevention

Prevention refers to any intervention that forestalls an unpleasant or undesirable event or makes it impossible for that event to occur in the future or increases the likelihood of desirable future outcomes, such as health and well-being (Albee & Ryan-Finn, 1993; Vera & Reese, 2000). In essence, prevention efforts target specific populations that have not yet been affected by a problem.

Romano and Hage (2000) conceptualize prevention in relation to mental health as any intervention that has one or more of the following characteristics: stops problem behaviors from ever occurring; delays the onset of problem behaviors; reduces the impacts of existing problem behaviors; strengthens knowledge, attitudes, and behaviors that promote emotional and physical well-being; and supports institutional, community, and government policies that promote physical and emotional well-being. A defining feature of sound prevention practice is intentionality (Cowen, 1980). That is, professionals should apply theory and research to design interventions that have as their purpose, or intention, the interception of "pathways" to disorder and adaptation (Felner & Felner, 1989).

Prevention may be especially useful in overcoming some of the unintentional racism in mental health services in low-income, minority comunities. Effective prevention programs can help reduce the incidence, prevalence, and duration of actual psychopathology. The reduction in the rates of disorders not only benefits the communities as a whole but decreases the numbers of individuals who are in need of remediation or tertiary interventions. This would mean fewer consumers are exposed to practitioners and agencies that are unintentionally racist.

A Formula

Given that many factors contribute to the precipitation of psychological problems, it follows that many factors also contribute to prevention of such problems. Some of the factors that contribute to or help prevent psychological problems are obvious, whereas others are less so. To design an effective prevention program, one first must identify and account for both kinds of factors. The Carter Commission on Mental Health's Task Panel on Prevention has developed the following formula to clarify the relationship between factors that can precipitate psychological problems and factors that can prevent them:

$$\frac{\text{Organic Factors} + \text{Stress} + \text{Exploitation}}{\text{Coping Skills} + \text{Self-Esteem} + \text{Support Groups}}$$

This formula illustrates how prevention reduces the noxious agents that adversely affect human development and strengthens a target population's resistance to stressful events (Albee & Ryan-Finn, 1993). In the numerator are the noxious agents that prevention programs seek to reduce, in this case, organic factors, stress, and exploitation. For ethnic minorities, such agents would include racism (Clark et al., 1999), minority status (Moritsugu & Sue, 1983), and acculturative stress (Anderson, 1991). In the denominator are the factors that prevention seeks to strengthen, in this case, coping skills, self-esteem, and support groups. For Native Americans, for example, bicultural competence has been demonstrated to be a coping skill (LaFromboise & Rowe, 1983). Essentially, prevention strategies aim to encourage voluntary lifestyle changes in at-risk individuals and to mobilize social support.

Parameters of Prevention Programs

To design effective prevention programs, professionals must understand the two parameters of such programs: categories and factors.

Categories. Traditionally, prevention efforts have been divided into three categories: primary, secondary, and tertiary. *Primary prevention* efforts are intended to reduce the number of future incidents of a problem (Albee, 2000). The success of a primary prevention program rests exclusively on a decrease in the rate of occurrence of the targeted problem—whether emotional disturbance or consumption of potentially harmful substances—in the target population (Albee & Ryan-Finn, 1983). *Secondary prevention* efforts involve the early detection and treatment of a problem in a population (Vera & Reese, 2000). Secondary prevention emphasizes keeping an identified problem from escalating to debilitating proportions. *Tertiary prevention* efforts focus on reducing the future consequences or the duration of established problems that may lead to diagnosable disorders (Vera & Reese, 2000). This type of prevention is often confused with psychotherapy or rehabilitation, but it is different in that tertiary prevention occurs before a diagnosable disorder is determined, whereas psychotherapy follows diagnosis of a disorder (Vera & Reese, 2000).

Factors. Professionals must consider two factors in designing prevention programs: risk factors and protective factors. Preventive interventions usually attempt to identify risk factors that may contribute to negative outcomes in the future. The literature is replete with discussions of at-risk individuals, but researchers have devoted little attention to individuals who otherwise would be considered at risk but have overcome obstacles without professional intervention. Protective factors contribute to individuals' likelihood of staving off mental health problems (Vera & Reese, 2000). Effective prevention programs seek to overcome risk factors and accentuate protective factors in a population.

Prevention in Action

Of the three categories of prevention efforts, primary prevention offers the greatest potential for overcoming unintentional racism in the mental health system. The very nature of primary prevention, with its emphasis on reducing risk factors and strengthening protective factors, is well suited to changing the social system dynamics that perpetuate racism and oppression as well as the personal dynamics that help people negotiate social system dynamics. Practitioners can draw upon the behavioral model of racism to identify what they otherwise would not recognize as risk factors in their communities and protective factors in their clients.

An Exemplar

Schinke et al. (1988) examined the effectiveness of a program designed to prevent tobacco, alcohol, and drug abuse among Native American adolescents. Participants in their study lived on two reservation sites in western Washington state. The preventive intervention was based on the theory of bicultural competence posited by LaFromboise and Rowe (1983), who describe bicultural competence in a Native American as the individual's ability to make his or her desires or preferences known in an Indian or non-Indian setting (p. 592). Schinke et al. describe three components of bicultural competence: communication skills, coping skills, and discrimination skills. They found that study participants who received an intervention based on these skills showed better posttest and follow-up outcomes than did participants in a no-intervention control group.

Action Research

In relation to mental health care, action research is research that is conducted to apply the local data gathered to the redesign and improvement of service delivery. Chin (2003) calls a system's responsiveness to action research efforts the system's "cultural competence." She notes that service delivery systems, in attempting to be unbiased and equitable, often ignore racial and ethnic differences among service consumers. As I have noted in earlier chapters, this color blindness is a type of defensiveness that leads to bias and inequity—the very outcomes that color-blind professionals seek to avoid. Below, I present some guidelines for mental health professionals who undertake action research.

Maintain a population focus. Chin (2003) notes that action research should focus on local populations and offers the following recommendations:

- *Collect data on population demographics.* Service delivery systems must determine the racial/ethnic composition of their target areas. They also need accurate data on population distributions for planning and resource allocation purposes.
- *Collect data on changing demographics.* As the racial/ethnic groups within an area's population change, the service delivery system also must change to be culturally responsive. If a given group experiences rapid growth (more than 10%), the system should respond by demonstrating how its services are appropriate and adequate for that group.
- *Plan for specific services.* When a racial/ethnic group reaches a benchmark of 1,500 persons or 3% of the area population, the service delivery system should conduct a needs assessment to determine the services that should be available to the group's members.
- *Establish representative governance.* A service delivery system achieves cultural competence in part by including the voices of various local population segments in the system's governance. To this end, the system's governance committees should reflect the racial/ethnic demographics of the service area's population.

Collect race/ethnicity data on consumers. Collecting race/ethnicity data on clients is the only way for service delivery systems to determine whether they are meeting the needs of various groups. However, collecting such data may be threatening to some system members, who may fear the possible exposure of enrollment biases such as inadequate services or utilization disparities. Chin (2003) recommends that service delivery systems adopt the following three guidelines in collecting race/ethnicity data:

- *Employ a federal and common standard.* The most recent U.S. census data should provide a standard for collecting race/ethnicity data. The data should be broken down into the five major racial/ethnic groups. A timetable for implementation should be set.
- *Ensure equitable representation in research.* Research findings are meaningful only if they are based on representative samples and can be generalized to the population of interest. In conducting consumer satisfaction surveys and needs assessments, service delivery systems should ensure that all local racial/ethnic groups are adequately represented.
- *Use language-appropriate methodology.* Considerable miscommunication and misinterpretation can occur when a survey instrument is in English and English is not the respondent's primary language. Consumer satisfaction surveys should be conducted in the clients' primary languages and, as much as possible, by professionals who are members of the clients' racial/ethnic groups.

Establish performance indicators for cultural competence. The level of a service delivery system's cultural competence cannot be measured without valid performance indicators. Such indicators should be integral to a system's quality assurance monitoring. Chin (2003) makes the following recommendations:

- *Determine utilization patterns.* Service delivery systems should determine the extent to which ethnic minority clients are covered by insurance or are uninsured. They also should determine whether there are differences among client groups in referrals, types of interventions, and other utilization patterns.
- *Measure utilization by service type or penetration rates.* If there are disparities in utilization or penetration among racial/ethnic groups within target areas, service delivery systems must develop plans to eliminate those disparities.
- *Identify cultural/linguistic needs.* Every cultural group faces psychological challenges that are unique to members of that group. Service delivery systems should identify the needs of specific groups and establish how they will determine how well they are meeting those needs.

Promote workforce development. Acquiring cultural competence is demanding, and it is understandable that many mental health professionals are inadequately prepared to meet this challenge. Chin (2003) suggests four ways in which service delivery systems can encourage professionals' development of cultural competence:

- *Provide access to a diverse network of professionals.* Service delivery systems should make directories of culturally specific resources available to all staff. These directories should include the names of local mental health care providers along with their geographic locations and information on their races/ethnicities, the languages they speak, and their areas of expertise.

- *Offer credentialing.* Service delivery systems should offer to certify as multiculturally competent those professionals who can demonstrate essential multicultural competencies as well as document relevant multicultural training.
- *Redesign contracts.* Service delivery systems should contract with providers to expand their cultural competence objectives. They also should contract with more culturally competent providers who are racial/ethnic minorities.
- *Require cultural competency plans.* Service delivery systems should require cultural competency plans from the professionals with whom they contract, and they should have enforcement mechanisms and incentives in place to ensure the success of these plans.

Affirmative Action

Minorities are greatly underrepresented in the various mental health professions in the United States, and applied psychology is no exception (Leong, Kohout, Smith, & Wicherski, 2003). This underrepresentation has many costs. The field forgoes the enrichment that diversity of membership can offer through expanded perspectives, varied treatment approaches, and legitimate challenges to the status quo. Without the diversity of membership, many minority consumers are deprived of treatment by professionals whose races or cultures are the same as theirs. Graduate students in training miss out on the benefits of more heterogeneous learning environments, such as exposure to other perspectives and interactions with people of diverse backgrounds.

To combat this situation, the mental health system needs a broad-based strategy for recruiting, retaining, and advancing the careers of minorities in the profession. As Myers, Echemendia, and Trimble (1991) note, the key to achieving parity in the profession lies in the equity of training programs. That achievement is possible only through active and affirmative action.

Definition

What is affirmative action? The Equal Employment Opportunity Act of 1972 (P.L. 92-261) defines affirmative action as "those actions appropriate to overcome the effects of past or present practices, policies, or other barriers to equal employment opportunity." Another noteworthy definition is supplied by the American Psychological Association (1996):

> Voluntary and mandatory efforts undertaken by federal, state, and local governments; private employers; and schools to combat discrimination and to promote equal opportunity in education and employment for all. (p. 2)

As these definitions suggest, affirmative action is directed toward institutional policies and practices. Kravitz et al. (1997) explain affirmative action's two fundamental purposes: (a) elimination of discriminatory behavior against women and ethnic minorities and (b) redress of the effects of past discrimination. Both purposes are essential to effective affirmative action policy.

A number of scholars have pointed out that affirmative action policy differs from a passive policy of equal opportunity (Crosby, 1994; Holloway, 1989; Konrad & Linnehan, 1999). Although both have the goal of equality, a passive policy assumes that fair and equitable treatment exists for all groups when there is no evidence of overt, intentional discrimination. As Crosby and Cordova (1996) explain, because equal opportunity is a passive policy, no action is taken until there is evidence of explicit discrimination.

The distinction between active policy and passive policy strikes right at the heart of the issue of unintentional racism in institutions. In Chapter 12, I explained how inaction, regardless of the intentions of the person or organization that does not act, can be inherently racist. Before I address the challenges of constructive change, I first must identify and critique the presuppositions on which both active and passive policies rest. As mentioned above, the passive policy of equal opportunity assumes that action is not necessary unless overt, intentional discrimination exists. As Crosby, Iyer, Clayton, and Downing (2003) observe:

> In contrast to equal opportunity, affirmative action is an active policy, calling for actions to ensure that equal opportunity exists. An underlying presupposition of affirmative action is that structural impediments to true equality do not always take the form of overt discrimination. Even policies that appear to be neutral with regard to ethnicity or gender can operate in ways that advantage individuals from one group over individuals from another group. (p. 95)

This point of view accords with the perspective on institutional racism presented in this book. Mental health professionals must examine the institutional policies and behaviors of the mental health system to determine which of these policies and practices perpetuate unequal access and opportunities for minority group members. When they find inequities, they must eliminate barriers so true equality can prevail (Crosby & Cordova, 1996).

A Three-Tiered Process

To confront the problem of institutional racism in the mental health system, institutions within the system must undertake a three-tiered process of affirmative action that includes attention to recruitment, selection, and mentoring. Institutions that successfully implement this process will find that they are more effective in attracting and retaining minority professionals.

Recruitment. Recruitment is a prelude to selection. Before minority individuals can be accepted into graduate programs or hired into mental health care positions, they first must enter the applicant pool. Gatewood and Field (2001) note that affirmative action recruitment serves three purposes: (a) It increases the size of the pool of applicants at minimal cost, (b) it helps organizations meet their legal and social responsibilities regarding the demographic composition of their workforces, and (c) it improves the hit rate for minorities in the selection process.

Seligman (1973) identifies four recruitment strategies that organizations use to avoid discrimination in hiring:

- *Passive nondiscrimination:* The organization demonstrates equity in all personnel decisions, which include hiring, promotion, and compensation. However, the organization does not make an assertive attempt to recruit minority applicants.
- *Pure affirmative action:* The organization makes an assertive effort to expand its pool of minority applicants. Once the pool is expanded, the organization hires or promotes on the basis of merit and impartial treatment of qualifications, regardless of applicant race.
- *Affirmative action with preferential selection:* The organization not only expands the pool of minority applicants, it also favors minority individuals in the selection process. This practice is referred to as a "soft quota" system.
- *Hard quotas:* The organization mandates the selection of a specific number or a specific proportion of minority applicants.

Cascio and Aguinis (2005) conclude that in the fairest of all possible worlds, pure affirmative action is the best option; I share their opinion. Special measures are needed to expand the pool of minorities who apply to graduate programs in mental health and who ultimately apply for professional positions in the field. To recruit effectively, an organization must plan a recruitment strategy, manage that recruitment strategy, and then evaluate the outcomes of the recruitment strategy.

Selection. Once an organization has recruited a representative pool of applicants, its next step is to select wisely from that pool. Reliance on standardized test scores for help in selection decisions, as is traditional in graduate admissions, is problematic because of the presence of selective system bias. This form of bias is introduced whenever the standardized racial gap in academic performance is smaller than the standardized gap in test performance (Jencks, 1998). Minorities that have lower test scores than Whites may perform nearly as well as Whites in their training programs. This fact suggests that the use of standardized tests in selection decisions leads to a disproportionate number of false negative decisions about minority applicants. To make valid decisions more consistently, organizations should adjust test score cutoffs according to the differential validities of the tests for different populations. They also should develop behavioral predictors that are related to performance criteria.

Mentoring. The mentoring process involves professionals helping others to develop in their profession. In the relationship between mentor and protégé, the experienced, accomplished, and competent professional guides, advises, and supports a less experienced and knowledgeable colleague (Johnson & Ridley, 2004).

Minority professionals sometimes are unable to reap the maximum benefits of good mentoring relationships for two reasons. First, junior professionals from minority groups often have limited access to mentors of their own races. Second, minority professionals often face special challenges in placement and promotion; they may have to prove themselves more than their White counterparts do to get the same rewards, may have to cope with unfair innuendos about their qualifications, and may be excluded from the informal network of decision making. Therefore, all senior professionals in the mental health field—not just those who are minority group members—should assume collective responsibility for the mentoring of minority professionals. As Atkinson, Neville, and Casas (1991) observe, because minority professionals are underrepresented in the field of applied psychology, White professors and senior professionals must mentor ethnic minority students and novice professionals. Their research suggests that cross-racial mentoring can be successful. Thomas (2001) suggests that mentors take the following actions to provide minority professionals with effective mentoring: create challenging assignments, put minority protégés in high-trust positions, provide crucial career advice, sponsor and recruit minority protégés into new positions, and protect minority protégés by confronting their critics, especially when the criticism carries racial overtones.

As in a counseling relationship, race should be addressed early in a mentoring relationship. A frank discussion of race provides mentor and protégé with the opportunity to address issues that may be sensitive. If such issues are left unresolved, the mentoring relationship may be undermined. It is important to note that the mentor should take the lead in broaching the issue of race. Thomas (1993) identifies two basic strategies for handling racial differences in mentoring relationships: direct engagement and denial and suppression. In *direct engagement,* the mentor and protégé openly discuss race. In *denial and suppression,* they avoid open discussion of race. Research indicates that it is important for mentor and protégé to agree on a strategy, but it is obvious that the most honest and potentially productive strategy is direct engagement, which allows both parties to explore their fears, apprehensions, and misgivings as well as the benefits of multicultural collaboration.

Overall, the most important guideline that senior mental health professionals should follow in mentoring minority professionals is to appreciate the similarities and differences between minority and nonminority professionals. Mentors must realize that junior minority professionals have the same aspirations, needs, and potential as their nonminority counterparts. On the other hand, junior minority professionals face challenges that nonminority professionals do not face. Among the most prominent of these challenges are the covert, unintentional institutional barriers that interfere with their advancement in the mental health system.

An Exemplar

The combined psychology program at the University of California, Santa Barbara, is an exemplar of the achievement of racial/ethnic equity in graduate training. Atkinson, Brown, and Casas (1996) describe the program, which undertook systematic efforts to increase diversity over a period of 25 years. As of 1996, 54% of the students in the graduate program were ethnic minorities, and the proportion of minority students in the program with a counseling psychology emphasis was 72%. Of the program's 10 faculty members, 3 were persons of color. In addition, the program is widely known for its significant contributions to the multicultural literature and for graduates who have become leaders in the field.

Atkinson et al. (1996) maintain that two preconditions are essential to the successful building of a racially/ethnically equitable graduate training program. First, the administration and faculty of the institution must commit to achieving racial/ethnic parity. Second, the program's faculty and students truly must appreciate ethnic and cultural diversity. Once a program meets these preconditions, it must implement two major activities: (a) the recruitment, selection, and support of ethnic minority students; and (b) the recruitment, hiring, and retention/advancement of ethnic minority faculty. Atkinson et al. provide a detailed discussion of these activities and note their belief that other programs can benefit from the UCSB program's experiences. In their epilogue, they give a word of warning: Passive recruitment efforts only maintain the status quo.

Chapter Summary

In the final analysis, mental health policies and procedures are implemented at treatment service centers. Therefore, regardless of where policies and procedural guidelines originate, the elimination of institutional racism requires constructive changes in actual service delivery at the local level. In this chapter, I have discussed six microsystem interventions: the establishment of a core ideology that embraces diversity, integrated service networks, consultation, prevention and health promotion, action research, and affirmative action. If mental health professionals take such interventions to heart, as well as implement the other individual and institutional strategies proposed in this book, there is hope that one day clients of all races and cultures will receive the competent treatment they deserve.

References

Abe-Kim, J. S., & Takeuchi, D. T. (1996). Cultural competence and quality care: Issues for mental health service delivery in managed care. *Clinical Psychology: Science and Practice, 3,* 273–295.

Abreu, J. M., Chung, R. H. G., & Atkinson, D. R. (2000). Multicultural counseling training. *The Counseling Psychologist, 28,* 641–656.

Acosta, F. (1979). Barriers between mental health services and Mexican Americans: An examination of a paradox. *American Journal of Community Psychology, 7,* 503–520.

Adams, P. L. (1970). Dealing with racism in biracial psychiatry. *Journal of the American Academy of Child Psychiatry, 9,* 33–43.

Adams, W. A. (1950). The Negro patient in psychiatric treatment. *American Journal of Orthopsychiatry, 20,* 305–310.

Adebimpe, V. R. (1981). Overview: White norms and psychiatric diagnosis of Black patients. *American Journal of Psychiatry, 138,* 279–285.

Adebimpe, V. R. (1982). Psychiatric symptoms in Black patients. In S. M. Turner & R. T. Jones (Eds.), *Behavior modification in Black populations: Psychosocial issues and empirical findings* (pp. 57–71). New York: Plenum.

Adebimpe, V. R., & Cohen, E. (1989). Schizophrenia and affective disorder in Black and White patients: A methodologic note. *Journal of the National Medical Association, 81,* 761–765.

Adebimpe, V. R., Gigandet, J., & Harris, E. (1979). MMPI diagnosis of Black psychiatric patients. *American Journal of Psychiatry, 136,* 85–87.

Adebimpe, V. R., Klein, H. E., & Fried, J. (1981). Hallucinations and delusions in Black psychiatric patients. *Journal of the National Medical Association, 73,* 517–520.

Albee, G. W. (2000). Commentary on prevention and counseling psychology. *The Counseling Psychologist, 28,* 845–853.

Albee, G. W., & Ryan-Finn, K. D. (1993). An overview of primary prevention. *Journal of Counseling and Development, 72,* 115–123.

Allport, G. W. (1946). Personalistic psychology as a science: A reply. *Psychological Review, 53,* 132–135.

American Association for Marriage and Family Therapy. (2001). *AAMFT code of ethics.* Washington, DC: Author.

American Counseling Association. (1995). *Code of ethics and standards of practice.* Alexandria, VA: Author.

American Psychiatric Association. (1987). *Diagnostic and statistical manual of mental disorders* (3rd ed., rev.). Washington, DC: Author.

American Psychiatric Association. (2000). *Diagnostic and statistical manual of mental disorders* (4th ed., text rev.). Washington, DC: Author.

American Psychological Association. (1996). *Affirmative action: Who benefits?* Washington, DC: Author.

American Psychological Association. (1997). *Visions and transformations: The final report of the Commission on Ethnic Minority Recruitment, Retention, and Training in Psychology.* Washington, DC: Author.

American Psychological Association. (2002). Ethical principles of psychologists and code of conduct. *American Psychologist, 57,* 1060–1073.

American Psychological Association. (2003). Guidelines on multicultural education, training, research, practice, and organizational change for psychologists. *American Psychologist, 58,* 377–402.

American Psychological Association, Task Force on Education, Training, and Service in Psychology. (1982). *Summary report.* Washington, DC: Author.

Anastasi, A. (1992). What counselors should know about the use and interpretation of psychological tests. *Journal of Counseling and Development, 70,* 610–615.

Anderson, L. P. (1991). Acculturative stress: A theory of relevance to Black Americans. *Clinical Psychology Review, 11,* 685–702.

Arax, M. (1987, April 12). Clash of two worlds leaves many in pain: Pt. 2. Asian impact. *Los Angeles Times,* San Gabriel Valley sec.

Aristotle. (1952). *Metaphysics* (R. Hope, Trans.). New York: Columbia University Press.

Arkes, H. R. (1981). Impediments to accurate clinical judgment and possible ways to minimize their impact. *Journal of Consulting and Clinical Psychology, 49,* 323–330.

Armstrong, H. E., Ishiki, D., Heiman, J., Mundt, J., &Womack, W. (1984). Service utilization by Black and White clientele in an urban community mental health center: Revised assessment of an old problem. *Community Mental Health Journal, 20,* 269–281.

Arredondo, P., & Reinoso, J. G. (2003). Multicultural competencies in consultation. In D. B. Pope-Davis, H. L. K. Coleman, W. M. Liu, & R. L. Toporek (Eds.), *Handbook of multicultural competencies in counseling and psychology* (pp. 330–346). Thousand Oaks, CA: Sage.

Arredondo, P., & Rice, T. M. (2004). Working from within: Contextual mental health and organizational competence. In T. B. Smith (Ed.), *Practicing multiculturalism: Affirming diversity in counseling and psychology* (pp. 76–96). Boston: Pearson/Allyn & Bacon.

Atkinson, D. R., Brown, M. T., & Casas, J. M. (1996). Achieving ethnic parity in counseling psychology. *The Counseling Psychologist, 24,* 230–258.

Atkinson, D. R., Casas, J. M., & Abreu, J. (1992). Mexican American acculturation, counselor ethnicity and cultural sensitivity, and perceived counselor competence. *Journal of Counseling Psychology, 39,* 515–520.

Atkinson, D. R., & Lowe, S. M. (1995). The role of ethnicity, cultural knowledge, and conventional techniques in counseling and psychotherapy. In J. G. Ponterotto, J. M. Casas, L. A. Suzuki, & C. M. Alexander (Eds.), *Handbook of multicultural counseling* (pp. 387–414). Thousand Oaks, CA: Sage.

Atkinson, D. R., Maruyama, M., & Matsui, S. (1978). Effects of counselor race and counseling approach on Asian Americans' perceptions of counselor credibility and utility. *Journal of Counseling Psychology, 25,* 76–83.

Atkinson, D. R., & Matsushita, Y. J. (1991). Japanese-American acculturation, counseling style, counselor ethnicity, and perceived counselor credibility. *Journal of Counseling Psychology, 38,* 473–478.

Atkinson, D. R., Morten, G., & Sue, D. W. (Eds.). (1993). *Counseling American minorities: A cross-cultural perspective* (4th ed.). Madison, WI: W. C. Brown & Benchmark.

Atkinson, D. R., Morten, G., & Sue, D. W. (Eds.). (1998a). *Counseling American minorities: A cross-cultural perspective* (5th ed.). New York: McGraw-Hill.

Atkinson, D. R., Morten, G., & Sue, D. W. (1998b). Defining populations and terms. In D. R. Atkinson, G. Morten, & D. W. Sue (Eds.), *Counseling American minorities: A cross-cultural perspective* (5th ed., pp. 3–20). New York: McGraw-Hill.

Atkinson, D. R., Morten, G., & Sue, D. W. (1998c). Within-group differences among racial/ethnic minorities. In D. R. Atkinson, G. Morten, & D. W. Sue (Eds.), *Counseling American minorities: A cross-cultural perspective* (5th ed., pp. 21–50). New York: McGraw-Hill.

Atkinson, D. R., Neville, H. A., & Casas, A. (1991). The mentorship of ethnic minorities in professional psychology. *Professional Psychology: Research and Practice, 22,* 336–338.

Atkinson, D. R., Thompson, C. E., & Grant, S. K. (1993). A three-dimensional model for counseling racial/ethnic minorities. *The Counseling Psychologist, 21,* 257–277.

Axelson, J. A. (1999). *Counseling and development in a multicultural society* (3rd ed.). Pacific Grove, CA: Brooks/Cole.

Babigian, H. M. (1976). Schizophrenia: Epidemiology. In A. M. Freedman, H. I. Kaplan, & B. J. Sadock (Eds.), *Comprehensive textbook of psychiatry* (2nd ed., pp. 423–426). Baltimore, MD: Williams & Wilkins.

Baker, D. B., & Benjamin, L. T. (2000). The affirmation of the scientist-practitioner: A look back at Boulder. *American Psychologist, 55,* 241–247.

Barlow, D. H. (1996). Health care policy, psychotherapy research, and the future of psychotherapy. *American Psychologist, 51,* 1050–1058.

Baron, R. S., Kerr, N. L., & Miller, N. (1993). *Group process, group decision, group action.* Pacific Grove, CA: Brooks/Cole.

Bartlett, F. C. (1932). *Remembering: A study in experimental and social psychology.* Cambridge: Cambridge University Press.

Baruth, L. G., & Huber, C. H. (1985). *Counseling and psychotherapy: Theoretical analyses and skills applications.* Columbus, OH: Charles E. Merrill.

Baskin, D. (1984). Cross-cultural categorization of mental illness. *Psychiatric Forum, 12,* 36–44.

Baskin, D., Bluestone, H., & Nelson, M. (1981). Ethnicity and psychiatric diagnosis. *Journal of Clinical Psychology, 37,* 529–537.

Batson, C. D., Jones, C. H., & Cochran, P. J. (1979). Attributional bias in counselors' diagnoses: The effects of resources. *Journal of Applied Social Psychology, 9,* 377–393.

Beck, E. M. (1980). Preface. In *Bartlett's familiar quotations* (15th ed.). Boston: Little, Brown.

Beebe, S. A., Mottet, T. P., & Roach, K. D. (2004). *Training and development: Enhancing communication and leadership skills.* Boston: Pearson/Allyn & Bacon.

Belar, C. D. (2000). Scientist-practitioner ≠ science + practice: Boulder is bolder. *American Psychologist, 55,* 249–250.

Belkin, G. S. (1984). *Introduction to counseling* (2nd ed.). Dubuque, IA: William C. Brown.

Bell, C. C., & Mehta, H. (1980). The misdiagnosis of Black patients with manic depressive illness. *Journal of the National Medical Association, 72,* 141–145.

Bell, C. C., & Mehta, H. (1981). The misdiagnosis of Black patients with manic depressive illness: Second in a series. *Journal of the National Medical Association, 73,* 101–107.

Bemporad, J. R., Smith, H. F., Hanson, G., & Cicchetti, D. (1982). Borderline syndromes in childhood: Criteria for diagnosis. *American Journal of Psychiatry, 139,* 596–602.

Benjamin, A. (1981). *The helping interview* (3rd ed.). Boston: Houghton Mifflin.

Bernard, V. W. (1953). Psychoanalysis and members of minority groups. *Journal of the American Psychoanalytic Association, 1,* 256–267.

Betancourt, H., & López, S. R. (1993). The study of culture, ethnicity, and race in American psychology. *American Psychologist, 48,* 629–637.

Beverly, C. (1989). Treatment issues for Black, alcoholic clients. *Social Casework, 70,* 370–374.

Bieri, J., Lobeck, R., & Galinsky, M. D. (1959). A comparison of direct, indirect, and fantasy measures of identification. *Journal of Abnormal and Social Psychology, 58,* 253–258.

Blake, W. (1973). The influence of race on diagnosis. *Smith College Studies in Social Work, 43,* 184–192.

Blazer, D. G., Hybels, C. F., Simonsick, E. G., & Hanlon, J. T. (2000). Marked difference in antidepressant use by race in an elderly community sample: 1986–1996. *American Journal of Psychiatry, 157,* 1089–1094.

Block, C. B. (1981). Black Americans and the cross-cultural counseling and psychotherapy experience. In A. J. Marsella & P. B. Pedersen (Eds.), *Cross-cultural counseling and psychotherapy: Foundations, evaluation, and cultural considerations* (pp. 177–194). Elmsford, NY: Pergamon.

Bloombaum, M., Yamamoto, J., & James, Q. (1968). Cultural stereotyping among psychotherapists. *Journal of Consulting and Clinical Psychology, 32,* 99.

Bond, C. F., DiCandia, C. G., & MacKinnon, J. R. (1988). Response to violence in a psychiatric setting: The role of the patient's race. *Personality and Social Psychology Bulletin, 14,* 448–458.

Boyd-Franklin, N. (1989). *Black families in therapy: A multisystems approach.* New York: Guilford.

Brantley, T. (1983). Racism and its impact on psychotherapy. *American Journal of Psychiatry, 140,* 1605–1608.

Brody, E. L., Derbyshire, R. L., & Schleifer, C. B. (1967). How the young adult Baltimore Negro male becomes a Maryland mental hospital statistic. In R. R. Monroe, G. D. Klee, & E. L. Brody (Eds.), *Psychiatric epidemiology and mental health planning.* Washington, DC: American Psychiatric Association.

Broman, C. L. (1987). Race differences in professional help seeking. *American Journal of Community Psychology, 15,* 473–489.

Bronstein, P. A., & Quina, K. (Eds.). (1988). *Teaching a psychology of people: Resources for gender and sociocultural awareness.* Washington, DC: American Psychological Association.

Brown, R. (1965). *Social psychology.* New York: Free Press.

Brown, S. P., Parham, T. A., & Yonker, R. (1996). Influence of a cross-cultural training course on racial identity attitudes of White women and men: Preliminary perspectives. *Journal of Counseling and Development, 74,* 510–516.

Brownell, K. D., Marlatt, G. A., Lichtenstein, E., & Wilson, G. T. (1986). Understanding and preventing relapse. *American Psychologist, 41,* 765–782.

Burlew, A. K. (2003). Research with ethnic minorities: Conceptual, methodological, and analytical issues. In G. Bernal, J. E. Trimble, A. K. Burlew, & F. T. L. Leong (Eds.), *Handbook of racial and ethnic minority psychology* (pp. 179–197). Thousand Oaks, CA: Sage.

Butts, H. F. (1969). White racism: Its origins, institutions and implications for professional practice in mental health. *International Journal of Psychiatry, 8,* 914–928.

Butts, H. F. (1971). Psychoanalysis and unconscious racism. *Journal of Contemporary Psychotherapy, 3*(2), 67–81.

Calnek, M. (1970). Racial factors in the counter-transference: The Black therapist and the Black client. *American Journal of Orthopsychiatry, 40,* 39–46.

Carter, J. H. (1979). Frequent mistakes made with Black patients in psychotherapy. *Journal of the National Medical Association, 71,* 1007–1009.

Carter, J. H. (1983). Sociocultural factors in the psychiatric assessment of Black patients: A case study. *Journal of the National Medical Association, 75,* 817–820.

Casas, J. M. (1984). Policy, training, and research in counseling psychology: The racial/ethnic minority perspective. In S. D. Brown & R. W. Lent (Eds.), *Handbook of counseling psychology* (pp. 785–831). New York: John Wiley.

Casas, J. M., Pavelski, R., Furlong, M. J., & Zanglis, I. (2001). Addressing the mental health needs of Latino youths with emotional and behavioral disorders: Practical perspectives and policy implications. *Harvard Journal of Hispanic Policy, 12,* 47–69.

Cascio, W. F., & Aguinis, H. (2005). *Applied psychology in human resource management* (6th ed.). Upper Saddle River, NJ: Prentice Hall.

Casimir, G. J., & Morrison, B. J. (1993). Rethinking work with multicultural populations. *Community Mental Health Journal, 29,* 547–559.

Castro, F. G. (1998). Cultural competence training in clinical psychology: Assessment, clinical intervention, and research. In C. D. Belar (Ed.), *Comprehensive clinical psychology: Vol. 10. Sociocultural and individual differences* (pp. 127–140). Elmsford, NY: Pergamon/Elsevier Science.

Cauce, A. M., Ryan, K. D., & Grove, K. (1998). Children and adolescents of color, where are you? Participation, selection, recruitment, and retention in developmental research. In V. C. McLoyd & L. Steinberg (Eds.), *Studying minority adolescents: Conceptual, methodological, and theoretical issues* (pp. 147–166). Mahwah, NJ: Lawrence Erlbaum.

Cavanagh, M. E. (1982). *The counseling experience: A theoretical and practical approach.* Pacific Grove, CA: Brooks/Cole.

Centers for Disease Control and Prevention. (1992). *HIV/AIDS surveillance report.* Atlanta, GA: Author.

Cervantes, R. C., & Arroyo, W. (1994). *DSM-IV:* Implications for Hispanic children and adolescents. *Hispanic Journal of Behavioral Science, 16,* 8–27.

Chess, S., Clark, K. B., & Thomas, A. (1953). The importance of cultural evaluation in psychiatric diagnosis and treatment. *Psychiatric Quarterly, 27,* 102–114.

Chin, J. L. (2003). Multicultural competencies in managed health care. In D. B. Pope-Davis, H. L. K. Coleman, W. M. Liu, & R. L. Toporek (Eds.), *Handbook of multicultural competencies in counseling and psychology* (pp. 347–364). Thousand Oaks, CA: Sage.

Christoff, K. A., & Kelly, J. A. (1985). A behavioral approach to social skills training with psychiatric patients. In L. L'Abate & M. A. Milan (Eds.), *Handbook of social skills training and research* (pp. 361–387). New York: John Wiley.

Clark, A. J. (1991). The identification and modification of defense mechanisms in counseling. *Journal of Counseling and Development, 69,* 231–236.

Clark, R., Anderson, N. B., Clark, V. R., & Williams, D. R. (1999). Racism as a stressor for African Americans: A biopsychosocial model. *American Psychologist, 54,* 805–816.

Coleman, D., & Baker, F. M. (1994). Misdiagnosis of schizophrenia in older, Black veterans. *Hospital and Community Psychiatry, 45,* 527–528.

Collins, J. C., & Porras, J. I. (2002). *Built to last: Successful habits of visionary companies.* New York: HarperCollins.

Collins, J. C., Rickman, L. E., & Mathura, C. B. (1980). Frequency of schizophrenia and depression in Black inpatient populations. *Journal of the National Medical Association, 72,* 851–856.

Committee for Economic Development. (1987). *Children in need: Investment strategies for the educationally disadvantaged: A statement.* New York: Author.

Constantine, M. G., & Ladany, N. (2000). Self-report multicultural counseling competence scales: Their relation to social desirability attitudes and multicultural case conceptualization ability. *Journal of Counseling Psychology, 47,* 155–164.

Cook, D. A., & Helms, J. E. (1988). Visible racial/ethnic group supervisees' satisfaction with cross-cultural supervision as predicted by relationship characteristics. *Journal of Counseling Psychology, 35,* 268–274.

Coonerty, S. M. (1991). Change in the change agents: Growth in the capacity to heal. In R. C. Curtis & G. Stricker (Eds.), *How people change: Inside and outside therapy* (pp. 81–97). New York: Plenum.

Cooper, J. E., Kendell, R. E., Gurland, B. J., Sharpe, I., Copeland, J., & Simon, R. (1972). *Psychiatric diagnosis in New York and London: A comparative study of mental hospital admissions.* London: Oxford University Press.

Cooper, R. P., & Werner, P. D. (1990). Predicting violence in newly admitted inmates: A lens model analysis of staff decision making. *Criminal Justice and Behavior, 17,* 431–447.

Cooper, S. (1973). A look at the effect of racism on clinical work. *Social Casework, 54*(2), 76–84.

Corey, G. (2005). *Theory and practice of counseling and psychotherapy* (7th ed.). Pacific Grove, CA: Brooks/Cole-Wadsworth.

Corey, G., Corey, M. S., & Callanan, P. (2003). *Issues and ethics in the helping professions* (6th ed.). Pacific Grove, CA: Brooks/Cole.

Cormier, L. S., & Hackney, H. (1993). *The professional counselor: A process guide to helping* (2nd ed.). Boston: Allyn & Bacon.

Cormier, W. H., & Cormier, L. S. (1991). *Interviewing strategies for helpers: Fundamental skills and cognitive behavioral interventions* (3rd ed.). Pacific Grove, CA: Brooks/Cole.

Corvin, S. A., & Wiggins, F. (1989). An antiracism training model for White professionals. *Journal of Multicultural Counseling and Development, 17,* 105–114.

Cottone, R. R., & Tarvydas, V. M. (1998). *Ethical and professional issues in counseling.* Upper Saddle River, NJ: Prentice Hall.

Cowen, E. L. (1980). The wooing of primary prevention. *American Journal of Community Psychology, 8,* 258–284.

Cronbach, L. J. (1970). *Essentials of psychological testing* (3rd ed.). New York: Harper & Row.

Crosby, F. J. (1994). Understanding affirmative action. *Basic and Applied Social Psychology, 15,* 13–41.

Crosby, F. J., & Cordova, D. I. (1996). Words worth of wisdom: Toward an understanding of affirmative action. *Journal of Social Issues, 52*(4), 33–49.

Crosby, F. J., Iyer, A., Clayton, S., & Downing, R. A. (2003). Affirmative action: Psychological data and policy debate. *American Psychologist, 58,* 93–115.

Cuffe, S. P., Waller, J. L., Cuccaro, M. L., Pumariega, A. J., & Garrison, C. Z. (1995). Race and gender difference in the treatment of psychiatric disorders in young adolescents. *Journal of the American Academy of Child and Adolescent Psychology, 34,* 1536–1543.

Dana, R. H. (1993). *Multicultural assessment perspectives for professional psychology.* Boston: Allyn & Bacon.

d'Ardenne, P. (1993). Transcultural counseling and psychotherapy in the 1990s. *British Journal of Guidance and Counseling, 21*(1), 1–7.

Darwin, C. (1859). *On the origin of species by means of natural selection.* London: J. Murray.

Dauphinais, P., Dauphinais, L., & Rowe, W. (1981). Effects of race and communication style on Indian perceptions of counselor effectiveness. *Counselor Education and Supervision, 21,* 72–80.

Davis, F. J. (1978). *Minority-dominant relations: A sociological analysis.* Arlington Heights, IL: AHM.

de Anda, D. (1984). Bicultural socialization: Factors affecting the minority experience. *Social Work, 29,* 101–107.

De La Cancela, V., Chin, J. L., & Jenkins, Y. M. (1998). *Community health psychology: Empowerment for diverse communities.* New York: Routledge.

deGobineau, A. (1915). *The inequality of human races.* New York: Putman.

DeHoyos, A., & DeHoyos, G. (1965). Symptomatology differential between Negro and White schizophrenics. *International Journal of Social Psychiatry, 11,* 245–255.

Dixon, V. (1971). Two approaches to Black-White relations. In V. Dixon & B. Foster (Eds.), *Beyond Black or White: An alterna America* (pp. 23–66). Boston: Little, Brown.

Dobbins, J. E., & Skillings, J. H. (2000). Racism as a clinical syndrome. *American Journal of Orthopsychiatry, 70,* 14–27.

Dollinger, S. J. (1989). Predictive validity of the Graduate Record Examination in a clinical psychology program. *Professional Psychology: Research and Practice, 20,* 56–58.

Dougherty, A. M. (2000). *Psychological consultation and collaboration in schools and community settings* (3rd ed.). Belmont, CA: Wadsworth.

Douglass, F. (1950). West India emancipation. In P. S. Foner (Ed.), *The life and writings of Frederick Douglass* (Vol. 2, pp. 426–439). New York: International. (Original work published 1857)

Dovidio, J. F., & Gaertner, S. L. (Eds.). (1986). *Prejudice, discrimination, and racism.* Orlando, FL: Academic Press.

Doyle, A. B. (1998). Are empirically validated treatments valid for culturally diverse populations? In K. S. Dobson & D. D. Craig (Eds.), *Empirically supported therapies: Best practice in professional psychology* (pp. 93–103). Thousand Oaks, CA: Sage.

Draguns, J. G. (1976). Counseling across cultures: Common themes and distinct approaches. In P. B. Pedersen, W. J. Lonner, & J. G. Draguns (Eds.), *Counseling across cultures* (pp. 1–16). Honolulu: University Press of Hawaii.

Draguns, J. G. (1989). Dilemmas and choices in cross-cultural counseling: The universal versus the culturally distinctive. In P. B. Pedersen, J. G. Draguns, W. J. Lonner, & J. E. Trimble (Eds.), *Counseling across cultures* (3rd ed., pp. 3–21). Honolulu: University of Hawaii Press.

Draguns, J. G. (2002). Universal and cultural aspects of counseling and psychotherapy. In P. B. Pedersen, J. G. Draguns, W. J. Lonner, & J. E. Trimble (Eds.), *Counseling across cultures* (5th ed., pp. 29–50). Thousand Oaks, CA: Sage.

Dreger, R. M., & Miller, K. S. (1960). Comparative psychological studies of Negroes and Whites in the United States. *Psychological Bulletin, 57,* 361–402.

Du Bois, W. E. B. (1969). *The souls of Black folk.* New York: New American Library. (Original work published 1903)

Dumont, F., & Lecomte, C. (1987). Inferential processes in clinical work: Inquiry into logical errors that affect diagnostic judgments. *Professional Psychology: Research and Practice, 18,* 433–438.

Edwards, A. W. (1982). The consequences of error in selecting treatment for Blacks. *Social Casework, 63,* 429–433.

Egan, C. (2002). *The skilled helper: A problem-management approach to helping* (7th ed.). Pacific Grove, CA: Brooks/Cole.

Einhorn, H. J., & Hogarth, R. M. (1978). Confidence in judgment: Persistence of the illusion of validity. *Psychological Review, 85,* 395–416.

Eisenberg, L. (1962). If not now, when? *American Journal of Orthopsychiatry, 32,* 781–793.

Engel, G. L. (1977). The need for a new medical model: A challenge for biomedicine. *Science, 196*(4286), 129–136.

Espin, O. M. (1985). Psychotherapy with Hispanic women: Some considerations. In P. B. Pedersen (Ed.), *Handbook of cross-cultural counseling and therapy* (pp. 165–171). Westport, CT: Greenwood.

Everett, F., Proctor, N., & Cartmell, B. (1983). Providing psychological services to American Indian children and families. *Professional Psychology: Research and Practice, 14,* 588–603.

Fairchild, H. H. (1991). Scientific racism: The cloak of objectivity. *Journal of Social Issues, 47*(3), 101–115.

Faris, R. E., & Dunham, H. W. (1967). *Mental disorders in urban areas: An ecological study of schizophrenia and other psychoses.* Chicago: University of Chicago Press. (Original work published 1939)

Faust, D. (1986). Research on human judgment and its application to clinical practice. *Professional Psychology: Research and Practice, 17,* 420–430.

Felner, R. D., & Felner, T. Y. (1989). Prevention programs in the educational context: A transactional-ecological framework for program models. In L. Bond & B. Compas (Eds.), *Primary prevention in the schools* (pp. 13–49). Newbury Park, CA: Sage.

Fernando, S. (1988). *Race and culture in psychiatry.* London: Croom Helm.

Fields, S. (1979). Mental health and the melting pot. *Innovations, 6*(2), 2–3.

Finkelhor, D. (1984). *Child sexual abuse: New theory and research.* New York: Free Press.

Flaherty, J., & Meagher, R. (1980). Measuring racial bias in inpatient treatment. *American Journal of Psychiatry, 137,* 679–682.

Flaskerud, J. H., & Hu, L.-T. (1992a). Racial/ethnic identity and amount and type of psychiatric treatment. *American Journal of Psychiatry, 149,* 379–384.

Flaskerud, J. H., & Hu, L.-T. (1992b). Relationship of ethnicity to psychiatric diagnosis. *Journal of Nervous and Mental Disease, 180,* 296–303.

Freire, P. (2000). *Pedagogy of the oppressed* (30th anniversary ed.; M. B. Ramos, Trans.). New York: Continuum.

Freud, S. (1949). *An outline of psychoanalysis* (J. Strachey, Trans.). New York: W. W. Norton. (Original work published 1940)

Freud, S. (1963). The dynamics of transference (J. Riviere, Trans.). In P. Rieff (Ed.), *Freud: Therapy and technique.* New York: Collier. (Original work published 1912)

Freud, S. (1989). *Inhibitions, symptoms, and anxiety.* New York: W. W. Norton. (Original work published 1926)

Frumkin, R. M. (1954). Race and major mental disorders: A research note. *Journal of Negro Education, 23,* 97–98.

Fuertes, J. N., Mueller, L. N., Chauhan, R. V., Walker, J. A., & Ladany, N. (2002). An investigation of European American therapists' approach to counseling African American clients. *The Counseling Psychologist, 30,* 763–788.

Galton, F. (1869). *Hereditary genius: An inquiry into its laws and consequences.* London: Macmillan.

Gambrill, E. (1990). *Critical thinking in clinical practice: Improving the accuracy of judgments and decisions about clients.* San Francisco: Jossey-Bass.

Garb, H. N. (1997). Race bias, social class bias, and gender bias in clinical judgment. *Clinical Psychology: Science and Practice, 4,* 99–120.

Gardner, L. H. (1971). The therapeutic relationship under varying conditions of race. *Psychotherapy: Theory, Research and Practice, 8,* 78–87.

Garland, A. F., & Zigler, E. (1993). Adolescent suicide prevention: Current research and social policy implications. *American Psychologist, 48,* 169–182.

Garretson, D. J. (1993). Psychological misdiagnosis of African Americans. *Journal of Multicultural Counseling and Development, 21,* 119–126.

Garza, A. (1981). Potential pitfalls in the diagnosis and treatment of minority groups. *Journal of Social Psychology, 114,* 9–22.

Gatewood, R. D., & Field, H. S. (2001). *Human resource selection* (5th ed.). Fort Worth, TX: Dryden.

Geller, J. D. (1988). Racial bias in the evaluation of patients for psychotherapy. In L. Comas-Díaz & E. E. H. Griffith (Eds.), *Clinical guidelines in cross-cultural mental health* (pp. 112–134). New York: John Wiley.

Gelso, C. J. (1979). Research in counseling: Methodological and professional issues. *The Counseling Psychologist, 8*(3), 7–35.

Gelso, C. J., & Carter, J. A. (1985). The relationship in counseling and psychotherapy: Components, consequences, and theoretical antecedents. *Counseling Psychologist, 13,* 155–243.

Gelso, C. J., & Fretz, B. R. (2001). *Counseling psychology* (2nd ed.). Fort Worth, TX: Harcourt Brace.

Gerrard, N. (1991). Racism and sexism, together, in counselling: Three women of colour tell their stories. *Canadian Journal of Counselling, 25,* 555–566.

Gim, R. H., Atkinson, D. R., & Kim, S. J. (1991). Asian-American acculturation, counselor ethnicity and cultural sensitivity, and ratings of counselors. *Journal of Counseling Psychology, 38,* 57–62.

Gladding, S. T. (1996). *Counseling: A comprehensive profession* (3rd ed.). Upper Saddle River, NJ: Merrill/Prentice Hall.

Gladding, S. T. (2004). *Counseling: A comprehensive profession* (5th ed.). Upper Saddle River, NJ: Merrill/Prentice Hall.

Goffman, E. (1961). *Asylums: Essays on the social situation of mental patients and other inmates.* Chicago: Aldine.

Gold, M. S., & Pearsall, H. R. (1983). Hypothyroidism—or is it depression? *Psychosomatics, 24,* 646–651, 654–656.

Goldstein, M. J., Baker, B. L., & Jamison, K. R. (1986). *Abnormal psychology* (2nd ed.). Boston: Little, Brown.

Gomez, E. A., Ruiz, P., & Laval, R. (1982). Psychotherapy and bilingualism: Is acculturation important? *Journal of Operational Psychiatry, 13*(1), 13–16.

Gong-Guy, E., Cravens, R. B., & Patterson, T. E. (1991). Clinical issues in mental health service delivery to refugees. *American Psychologist, 46,* 642–648.

Goodman, A. B., & Hoffer, A. (1979). Ethnic and class factors affecting mental health clinic service. *Journal of Evaluation and Program Planning, 2,* 159–171.

Goodman, A. B., & Siegel, C. (1978). Differences in White-nonwhite community mental health center utilization patterns. *Journal of Evaluation and Program Planning, 1,* 51–63.

Goodman, J. A. (Ed.). (1973). *Dynamics of racism in social work practice.* Washington, DC: National Association of Social Workers.

Goodwin, S. (1997). *Comparative mental health policy: From institutional to community care.* Thousand Oaks, CA: Sage.

Graham, S. (1992). Most of the subjects were White and middle class: Trends in published research on African Americans in selected APA journals, 1970–1989. *American Psychologist, 47,* 629–639.

Grantham, R. J. (1973). Effects of counselor sex, race, and language style on Black students in initial interviews. *Journal of Counseling Psychology, 20,* 553–559.

Greene, B. (1994a). African American women. In L. Comas-Díaz & B. Greene (Eds.), *Women of color: Integrating ethnic and gender identities in psychotherapy* (pp. 10–29). New York: Guilford.

Greene, B. (1994b). Ethnic-minority lesbians and gay men: Mental health and treatment issues. *Journal of Consulting and Clinical Psychology, 62,* 243–251.

Grier, W. H., & Cobbs, P. M. (1968). *Black rage.* New York: Basic Books.

Grier, W. H., & Cobbs, P. M. (1992). *Black rage* (2nd ed.). New York: Basic Books.

Griffin, J. (1961). *Black like me.* Boston: Houghton Mifflin.

Griffith, M. S. (1977). The influences of race on the psychotherapeutic relationship. *Psychiatry, 40,* 27–40.

Griffith, M. S., & Jones, E. E. (1978). Race and psychotherapy: Changing perspectives. In J. H. Masserman (Ed.), *Current psychiatric therapies* (Vol. 18, pp. 225–235). New York: Grune & Stratton.

Gross, H. S., Herbert, M. R., Knatterud, G. L., & Donner, L. (1969). The effect of race and sex on the variation of diagnosis and disposition in a psychiatric emergency room. *Journal of Nervous and Mental Disease, 148,* 638–642.

Gurland, B. J. (1972). The mislabeling of depressed patients in New York state hospitals. In J. Zubin & F. A. Freyhan (Eds.), *Disorders of mood* (pp. 17–31). Baltimore, MD: Johns Hopkins University Press.

Guthrie, R. V. (1976). *Even the rat was white: A historical view of psychology.* New York: Harper & Row.

Hackney, H., & Cormier, L. S. (1994). *Counseling strategies and interventions* (4th ed.). Boston: Allyn & Bacon.

Hackney, H., & Cormier, L. S. (2001). *The professional counselor: A process guide to helping* (4th ed.). Boston: Allyn & Bacon.

Haettenschwiller, D. L. (1971). Counseling Black college students in special programs. *Personnel and Guidance Journal, 50,* 29–35.

Haley, J. (1963). *Strategies of psychotherapy.* New York: Grune & Stratton.

Hall, C. C. I. (1997). Cultural malpractice: The growing obsolescence of psychology with the changing U.S. population. *American Psychologist, 52,* 642–651.

Hall, E. T. (1973). *The silent language.* Garden City, NY: Anchor.

Hall, G. C. N. (2001). Psychotherapy research with ethnic minorities: Empirical, ethical, and conceptual issues. *Journal of Consulting and Clinical Psychology, 69,* 502–510.

Hall, G. S. (1904). *Adolescence: Its psychology and its relations to physiology, anthropology, sociology, sex, crime, religion, and education* (Vol. 2). New York: D. Appleton.

Halleck, S. L. (1971, April). Therapy is the handmaiden of the status quo. *Psychology Today,* pp. 30–34, 98–100.

Hampton, R. L., & Newberger, E. H. (1985). Child abuse incidence and reporting by hospitals: Significance of severity, class, and race. *American Journal of Public Health, 75,* 56–60.

Hanson, B., & Klerman, G. (1974). Interracial problems in the assessment of clinical depression: Concordance differences between Black and White psychiatrists and Black and White patients. *Psychopharmacology Bulletin, 10,* 65–66.

Harrison, D. K. (1975). Race as a counselor-client variable in counseling and psychotherapy: A review of the research. *The Counseling Psychologist, 5*(1), 124–133.

Hayes, C. (1982). *Making policies for children: A study of the federal process.* Washington, DC: National Academy of Sciences.

Helms, J. E. (1992). Why is there no study of cultural equivalence in standardized cognitive ability testing? *American Psychologist, 47,* 1083–1101.

Helms, J. E. (1994). How multiculturalism obscures racial factors in the therapy process: Comment on Ridley et al. (1994), Sodowsky et al. (1994), Ottavi et al. (1994), and Thompson et al. (1994). *Journal of Counseling Psychology, 41,* 162–165.

Helzer, J. E. (1975). Bipolar affective disorder in Black and White men. *Archives of General Psychiatry, 32,* 1140–1143.

Herrnstein, R. (1971, September). I.Q. *Atlantic Monthly, 228*(3), 43–64.

Hersch, C. (1968). The discontent explosion in mental health. *American Psychologist, 23,* 497–506.

Highlen, P. S., & Hill, C. E. (1984). Factors affecting client change in individual counseling: Current status and theoretical speculations. In S. D. Brown & R. W. Lent (Eds.), *Handbook of counseling psychology* (pp. 334–396). New York: John Wiley.

Hills, H. I., & Strozier, A. L. (1992). Multicultural training in APA-approved counseling psychology programs: A survey. *Professional Psychology: Research and Practice, 23,* 43–51.

Hjelle, L. A., & Ziegler, D. J. (1992). *Personality theories: Basic assumptions, research, and applications* (3rd ed.). New York: McGraw-Hill.

Ho, M. K. (1992). *Minority children and adolescents in therapy.* Newbury Park, CA: Sage.

Hoffman, M. A. (1993). Multiculturalism as a force in counseling clients with HIV-related concerns. *The Counseling Psychologist, 21,* 712–731.

Hoffman, M. A., & Driscoll, J. M. (2000). Health promotion and disease prevention: A concentric biopsychosocial model of health status. In S. D. Brown & R. W. Lent (Eds.), *Handbook of counseling psychology* (3rd ed., pp. 532–567). New York: John Wiley.

Holcomb-McCoy, C. C. (2000). Multicultural counseling competencies: An exploratory factor analysis. *Journal of Multicultural Counseling and Development, 28,* 83–97.

Holiman, M., & Lauver, P. J. (1987). The counselor culture and client-centered practice. *Counselor Education and Supervision, 26,* 184–191.

Holland, J. G., & Skinner, B. F. (1961). *The analysis of behavior: A program for self-instruction.* New York: McGraw-Hill.

Hollingshead, A. B., & Redlich, F. C. (1958). *Social class and mental illness: A community study.* New York: John Wiley.

Holloway, F. A. (1989). What is affirmative action? In F. A. Blanchard & F. J. Crosby (Eds.), *Affirmative action in perspective* (pp. 9–19). New York: Springer.

Holsopple, J. Q., & Phelan, J. G. (1954). The skills of clinicians in analysis of projective tests. *Journal of Clinical Psychology, 10,* 307–320.

House, J. D., & Johnson, J. J. (1993). Predictive validity of the Graduate Record Examination Advanced Psychology Test for graduate grades. *Psychological Reports, 23,* 80–86.

Hu, T., Snowden, L., Jerrell, J., & Nguyen, T. (1991). Ethnic populations in public mental health: Services and level of use. *American Journal of Public Health, 81,* 1429–1434.

Ibrahim, F. A. (1991). Contribution of cultural worldview to generic counseling and development. *Journal of Counseling and Development, 70,* 13–19.

Ivey, A. E., Ivey, M. B., & Simek-Morgan, L. (1993). *Counseling and psychotherapy: A multicultural perspective* (3rd ed.). Boston: Allyn & Bacon.

Jackson, A. M. (1973). Psychotherapy: Factors associated with the race of the therapist. *Psychotherapy: Theory, Research and Practice, 10,* 273–277.

Jackson, A. M. (1976). Mental health center delivery systems and the Black client. *Journal of Afro-American Issues, 4*(1), 28–34.

Jackson, A. M. (1983). Treatment issues for Black patients. *Psychotherapy: Theory, Research and Practice, 20,* 143–151.

Jackson, A. M., Berkowitz, H., & Farley, G. K. (1974). Race as a variable affecting the treatment involvement of children. *Journal of the American Academy of Child Psychiatry, 13,* 20–31.

Jaco, G. (1960). *Social epidemiology of mental disorder.* New York: Russell Sage.

Janis, I. L. (1982). *Groupthink: Psychological studies of policy decisions and fiascoes.* Boston: Houghton Mifflin.

Janis, I. L. (1989). *Crucial decisions: Leadership in policymaking and crisis management.* New York: Free Press.

Jencks, C. (1998). Racial bias in testing. In C. Jencks & M. Phillips (Eds.), *The Black-White test score gap* (pp. 457–479). Washington, DC: Brookings Institution.

Jenkins-Hall, K., & Sacco, W. P. (1991). Effect of client race and depression on evaluations by White therapists. *Journal of Social and Clinical Psychology, 10,* 322–333.

Jensen, A. R. (1969). How much can we boost IQ and scholastic achievement? *Harvard Educational Review, 39,* 1–123.

Johns, G. (1992). *Organizational behavior: Understanding life at work* (3rd ed.). New York: HarperCollins.

Johnson, G., Gershon, S., & Hekimian, L. J. (1968). Controlled evaluation of lithium and chlorpromazine in the treatment of manic states: An interim report. *Comprehensive Psychiatry, 9,* 563–573.

Johnson, N. G. (2001). President's column: Will we be ready? *Monitor on Psychology, 32*(3). Retrieved December 13, 2004, from http://www.apa.org/monitor/ mar01/pc.htm

Johnson, W. B., & Ridley, C. R. (2004). *The elements of mentoring.* New York: Palgrave Macmillan.

Jones, A., & Seagull, A. A. (1977). Dimensions of the relationship between the Black client and the White therapist: A theoretical overview. *American Psychologist, 32,* 850–855.

Jones, B. E., & Gray, B. A. (1983). Black males and psychotherapy: Theoretical issues. *American Journal of Psychotherapy, 37,* 77–85.

Jones, B. E., & Gray, B. A. (1986). Problems in diagnosing schizophrenia and affective disorders among Blacks. *Hospital and Community Psychiatry, 37,* 61–65.

Jones, B. E., Lightfoot, O. B., Palmer, D., Wilkerson, R. G., & Williams, D. H. (1970). Problems of Black psychiatric residents in White training institutes. *American Journal of Psychiatry, 127,* 798–803.

Jones, C. P., LaVeist, T. A., & Lillie-Blanton, M. (1991). "Race" in the epidemiologic literature: An examination of the *American Journal of Epidemiology, 1921–1990. American Journal of Epidemiology, 134,* 1079–1083.

Jones, D. L. (1979). African-American clients: Clinical practice issues. *Social Work, 24,* 112–118.

Jones, E. E. (1985). Psychotherapy and counseling with Black clients. In P. B. Pedersen (Ed.), *Handbook of cross-cultural counseling and therapy* (pp. 173–179). Westport, CT: Greenwood.

Jones, E. E., & Korchin, S. J. (Eds.). (1982). *Minority mental health.* New York: Praeger.

Jones, E. E., & Thorne, A. (1987). Rediscovery of the subject: Intercultural approaches to clinical assessment. *Journal of Consulting and Clinical Psychology, 55,* 488–495.

Jones, J. H. (1981). *Bad blood: The Tuskegee syphilis experiment.* New York: Free Press.

Jones, J. M. (1972). *Prejudice and racism.* Reading, MA: Addison-Wesley.

Jones, J. M. (1992). Understanding the mental health consequences of race: Contributions of basic social psychological processes. In D. N. Ruble, P. R. Costanzo, & M. E. Oliveri (Eds.), *The social psychology of mental health: Basic mechanisms and applications* (pp. 199–240). New York: Guilford.

Kadushin, A. (1963). Diagnosis and evaluation for (almost) all occasions. *Social Work, 8*(1), 12–19.

Kadushin, A. (1972). The racial factor in the interview. *Social Work, 17*(3), 88–98.

Kaplan, R. M., & Saccuzzo, D. P. (1993). *Psychological testing: Principles, applications, and issues* (3rd ed.). Pacific Grove, CA: Brooks/Cole.

Kardiner, A., & Ovesey, L. (1951). *The mark of oppression: Explorations in the personality of the American Negro.* Cleveland, OH: World.

Karno, M. (1966). The enigma of ethnicity in a psychiatric clinic. *Archives of General Psychiatry, 14,* 516–520.

Katz, D., & Kahn, R. L. (1978). *The social psychology of organizations* (2nd ed.). New York: John Wiley.

Katz, J. H. (1985). The sociopolitical nature of counseling. *The Counseling Psychologist, 13,* 615–624.

Katz, P. A., & Taylor, D. A. (Eds.). (1988). *Eliminating racism: Profiles in controversy.* New York: Plenum.

Keefe, S. E., & Casas, J. M. (1980). Mexican-Americans and mental health: A selected review and recommendations for mental health service delivery. *American Journal of Community Psychology, 8,* 303–326.

Keisling, R. (1981). Underdiagnosis of manic-depressive illness in a hospital unit. *American Journal of Psychiatry, 138,* 672–673.

Keith-Spiegel, P., & Koocher, G. P. (1985). *Ethics in psychology: Professional standards and cases*. New York: McGraw-Hill.

Kelly, T. A. (1990). The role of values in psychotherapy: A critical review of process and outcome effects. *Clinical Psychology Review, 10,* 171–186.

Kessler, R. C. (1979). Stress, social status and psychological distress. *Journal of Health and Social Behavior, 20,* 259–272.

Kiesler, C. A. (1980). Mental health policy as a field of inquiry for psychology. *American Psychologist, 35,* 1066–1080.

King, J. E. (1991). Dysconscious racism: Ideology, identity, and the miseducation of teachers. *Journal of Negro Education, 60,* 133–146.

Kiselica, M. S. (1998). Preparing Anglos for the challenges and joys of multiculturalism. *The Counseling Psychologist, 26,* 5–21.

Kiselica, M. S., Maben, P., & Locke, D. C. (1999). Do multicultural education and diversity appreciation training reduce prejudice among counseling trainees? *Journal of Mental Health Counseling, 21,* 240–254.

Kleiner, R. J., Tuckman, J., & Lavell, M. (1960). Mental disorder and status based on race. *Psychiatry, 23,* 271–274.

Knowles, L. L., & Prewitt, K. (Eds.). (1969). *Institutional racism in America.* Englewood Cliffs, NJ: Prentice Hall.

Knox, S., Burkard, A. W., Johnson, A. J., Suzuki, L. A., & Ponterotto, J. G. (2003). African American and European American therapists' experiences of addressing race in cross-racial psychotherapy dyads. *Journal of Counseling Psychology, 50,* 466–481.

Komoroff, A. L., Masuda, M., & Holmes, T. (1968). The Social Readjustment Rating Scale: A comparative study of Negro, Mexican, and White Americans. *Journal of Psychosomatic Research, 12,* 121–128.

Konrad, A. M., & Linnehan, F. (1999). Affirmative action: History, effects, and attitudes. In G. N. Powell (Ed.), *Handbook of gender and work* (pp. 429–452). Thousand Oaks, CA: Sage.

Korchin, S. J. (1980). Clinical psychology and minority problems. *American Psychologist, 35,* 262–269.

Koriat, A., Lichtenstein, S., & Fischhoff, B. (1980). Reasons for confidence. *Journal of Experimental Psychology: Human Learning and Memory, 6*(2), 107–118.

Korman, M. (1974). National conference on levels and patterns of professional training in psychology: The major themes. *American Psychologist, 29,* 441–449.

Kramer, B. M. (1973). Racism and mental health as a field of thought. In C. V. Willie, B. M. Kramer, & B. S. Brown (Eds.), *Racism and mental health: Essays* (pp. 3–23). Pittsburgh, PA: University of Pittsburgh Press.

Krantz, D. S., Grunberg, N. E., & Baum, A. (1985). Health psychology. *Annual Review of Psychology, PA 36,* 349–383.

Kravitz, D. A., Harrison, D. A., Turner, M. E., Levine, E. L., Chaves, W., Brannick, M. T., et al. (1997). *Affirmative action: A review of psychological and behavioral research.* Bowling Green, OH: Society for Industrial and Organizational Psychology.

Kuriloff, P. J. (1970). *Toward a viable public practice of psychology: A psychoecological model.* Unpublished doctoral dissertation, Harvard University.

Kurpius, D. J., & Lewis, J. E. (1988). Introduction to consultation: An intervention for advocacy and outreach. In D. J. Kurpius & D. Brown (Eds.), *Handbook of consultation: An intervention for advocacy and outreach* (pp. 1–4). Alexandria, VA: American Association for Counseling and Development.

LaFromboise, T. D. (1988). American Indian mental health policy. *American Psychologist, 43,* 388–397.

LaFromboise, T. D., Coleman, H. L. K., & Gerton, J. (1993). Psychological impact of biculturalism: Evidence and theory. *Psychological Bulletin, 114,* 395–412.

LaFromboise, T. D., & Rowe, W. (1983). Skills training for bicultural competence: Rationale and application. *Journal of Counseling Psychology, 30,* 589–595.

Larson, P. C. (1982). Counseling special populations. *Professional Psychology, 13,* 843–858.

Lasser, K. E., Himmelstein, D. V., Woolhandler, S. J., McCormick, D., & Bor, D. H. (2002). Do minorities in the United States receive fewer mental health services than Whites? *International Journal of Health Services, 32,* 567–578.

Lawson, W. B., Hepler, N., Holladay, J., & Cuffel, B. (1994). Race as a factor in inpatient and outpatient admissions and diagnosis. *Hospital and Community Psychiatry, 45,* 72–74.

Lazarus, A. A. (1989). *The practice of multimodal therapy: Systematic, comprehensive, and effective psychotherapy.* Baltimore, MD: Johns Hopkins University Press.

Lazowick, L. M. (1955). On the nature of identification. *Journal of Abnormal and Social Psychology, 51,* 175–183.

Lefley, H. P., & Bestman, E. W. (1984). Community mental health and minority populations: A multi-ethnic approach. In S. Sue & T. Moore (Eds.), *The pluralistic society: A community mental health perspective* (pp. 116–148). New York: Human Sciences.

Leigh, J. W. (1984). *Empowerment strategies for work with multi-ethnic populations.* Paper presented at the annual meeting of the Council on Social Work Education, Detroit, MI.

Leong, F. T. L. (1992). Guidelines for minimizing premature termination among Asian American clients in group counseling. *Journal for Specialists in Group Work, 17,* 218–228.

Leong, F. T. L., & Brown, M. T. (1995). Theoretical issues in cross-cultural career development: Cultural validity and cultural specificity. In W. B. Walsh & S. H. Osipow (Eds.), *Handbook of vocational psychology* (2nd ed., pp. 143–180). Mahwah, NJ: Lawrence Erlbaum.

Leong, F. T. L., Kohout, J., Smith, J., & Wicherski, M. (2003). A profile of ethnic minority psychology: A pipeline perspective. In G. Bernal, J. E. Trimble, A. K. Burlew, & F. T. L. Leong (Eds.), *Handbook of racial and ethnic minority psychology* (pp. 76–99). Thousand Oaks, CA: Sage.

Lewis, D. O., Shanok, S. S., Cohen, R. J., Kligfeld, M., & Frisone, G. (1980). Race bias in the diagnosis and disposition of violent adolescents. *American Journal of Psychiatry, 137,* 1211–1216.

Lewis, J. A., Sperry, L., & Carlson, J. (1993). *Health counseling.* Pacific Grove, CA: Brooks/Cole.

Lichtenstein, S., Fischhoff, B., & Phillips, L. D. (1982). Calibration of probabilities: The state of the art to 1980. In D. Kahneman, P. Slovic, & A. Tversky (Eds.),

Judgment under uncertainty: Heuristics and biases (pp. 306–351). New York: Cambridge University Press.

Lindsey, K. P., & Paul, G. L. (1989). Involuntary commitments to public mental institutions: Issues involving the overrepresentation of Blacks and assessment of relevant functioning. *Psychological Bulletin, 106,* 171–183.

Lippitt, G., & Lippitt, R. (1986). *The consulting process in action* (2nd ed.). La Jolla, CA: University Associates.

Locke, D. C. (1998). *Increasing multicultural understanding: A comprehensive model* (2nd ed.). Thousand Oaks, CA: Sage.

Loftus, E. F., & Loftus, G. R. (1980). On the permanence of stored information in the human brain. *American Psychologist, 35,* 409–420.

Loo, C., Fong, K. T., & Iwamasa, G. (1988). Ethnicity and cultural diversity: An analysis of work published in community psychology journals, 1965–1985. *Journal of Community Psychology, 16,* 332–349.

López, S. R. (1989). Patient variable biases in clinical judgment: Conceptual overview and methodological considerations. *Psychological Bulletin, 106,* 184–203.

López, S. R. (2003). Reflections on the surgeon general's report on mental health, culture, race, and ethnicity. *Culture, Medicine and Psychiatry, 27,* 419–434.

Loring, M., & Powell, B. (1988). Gender, race, and *DSM-III:* A study of the objectivity of psychiatric diagnostic behavior. *Journal of Health and Social Behavior, 29,* 1–22.

Lu, F. G., Lim, R. F., & Mezzich, J. E. (1995). Issues in the assessment and diagnosis of culturally diverse individuals. In J. Oldham & M. Riba (Eds.), *American Psychiatric Press review of psychiatry* (Vol. 14, pp. 477–510). Washington, DC: American Psychiatric Press.

Lum, D. (2004). *Social work practice and people of color: A process-stage approach* (5th ed.). Pacific Grove, CA: Brooks/Cole-Wadsworth.

Mabry, M. (1988, April). Living in two worlds. *Newsweek on Campus,* p. 52.

MacPhee, D., Kreutzer, J. C., & Fritz, J. J. (1994). Infusing a diversity perspective into human development courses. *The Child Development, 65,* 699–715.

MacRae, D. (1976). *The social function of social science.* New Haven, CT: Yale University Press.

Malgady, R. G., Rogler, L. H., & Costantino, G. (1987). Ethnocultural and linguistic bias in mental health evaluation of Hispanics. *American Psychologist, 42,* 228–234.

Malzberg, B. (1963). Mental disorders in the U.S. In A. Deutsch & H. Fishman (Eds.), *Encyclopedia of mental health* (Vol. 3, pp. 1051–1066). New York: Franklin Watts.

Mancucella, H. (1985). Learning theory. In Association for Advanced Training in the Behavioral Sciences (Ed.), *Preparatory course for the national/state psychology licensure examination review* (20th series; Vol. 1, pp. 1–36). Los Angeles: Association for Advanced Training in the Behavioral Sciences.

Manderscheid, R. W., & Barrett, S. A. (Eds.). (1987). *Mental health, United States, 1987* (DHHS Publication No. ADM 87-1518). Washington, DC: Government Printing Office.

Manderscheid, R. W., & Henderson, M. J. (Eds.). (1998). *Mental health, United States: 1998.* Rockville, MD: Center for Mental Health Services.

Manly, J. (2001, March). *Diversity in neuropsychological testing: Issues with African American populations.* Paper presented at the meeting of Northern California Neuropsychology Forum, San Francisco.

Marín, G., Organista, P. B., & Chun, K. M. (2003). Acculturation research: Current issues and findings. In G. Bernal, J. E. Trimble, A. K. Burlew, & F. T. L. Leong (Eds.), *Handbook of racial and ethnic minority psychology* (pp. 208–219). Thousand Oaks, CA: Sage.

Marlatt, G. A. (1982). Relapse prevention: A self-control program for the treatment of addictive behaviors. In R. B. Stuart (Ed.), *Adherence, compliance and generalization in behavioral medicine* (pp. 329–378). New York: Brunner/Mazel.

Marlatt, G. A., & Gordon, J. R. (Eds.). (1985). *Relapse prevention: Maintenance strategies in the treatment of addictive behaviors.* New York: Guilford.

Marston, A. R. (1971). It is time to reconsider the Graduate Record Examination. *American Psychologist, 26,* 653–655.

Martinez, C. (1988). Mexican-Americans. In L. Comas-Díaz & E. E. H. Griffith (Eds.), *Clinical guidelines in cross-cultural mental health* (pp. 182–203). New York: John Wiley.

Mass, J. (1967). Incidence and treatment variations between Negroes and Caucasians in mental illness. *Community Mental Health, 3*(1), 61–65.

Masserman, J. (1960). *Psychoanalysis and human values.* New York: Grune & Stratton.

Masters, J. C., & Burish, T. G. (1987). *Behavior therapy: Techniques and empirical findings* (3rd ed.). San Diego, CA: Harcourt Brace Jovanovich.

Matarazzo, J. D. (1980). Behavioral health and behavioral medicine: Frontiers for a new health psychology. *American Psychologist, 35,* 807–817.

Maultsby, M. C. (1982). A historical view of Blacks' distrust of psychiatry. In S. M. Turner & R. T. Jones (Eds.), *Behavior modification in Black populations: Psychosocial issues and empirical findings* (pp. 39–55). New York: Plenum.

Mayo, J. A. (1974). The significance of sociocultural variables in psychiatric treatment of Black outpatients. *Comprehensive Psychiatry, 15,* 471–482.

McCann, I. L., Sakheim, D. K., & Abrahamson, D. J. (1988). Trauma and victimization: A model of psychological adaptation. *The Counseling Psychologist, 16,* 531–594.

McCauley, C., Stitt, C. L., & Segal, M. (1980). Stereotyping: From prejudice to prediction. *Psychological Bulletin, 87,* 195–208.

McGoldrick, M., Pearce, J. K., & Giordano, J. (Eds.). (1982). *Ethnicity and family therapy.* New York: Guilford.

McNeil, D. E., & Binder, R. L. (1995). Correlates of accuracy in the assessment of psychiatric inpatients' risk of violence. *American Journal of Psychiatry, 152,* 901–906.

Mechanic, D. (1999). *Mental health and social policy: The emergence of managed care* (4th ed.). Boston: Allyn & Bacon.

Meehl, P. E. (1960). The cognitive activity of the clinician. *American Psychologist, 15,* 19–27.

Melfi, C., Croghan, T. W., Hanna, M. P., & Robinson, R. L. (2000). Racial variation in antidepressant treatment in a Medicaid population. *Journal of Clinical Psychiatry, 61,* 16–21.

Melzack, R., & Wall, P. (1982). *The challenge of pain.* New York: Basic Books.

Mercer, K. (1984). Black communities' experience of psychiatric services. *International Journal of Social Psychiatry, 30,* 22–27.

Miles, R. (1989). *Racism.* London: Routledge.

Miles, R. (1993). *Racism after "race relations."* London: Routledge.

Miranda, J., Azocar, F., Organista, K. C., Muñoz, R. F., & Lieberman, A. (1996). Recruiting and retaining low-income Latinos in psychotherapy research. *Journal of Consulting and Clinical Psychology, 64,* 868–874.

Miranda, J., Nakamura, R., & Bernal, G. (2003). Including ethnic minorities in mental health intervention research: A practical approach to a long-standing problem. *Culture, Medicine and Psychiatry, 27,* 467–486.

Mollen, D., Ridley, C. R., & Hill, C. L. (2003). Models of multicultural counseling competence: A critical evaluation. In D. B. Pope-Davis, H. L. K. Coleman, W. M. Liu, & R. L. Toporek (Eds.), *Handbook of multicultural competencies in counseling and psychology* (pp. 21–37). Thousand Oaks, CA: Sage.

Mollica, R. F. (1990, March). *A look to the future.* Paper presented at the Conference on Mental Health of Immigrants and Refugees, World Federation for Mental Health and Hogg Foundation for Mental Health, Houston, TX.

Mollica, R. F., Blum, J. D., & Redlich, F. (1980). Equity and the psychiatric core of the Black patient, 1950–1970. *Journal of Nervous and Mental Disease, 168,* 279–286.

Montagu, A. (Ed.). (1964). *The concept of race.* New York: Free Press.

Moritsugu, J., & Sue, S. (1983). Minority status as a stressor. In R. D. Felner, L. A. Jason, J. Moritsugu, & S. S. Farber (Eds.), *Preventive psychology: Theory, research, and practice* (pp. 162–174). Elmsford, NY: Pergamon.

Morrow, K. A., & Deidan, C. T. (1992). Bias in the counseling process: How to recognize and avoid it. *Journal of Counseling and Development, 70,* 571–577.

Moses-Zirkes, S. (1993, August). APA asks Congress to fund more training for minorities. *APA Monitor,* p. 57.

Moy, S. (1992). A culturally sensitive, psychoeducational model for understanding and treating Asian-American clients. *Journal of Psychology and Christianity, 11,* 358–367.

Mueller, D. P., Edwards, D. W., & Yarvis, R. M. (1977). Stressful life events and psychiatric symptomatology: Change or undesirability? *Journal of Health and Social Behavior, 18,* 307–317.

Mukherjee, S., Shukla, S., Woodle, J., Rosen, A. M., & Olarte, S. (1983). Misdiagnosis of schizophrenia in bipolar patients: A multiethnic comparison. *American Journal of Psychiatry, 140,* 1571–1574.

Murphy, K. R., & Cleveland, J. N. (1995). *Understanding performance appraisal: Social, organizational, and goal-based perspectives.* Thousand Oaks, CA: Sage.

Myers, H. F., Echemendia, R. J., & Trimble, J. E. (1991). The need for training ethnic minority psychologists. In H. F. Myers, P. Wohlford, L. P. Guzman, & R. J. Echemendia (Eds.), *Ethnic minority perspectives on clinical training and services in psychology* (pp. 3–11). Washington, DC: American Psychological Association.

National Association of Social Workers. (1996). *Code of ethics.* Washington, DC: Author.

National Institutes of Health. (1994). *NIH guidelines on the inclusion of women and minorities as subjects in clinical research.* Retrieved November 10, 2004, from http://grants.nih.gov/grants/guide/notice-files/not94-100.html

Neighbors, H. W., Bashshur, R., Price, R., Donavedian, A., Selig, S., & Shannon, G. (1992). Ethnic minority health service delivery: A review of the literature. *Research in Community and Mental Health, 7,* 55–71.

Neighbors, H. W., Jackson, J. S., Campbell, L., & Williams, D. (1989). The influence of racial factors on psychiatric diagnosis: A review and suggestion for research. *Community Mental Health Journal, 25,* 301–311.

Neighbors, H. W., Trierweiler, S. J., Munday, C., Thompson, E. E., Jackson, J. S., Binion, V. J., et al. (1999). Psychiatric diagnosis of African Americans: Diagnostic divergence in clinician-structured and semistructured interviewing conditions. *Journal of the National Medical Association, 91,* 601–612.

Neville, H. A., Heppner, M. J., Louie, C. E., Thompson, C. E., Brooks, L., & Baker, C. E. (1996). The impact of multicultural training on White racial identity attitudes and therapy competencies. *Professional Psychology: Research and Practice, 27,* 83–89.

Nietzel, M. T., Bernstein, D. A., Kramer, G. P., & Milich, R. (2003). *Introduction to clinical psychology* (6th ed.). Upper Saddle River, NJ: Prentice Hall.

Norton, I. M., & Manson, S. M. (1996). Research in American Indian and Alaska Native communities: Navigating the cultural universe of values and process. *Journal of Consulting and Clinical Psychology, 64,* 856–860.

Okun, B. F. (2002). *Effective helping: Interviewing and counseling techniques* (6th ed.). Pacific Grove, CA: Brooks/Cole.

O'Sullivan, M. J., Peterson, P. D., Cox, G. B., & Kirkeby, J. (1989). Ethnic populations: Community mental health services ten years later. *American Journal of Community Psychology, 17,* 17–30.

Padilla, A. M., & Lindholm, K. J. (1995). Quantitative educational research with ethnic minorities. In J. A. Banks & C. A. McGee-Banks (Eds.), *Handbook of research on multicultural education* (pp. 97–113). New York: Macmillan.

Pavkov, T. W., Lewis, D. A., & Lyons, J. S. (1989). Psychiatric diagnoses and racial bias: An empirical investigation. *Professional Psychology: Research and Practice, 20,* 364–368.

Pedersen, P. B. (1987). Ten frequent assumptions of cultural bias in counseling. *Journal of Multicultural Counseling and Development, 15,* 16–24.

Pedersen, P. B. (1990a, August). Interracial collaboration among counseling psychologists. In J. G. Ponterotto (Chair), *The White American researcher in multicultural counseling: Significance and challenges.* Symposium conducted at the 98th Annual Meeting of the American Psychological Association, Boston.

Pedersen, P. B. (1990b). The multicultural perspective as a fourth force in counseling. *Journal of Mental Health Counseling, 12,* 93–95.

Pedersen, P. B. (1994). *A handbook for developing multicultural awareness* (2nd ed.). Alexandria, VA: American Counseling Association.

Pedersen, P. B. (Eds.). (1999). *Multiculturalism as a fourth force.* Philadelphia: Brunner/Mazel.

Pedersen, P. B. (2003). Reducing prejudice and racism through counselor training as a primary prevention strategy. In G. Bernal, J. E. Trimble, A. K. Burlew, &

F. T. L. Leong (Eds.), *Handbook of racial and ethnic minority psychology* (pp. 621–632). Thousand Oaks, CA: Sage.

Peoples, V. Y., & Dell, D. M. (1975). Black and White student preferences for counselor roles. *Journal of Counseling Psychology, 22,* 529–534.

Peterson, D. R. (2000). Scientist-practitioner or scientific practitioner? *American Psychologist, 55,* 252–253.

Phares, E. J. (1992). *Clinical psychology: Concepts, methods, and profession* (4th ed.). Pacific Grove, CA: Brooks/Cole.

Phillips, D. A. (2000). Social policy and community psychology. In J. Rappaport & E. Seidman (Eds.), *Handbook of community psychology* (pp. 397–419). New York: Kluwer Academic/Plenum.

Phinney, J. S., Lochner, B. T., & Murphy, R. (1990). Ethnic identity development and psychological adjustment in adolescence. In A. R. Stiffman & L. E. Davis (Eds.), *Ethnic issues in adolescent mental health* (pp. 53–72). Newbury Park, CA: Sage.

Pietrofesa, J. J., Hoffman, A., & Splete, H. H. (1984). *Counseling: An introduction* (2nd ed.). Boston: Houghton Mifflin.

Pinderhughes, C. A. (1973). Racism and psychotherapy. In C. V. Willie, B. M. Kramer, & B. S. Brown (Eds.), *Racism and mental health: Essays* (pp. 61–121). Pittsburgh, PA: University of Pittsburgh Press.

Pinderhughes, E. (1989). *Understanding race, ethnicity, and power: The key to efficacy in clinical practice.* New York: Free Press.

Pomales, J., Claiborn, C. D., & LaFromboise, T. D. (1986). Effects of Black students' racial identity on perceptions of White counselors varying in cultural sensitivity. *Journal of Counseling Psychology, 34,* 123–131.

Ponce, F. Q., & Atkinson, D. R. (1989). Mexican-American acculturation, counselor ethnicity, counseling style, and perceived counselor credibility. *Journal of Counseling Psychology, 36,* 203–208.

Ponterotto, J. G. (1987). Counseling Mexican Americans: A multimodal approach. *Journal of Counseling and Development, 65,* 308–312.

Ponterotto, J. G. (1988). Racial/ethnic minority research in the *Journal of Counseling Psychology:* A content analysis and methodological critique. *Journal of Counseling Psychology, 35,* 410–418.

Ponterotto, J. G., & Casas, J. M. (1987). In search of multicultural competence within counselor education programs. *Journal of Counseling and Development, 65,* 430–434.

Ponterotto, J. G., & Casas, J. M. (1991). *Handbook of racial/ethnic minority counseling research.* Springfield, IL: Charles C Thomas.

Ponterotto, J. G., Costa, C. I., & Werner-Lin, A. (2002). Research perspectives in cross-cultural counseling. In P. B. Pedersen, J. G. Draguns, W. J. Lonner, & J. E. Trimble (Eds.), *Counseling across cultures* (5th ed., pp. 395–420). Thousand Oaks, CA: Sage.

Ponterotto, J. G., Fuertes, J. N., & Chen, E. C. (2000). Models of multicultural counseling. In S. D. Brown & R. W. Lent (Eds.), *Handbook of counseling psychology* (3rd ed., pp. 639–669). New York: John Wiley.

Ponterotto, J. G., & Pedersen, P. B. (1993). *Preventing prejudice: A guide for counselors and educators.* Newbury Park, CA: Sage.

Pope-Davis, D. B., & Coleman, H. L. K. (Eds.). (1997). *Multicultural counseling competencies: Assessment, education and training, and supervision.* Thousand Oaks, CA: Sage.

Poussaint, A. F. (1999, August 26). They hate. They kill. Are they insane? *New York Times,* p. A17.

Prange, A., & Vitols, M. (1962). Cultural aspects of the relatively low incidence of depression in southern Negroes. *International Journal of Social Psychiatry, 8,* 104–112.

President's Commission on Mental Health. (1978). *Task panel report to the president* (Vols. 1–4). Washington, DC: Government Printing Office.

Priest, R. (1991). Racism and prejudice as negative impacts on African American clients in therapy. *Journal of Counseling and Development, 70,* 213–215.

Prudhomme, C., & Musto, D. F. (1973). Historical perspectives on mental health and racism in the United States. In C. V. Willie, B. M. Kramer, & B. S. Brown (Eds.), *Racism and mental health: Essays* (pp. 25–57). Pittsburgh, PA: University of Pittsburgh Press.

Quintana, S. M. (1994). A model of ethnic perspective taking ability applied to Mexican-American children and youth. *International Journal of Intercultural Relations, 18,* 419–448.

Quintana, S. M., Troyano, N., & Taylor, G. (2001). Cultural validity and inherent challenges in quantitative methods for multicultural research. In J. G. Ponterotto, J. M. Casas, L. A. Suzuki, & C. M. Alexander (Eds.), *Handbook of multicultural counseling* (2nd ed., pp. 604–630). Thousand Oaks, CA: Sage.

Ramirez, M. (1983). *Psychology of the Americas: Mestizo perspectives on personality and mental health.* Elmsford, NY: Pergamon.

Ramos-McKay, J. M., Comas-Díaz, L., & Rivera, L. A. (1988). Puerto Ricans. In L. Comas-Díaz & E. E. H. Griffith (Eds.), *Clinical guidelines in cross-cultural mental health* (pp. 204–232). New York: John Wiley.

Rappaport, J. (1981). In praise of paradox: A social policy of empowerment over prevention. *American Journal of Community Psychology, 9,* 1–26.

Reed, R. (1988). Education and achievement of young Black males. In J. T. Gibbs (Ed.), *Young, Black and male in America: An endangered species* (pp. 37–96). Dover, MA: Auburn House.

Reiff, R. (1967). Mental health, manpower and institutional change. In E. L. Cowen, E. A. Gardner, & M. Zax (Eds.), *Emergent approaches to mental health problems* (pp. 74–88). New York: Appleton-Century-Crofts.

Reiss, S., & Szyszko, J. (1983). Diagnostic overshadowing and professional experience with mentally retarded persons. *American Journal of Mental Deficiency, 87,* 396–402.

Rendon, M. (1984). Myths and stereotypes in minority groups. *International Journal of Social Psychiatry, 30,* 297–309.

Reynolds, A. L., & Pope, R. L. (2003). Multicultural competence in counseling centers. In D. B. Pope-Davis, H. L. K. Coleman, W. M. Liu, & R. L. Toporek (Eds.), *Handbook of multicultural competencies in counseling and psychology* (pp. 365–382). Thousand Oaks, CA: Sage.

Reynolds, C. R., & Brown, R. T. (1984). Bias in mental testing: An introduction to the issues. In C. R. Reynolds & R. T. Brown (Eds.), *Perspectives on bias in mental testing* (pp. 1–39). New York: Plenum.

Reynolds, G. S. (1968). *A primer of operant conditioning.* Glenview, IL: Scott, Foresman.

Richardson, J., Anderson, T., Flaherty, J., & Bell, C. (2003). The quality of mental health care for African Americans. *Culture, Medicine, and Psychiatry, 27,* 487–498.

Ridley, C. R. (1978). Cross-cultural counseling: A multivariate analysis. *Viewpoints in Teaching and Learning, 54*(1), 43–50.

Ridley, C. R. (1984). Clinical treatment of the nondisclosing Black client: A therapeutic paradox. *American Psychologist, 39,* 1234–1244.

Ridley, C. R. (1985a). Imperatives for ethnic and cultural relevance in psychology training programs. *Professional Psychology: Research and Practice, 16,* 611–622.

Ridley, C. R. (1985b). Pseudo-transference in interracial psychotherapy: An operant paradigm. *Journal of Contemporary Psychotherapy, 15,* 29–36.

Ridley, C. R. (1986a). Cross-cultural counseling in theological context. *Journal of Psychology and Theology, 14,* 288–297.

Ridley, C. R. (1986b). Diagnosis as a function of race pairing and client self-disclosure. *Journal of Cross-Cultural Psychology, 17,* 337–351.

Ridley, C. R. (1986c). Optimum service delivery to the Black client. *American Psychologist, 41,* 226–227.

Ridley, C. R. (1989). Racism in counseling as an aversive behavioral process. In P. B. Pedersen, J. G. Draguns, W. J. Lonner, & J. E. Trimble (Eds.), *Counseling across cultures* (3rd ed., pp. 55–77). Honolulu: University of Hawaii Press.

Ridley, C. R., & Goodwin, S. J. (2003). *Overcoming resistance to change.* St. Charles, IL: ChurchSmart Resources.

Ridley, C. R., & Kleiner, A. J. (2003). Multicultural counseling competence: History, themes, and issues. In D. B. Pope-Davis, H. L. K. Coleman, W. M. Liu, & R. L. Toporek (Eds.), *Handbook of multicultural competencies in counseling and psychology* (pp. 3–20). Thousand Oaks, CA: Sage.

Ridley, C. R., Liddle, M. C., Hill, C. L., & Li, L. C. (2001). Ethical decision making in multicultural counseling. In J. G. Ponterotto, J. M. Casas, L. A. Suzuki, & C. M. Alexander (Eds.), *Handbook of multicultural counseling* (2nd ed., pp. 165–188). Thousand Oaks, CA: Sage.

Ridley, C. R., & Lingle, D. W. (1996). Cultural empathy in multicultural counseling: A multidimensional process model. In P. B. Pedersen, J. G. Draguns, W. J. Lonner, & J. E. Trimble (Eds.), *Counseling across cultures* (4th ed., pp. 21–46). Thousand Oaks, CA: Sage.

Ridley, C. R., & Mendoza, D. W. (1993). Putting organizational effectiveness into practice: The preeminent consultation task. *Journal of Counseling and Development, 72,* 168–177.

Ridley, C. R., Mendoza, D. W., & Kanitz, B. (1994). Multicultural training: Reexamination, operationalization, and integration. *Counseling Psychologist, 22,* 227–289.

Ridley, C. R., Mendoza, D. W., Kanitz, B. E., Angermeier, L., & Zenk, R. (1994). Cultural sensitivity in multicultural counseling: A perceptual schema model. *Journal of Counseling Psychology, 41,* 125–136.

Ridley, C. R., & Tan, S.-Y. (1986). Unintentional paradoxes and potential pitfalls in paradoxical psychotherapy. *The Counseling Psychologist, 14,* 303–308.

Ridley, C. R., & Thompson, C. E. (1999). Managing resistance to diversity training: A social systems perspective. In M. S. Kiselica (Ed.), *Confronting prejudice and racism during multicultural training.* Alexandria, VA: American Counseling Association.

Ridley, C. R., & Udipi, S. (2002). Putting cultural empathy into practice. In P. B. Pedersen, J. G. Draguns, W. J. Lonner, & J. E. Trimble (Eds.), *Counseling across cultures* (5th ed., pp. 317–333). Thousand Oaks, CA: Sage.

Riessman, F., & Miller, S. M. (1964). Social change versus the psychiatric world view. *American Journal of Orthopsychiatry, 34,* 29–38.

Rivers, L. W., Henderson, D. M., Jones, R. L., Ladner, J. A., & Williams, R. L. (1975). Mosaic of labels for Black children. In N. Hobbs (Ed.), *Issues in the classification of children* (Vol. 2, pp. 213–245). San Francisco: Jossey-Bass.

Roark, A. (1974). A tentative model for helping relationships with minorities. *Counseling and Values, 18,* 172–178.

Robinson, T. (1993). The intersections of gender, class, race, and culture: On seeing clients whole. *Journal of Multicultural Counseling and Development, 21,* 50–58.

Rogers, C. R. (1961). *On becoming a person: A therapist's view of psychotherapy.* Boston: Houghton Mifflin.

Rogler, L. H. (1989). Methodological source of cultural insensitivity in mental health research. *American Psychologist, 50,* 859–877.

Rogler, L. H. (1993). Culture in psychiatric diagnosis: An issue of scientific accuracy. *Psychiatry, 56,* 324–327.

Rogler, L. H., Santana-Cooney, R., Costantino, G., Earley, B., Grossman, B., Gurak, D., et al. (1983). *A conceptual framework for mental health research on Hispanic populations* (Hispanic Research Center Monograph No. 10). New York: Fordham University.

Rollock, D., & Gordon, E. W. (2000). Racism and mental health into the 21st century: Perspectives and parameters. *American Journal of Orthopsychiatry, 70,* 5–13.

Romano, J. L., & Hage, S. M. (2000). Prevention and counseling psychology: Revitalizing commitments for the 21st century. *The Counseling Psychologist, 28,* 733–763.

Romano, J. L., & Kachgal, M. M. (2004). Counseling psychology and school counseling: An underutilized partnership. *The Counseling Psychologist, 32,* 184–215.

Rosado, J. W., Jr., & Elias, M. J. (1993). Ecological and psychocultural mediators in the delivery of services for urban, culturally diverse Hispanic clients. *Professional Psychology: Research and Practice, 24,* 450–459.

Rosen, H., & Frank, J. D. (1962). Negroes in psychotherapy. *American Journal of Psychiatry, 119,* 456–460.

Rosenfield, S. (1984). Race differences in involuntary hospitalization: Psychiatric versus labeling perspectives. *Journal of Health and Social Behavior, 25,* 14–23.

Rosenhan, D. L. (1973). On being sane in insane places. *Science, 179*(4070), 250–258.

Rosenhan, D. L., & Seligman, M. E. P. (1995). *Abnormal psychology* (3rd ed.). New York: W. W. Norton.

Rosenstein, M. J., Milazzo-Sayre, L. J., MacAskill, R. L., & Manderscheid, R. W. (1987). Use of inpatient services by special populations. In R. W. Manderscheid & S. A. Barrett (Eds.), *Mental health, United States, 1987* (DHHS Publication No. ADM 87-1518). Washington, DC: Government Printing Office.

Ross, L. (1977). The intuitive psychologist and his shortcomings: Distortions in the attribution process. In L. Berkowitz (Ed.), *Advances in experimental social psychology* (Vol. 10, pp. 173–220). New York: Academic Press.

Rousseve, R. (1987, March/April). A Black American youth torn between cultures. *Humanist,* pp. 5–8.

Ruch, F. L. (1967). *Psychology and life* (7th ed.). Glenview, IL: Scott, Foresman.

Rushton, J. P. (1988). Race differences in behaviour: A review and evolutionary analysis. *Journal of Personality and Individual Differences, 9,* 1009–1024.

Ryan, W. (1971). *Blaming the victim.* New York: Vintage.

Rychlak, J. F. (1981). *A philosophy of science for personality theory.* Malabar, FL: Robert E. Krieger.

Sabshin, M., Diesenhaus, H., & Wilkerson, R. (1970). Dimensions of institutional racism in psychiatry. *American Journal of Psychiatry, 127,* 787–793.

Sager, C. J., Brayboy, T. L., & Waxenberg, B. R. (1972). Black patient-White therapist. *American Journal of Orthopsychiatry, 42,* 415–423.

Samuda, R. J. (1975). *Psychological testing of American minorities: Issues and consequences.* New York: Dodd, Mead.

Sandler, J., & Freud, A. (1985). *The analysis of defense: The ego and the mechanisms of defense revisited.* New York: International Universities Press.

Schaefer, R. T. (1988). *Racial and ethnic groups* (3rd ed.). Glenview, IL: Scott, Foresman.

Scheffler, R. M., & Miller, A. B. (1991). Differences in mental health service utilization among ethnic sub-populations. *International Journal of Law and Psychiatry, 14,* 363–376.

Schein, E. H. (1988). *Process consultation: Its role in organization development* (Vol. 1, 2nd ed.). Reading, MA: Addison-Wesley.

Schinke, S. P., Botvin, G. J., Trimble, J. E., Orlandi, M. A., Gilchrist, L. D., & Locklear, V. S. (1988). Preventing substance abuse among American-Indian adolescents. *Journal of Counseling Psychology, 35,* 87–90.

Schofield, W. (1964). *Psychotherapy: The purchase of friendship.* Englewood Cliffs, NJ: Prentice Hall.

Schonbachler, P., & Spengler, P. M. (1992). *Borderline personality disorder and signs of sexual abuse: Do psychologists test a sexual trauma hypothesis?* Unpublished manuscript.

Scissons, E. H. (1993). *Counseling for results: Principles and practices of helping.* Pacific Grove, CA: Brooks/Cole.

Sedlacek, W. E., & Brooks, G. C. (1976). *Racism in American education: A model for change.* Chicago: Nelson-Hall.

Segal, S. P., Bola, J. R., & Watson, M. A. (1996). Race, quality of care, and antipsychotic prescribing practices in psychiatric emergency services. *Psychiatric Services, 47,* 282–286.

Seligman, D. (1973, March). How "equal opportunity" turned into employment quotas. *Fortune,* pp. 160–168.

Seligman, M. E. P. (1995). The effectiveness of psychotherapy: The *Consumer Reports* study. *American Psychologist, 50,* 965–974.

Seligman, M. E. P. (1996). Science as an ally of practice. *American Psychologist, 51,* 1072–1079.

Shervington, W. W. (1976). Racism, professionalism, elitism: Their effect on the mental health delivery system. *Journal of the National Medical Association, 68,* 91–96.

Shockley, W. (1971). Negro IQ deficit: Failure of a malicious coincidence model warrants new research proposals. *Review of Educational Research, 41,* 227–248.

Shuey, A. M. (1966). *The testing of Negro intelligence.* New York: Social Science Press.

Shweder, R. A. (1990). Cultural psychology: What is it? In J. W. Stigler, R. A. Shweder, & G. Herdt (Eds.), *Cultural psychology: Essays on comparative human development.* New York: Cambridge University Press.

Simon, R. J., Fleiss, J. L., Gurland, B. J., Stiller, P. R., & Sharpe, L. (1973). Depression and schizophrenia in hospitalized Black and White mental patients. *Archives of General Psychiatry, 28,* 509–512.

Skillings, J., & Dobbins, J. E. (1991). Racism as a disease: Etiology and treatment implications. *Journal of Counseling and Development, 70,* 206–212.

Skinner, B. F. (1957). *Verbal behavior.* New York: Appleton-Century-Crofts.

Smart, D., & Smart, J. F. (1997). *DSM-IV* and culturally sensitive diagnosis: Some observations for counselors. *Journal of Counseling and Development, 75,* 392–398.

Smedes, L. B. (1984). *Forgive and forget: Healing the hurts we don't deserve.* San Francisco: Harper & Row.

Smedley, B. D., Stith, A. Y., & Nelson, A. R. (Eds.). (2003). *Unequal treatment: Confronting racial and ethnic disparities in healthcare.* Washington, DC: National Academies Press.

Smirnow, B. W., & Bruhn, A. R. (1984). Encopresis in a Hispanic boy: Distinguishing pathology from cultural differences. *Psychotherapy: Theory, Research and Practice, 21,* 24–30.

Smith, E. J. (1981). Cultural and historical perspectives in counseling Blacks. In D. W. Sue (Ed.), *Counseling the culturally different* (pp. 141–185). New York: John Wiley.

Snowden, L. R., & Cheung, F. K. (1990). Use of inpatient mental health services by members of ethnic minority groups. *American Psychologist, 45,* 347–355.

Snyder, M. (1982, July). Self-fulfilling stereotypes. *Psychology Today,* pp. 60, 65, 67–68.

Snyder, M., & Uranowitz, S. W. (1978). Reconstructing the past: Some cognitive consequences of person perception. *Journal of Personality and Social Psychology, 36,* 941–950.

Solomon, A. (1992). Clinical diagnosis among diverse populations: A multicultural perspective. *Families in Society, 73,* 371–377.

Solomon, P. (1988). Racial factors in mental health service utilization. *Psychosocial Rehabilitation Journal, 11*(3), 3–12.

Speight, S. L., Thomas, A. J., Kennel, R. G., & Anderson, M. E. (1995). Operationalizing multicultural training in doctoral programs and internships. *Professional Psychology: Research and Practice, 26,* 401–406.

Spengler, P. M. (1992, August). Application of scientist-professional assessment to practice and graduate curriculum. In P. M. Spengler (Chair), *Scientist-professional model of psychological assessment.* Symposium conducted at the annual meeting of the American Psychological Association, Washington, DC.

Spengler, P. M., Blustein, D. L., & Strohmer, D. C. (1990). Diagnostic and treatment overshadowing of vocational problems by personal problems. *Journal of Counseling Psychology, 37,* 372–381.

Spengler, P. M., Strohmer, D. C., Dorau, L. M., & Gard, T. L. (1994, August). *Psychological masquerade: Comparison of counseling and clinical psychologists, psychiatrists, and physicians.* Paper presented at the annual meeting of the American Psychological Association, Los Angeles.

Sperry, L. (1988). Biopsychosocial therapy: An integrative approach for tailoring treatment. *Individual Psychology, 44,* 225–235.

Spurlock, J. (1985). Assessment and therapeutic intervention of Black children. *Journal of the American Academy of Child Psychiatry, 24,* 168–174.

Stack, L. C., Lannon, P. B., & Miley, A. D. (1983). Accuracy of clinicians' expectancies for psychiatric rehospitalization. *American Journal of Community Psychology, 11,* 99–113.

Stanton, W. R. (1960). *The leopard's spots: Scientific attitudes toward race in America, 1815–1859.* Chicago: University of Chicago Press.

Steele, S. (1990). *The content of our character: A new vision of race in America.* New York: HarperPerennial.

Steinberg, L., & Fletcher, A. C. (1998). Data analytic strategies in research on ethnic minority youth. In V. C. McLoyd & L. Steinberg (Eds.), *Studying minority adolescents: Conceptual, methodological, and theoretical issues* (pp. 279–294). Mahwah, NJ: Lawrence Erlbaum.

Steinberg, M. D., Pardes, H., Bjork, D., & Sporty, L. (1977). Demographic and clinical characteristics of Black psychiatric patients in a private general hospital. *Hospital and Community Psychiatry, 28,* 128–132.

Stevenson, H. C., & Renard, G. (1993). Trusting ole' wise owls: Therapeutic use of cultural strengths in African-American families. *Professional Psychology: Research and Practice, 24,* 433–442.

Strakowski, S. M., Lonczak, H. S., Sax, K. W., West, S. A., Crist, A., Mehta, R., et al. (1995). The effects of race on diagnosis and disposition from a psychiatric emergency service. *Journal of Clinical Psychiatry, 56,* 101–107.

Strakowski, S. M., Shelton, R. C., & Kolbrener, M. L. (1993). The effects of race and comorbidity on clinical diagnosis in patients with psychosis. *Journal of Clinical Psychiatry, 54,* 96–102.

Strauss, M. E., Gynther, M. D., & Wallhermfechtel, J. (1974). Differential and misdiagnosis of Blacks and Whites by MMPI. *Journal of Personality and Assessment, 39,* 138–140.

Strohmer, D. C., & Shivy, V. A. (1992, August). Judgmental and inferential errors in counseling. In P. M. Spengler (Chair), *Scientist-professional model of psychological assessment.* Symposium conducted at the annual meeting of the American Psychological Association, Washington, DC.

Strong, S. R. (1964). Verbal conditioning and counseling research. *Personnel and Guidance Journal, 42,* 660–669.

Sue, D. W. (1977). Counseling the culturally different: A conceptual analysis. *Personnel and Guidance Journal, 55,* 422–425.

Sue, D. W. (1978). Eliminating cultural oppression in counseling: Toward a general theory. *Journal of Counseling Psychology, 25,* 419–428.

Sue, D. W., Arredondo, P., & McDavis, R. J. (1992). Multicultural competencies/standards: A pressing need. *Journal of Counseling and Development, 70,* 477–486.

Sue, D. W., Carter, R. T., Casas, J. M., Foad, N. A., Ivey, A. E., Jensen, M., et al. (1998). *Multicultural counseling competencies: Individual and organizational development.* Thousand Oaks, CA: Sage.

Sue, D. W., Ivey, A. E., & Pedersen, P. B. (1996). *A theory of multicultural counseling and therapy.* Pacific Grove, CA: Brooks/Cole.

Sue, D. W., & Sue, D. (1977). Barriers to effective cross-cultural counseling. *Journal of Counseling Psychology, 24,* 420–429.

Sue, D. W., & Sue, D. (2003). *Counseling the culturally diverse: Theory and practice* (4th ed.). New York: John Wiley.

Sue, D. W., & Sue, S. (1972). Counseling Chinese-Americans. *Personnel and Guidance Journal, 50,* 637–644.

Sue, S. (1977). Community mental health services to minority groups: Some optimism, some pessimism. *American Psychologist, 32,* 616–624.

Sue, S. (1992). Ethnicity and mental health: Research and policy issues. *Journal of Social Issues, 48*(2), 187–205.

Sue, S. (1998). In search of cultural competence in psychotherapy and counseling. *American Psychologist, 53,* 440–448.

Sue, S. (1999). Science, ethnicity, and bias: Where have we gone wrong? *American Psychologist, 54,* 1070–1077.

Sue, S. (2003). Ethnic research is good science. In G. Bernal, J. E. Trimble, A. K. Burlew, & F. T. L. Leong (Eds.), *Handbook of racial and ethnic minority psychology* (pp. 198–207). Thousand Oaks, CA: Sage.

Sue, S. (in press). Multicultural lessons learned from clinical psychology and implications for school psychology. In G. Esquivel, E. Lopez, & S. Nahari (Eds.), *Handbook of multicultural school psychology.* Mahwah, NJ: Lawrence Erlbaum.

Sue, S., Kurasaki, K. S., & Srinivasan, S. (1999). Ethnicity, gender, and cross-cultural issues in clinical research. In P. C. Kendall, J. N. Butcher, & G. N. Holmbeck (Eds.), *Handbook of research methods in clinical psychology* (2nd ed., pp. 54–71). New York: John Wiley.

Sue, S., & McKinney, H. (1975). Asian Americans in the community mental health care system. *American Journal of Orthopsychiatry, 45,* 111–118.

Sue, S., McKinney, H., Allen, D., & Hall, J. (1974). Delivery of community mental health services to Black and White clients. *Journal of Consulting and Clinical Psychology, 42,* 794–801.

Sue, S., & Zane, N. (1987). The role of culture and cultural techniques in psychotherapy: A critique and reformulation. *American Psychologist, 42,* 37–45.

Sutton, R. G., & Kessler, M. (1986). National study of the effects of clients' socioeconomic status on clinical psychologists' professional judgments. *Journal of Consulting and Clinical Psychology, 54,* 275–276.

Sykes, D. K. (1987). An approach to working with Black youth in cross-cultural therapy. *Clinical Social Work Journal, 15,* 260–270.

Szapocznik, J., & Kurtines, W. M. (1980). Acculturation, biculturalism, and adjustment among Cuban Americans. In A. Padilla (Ed.), *Acculturation: Theory, models, and some new findings* (pp. 27–42). Boulder, CO: Westview.

Szapocznik, J., & Kurtines, W. M. (1993). Family psychology and cultural diversity: Opportunities for theory, research, and application. *American Psychologist, 48,* 400–407.

Szapocznik, J., Scopetta, M. A., Arnalde, M. & Kurtines, W. M. (1978). Cuban value structure: Treatment implications. *Journal of Consulting and Clinical Psychology, 46,* 961–970.

Tajfel, H. (Ed.). (1978). *Differentiation between social groups: Studies in the social psychology of intergroup relations.* London: Academic Press.

Takeuchi, D. T., & Uehara, E. S. (1996). Ethnic minority mental health services: Current research and future conceptual directions. In B. L. Levin & J. Petrila (Eds.), *Mental health services: A public health perspective* (pp. 63–80). New York: Oxford University Press.

Taube, C. A. (1971). *Admission rates to state and county mental hospitals by age, sex, and color, United States, 1969* (Statistical Note 41). Rockville, MD: U.S. Department of Health, Education and Welfare, National Institute of Mental Health, Biometry Branch.

Taylor, S. E. (1990). Health psychology: The science and the field. *American Psychologist, 45,* 40–50.

Teichner, V., Cadden, J. J., & Berry, G. W. (1981). The Puerto Rican patient: Some historical, cultural and psychological aspects. *Journal of the American Academy of Psychoanalysis, 9,* 277–289.

Terman, L. M. (1916). *The measurement of intelligence: An explanation of and a complete guide for the use of the Stanford revision and extension of the Binet-Simon Intelligence Scale.* Boston: Houghton Mifflin.

Teyber, E. (2000). *Interpersonal process in psychotherapy: A guide for clinical practice* (4th ed.). Pacific Grove, CA: Wadsworth.

Tharp, R. G. (1991). Cultural diversity and treatment of children. *Journal of Consulting and Clinical Psychology, 59,* 799–812.

Thomas, A. (1962). Pseudo-transference reactions due to cultural stereotyping. *American Journal of Orthopsychiatry, 32,* 894–900.

Thomas, A., & Sillen, S. (1972). *Racism and psychiatry.* Secaucus, NJ: Citadel.

Thomas, C. S., & Comer, J. P. (1973). Racism and mental health services. In C. V. Willie, B. M. Kramer, & B. S. Brown (Eds.), *Racism and mental health: Essays* (pp. 165–181). Pittsburgh, PA: University of Pittsburgh Press.

Thomas, C. W. (1973). The system-maintenance role of the White psychologist. *Journal of Social Issues, 29*(1), 57–65.

Thomas, D. A. (1993). Racial dynamics in cross-race developmental relationships. *Administrative Science Quarterly, 38,* 169–194.

Thomas, D. A. (2001). The truth about mentoring minorities: Race matters. *Harvard Business Review, 79*(4), 98–111.

Thomason, T. C. (1991). Counseling Native Americans: An introduction for non-Native American counselors. *Journal of Counseling and Development, 69,* 321–327.

Thompson, C. E., & Jenal, S. T. (1994). Interracial and intraracial quasi-counseling interactions when counselors avoid discussing race. *Journal of Counseling Psychology, 41,* 484–491.

Thompson, C. E., & Neville, H. A. (1999). Racism, mental health, and mental health practice. *The Counseling Psychologist, 27,* 155–223.

Thompson, C. E., Worthington, R., & Atkinson, D. R. (1994). Counselor content orientation, counselor race, and Black women's cultural mistrust and self-disclosures. *Journal of Counseling Psychology, 41,* 155–161.

Thompson, E. E., Neighbors, H. W., Munday, C., & Jackson, J. S. (1996). Recruitment and retention of African American patients for clinical research: An exploration of response rates in an urban psychiatric hospital. *Journal of Consulting and Clinical Psychology, 64,* 861–867.

Thompson, J. W., Blueye, H. B., Smith, C. R., & Walker, R. D. (1983). Cross-cultural curriculum content in psychiatric residency training: An American Indian and Alaska Native perspective. In J. C. Chunn II, P. J. Dunston, & F. Ross-Sherrif (Eds.), *Mental health and people of color: Curriculum development and change* (pp. 269–288). Washington, DC: Howard University Press.

Thornton, G. C., & Zorich, S. (1980). Training to improve observer accuracy. *Journal of Applied Psychology, 65,* 351–354.

Thouless, R. H. (1974). *Straight and crooked thinking: Thirty-eight dishonest tricks of debate.* London: Pan.

Tinsley-Jones, H. A. (2001). Racism in our midst: Listening to psychologists of color. *Professional Psychology: Research and Practice, 32,* 573–580.

Tirozzi, G. N., & Uro, G. (1997). Education reform in the United States: National policy in support of local efforts for school improvement. *American Psychologist, 52,* 241–249.

Toch, H., Adams, K., & Greene, R. (1987). Ethnicity, disruptiveness, and emotional disorder among prison inmates. *Criminal Justice and Behavior, 14,* 93–109.

Tomlinson-Clarke, S., & Wang, V. O. (1999). A paradigm for racial-cultural training in the development of counselor cultural competencies. In M. S. Kiselica (Ed.), *Confronting prejudice and racism during multicultural training* (pp. 155–168). Alexandria, VA: American Counseling Association.

Townsend, J. (1995). Racial, ethnic, and mental illness stereotypes: Cognitive process and behavioral effects. In C. V. Willis, P. P. Rieker, B. M. Kramer, & B. S. Brown (Eds.), *Mental health, racism, and sexism* (pp. 119–147). Pittsburgh, PA: University of Pittsburgh Press.

Triandis, H. C., Malpass, R. S., & Davidson, A. R. (1973). Psychology and culture. *Annual Review of Psychology, 24,* 355–378.

Trierweiler, S. J., Neighbors, H. W., Munday, C., Thompson, E. E., Binion, V. J., & Gomez, J. P. (2000). Clinician attributions associated with the diagnosis of schizophrenia in African American and non–African American patients. *Journal of Consulting and Clinical Psychology, 68,* 171–175.

Tropman, J. E. (1995). Policy management in a social agency. In J. E. Tropman, J. L. Erlich, & J. Rothman (Eds.), *Tactics and techniques of community intervention* (3rd ed., pp. 288–295). Itasca, IL: F. E. Peacock.

Turner, C. B., & Kramer, B. M. (1995). Connections between racism and mental health. In C. V. Willie, P. P. Rieker, B. M. Kramer, & B. S. Brown (Eds.), *Mental health, racism, and sexism* (pp. 3–25). Pittsburgh, PA: University of Pittsburgh Press.

Turner, M. E., Pratkanis, A. R., Probasco, P., & Leve, C. (1992). Threat, cohesion, and group effectiveness: Testing a racial identity maintenance perspective on groupthink. *Journal of Personality and Social Psychology, 63,* 781–796.

Turner, R. J., & Cumming, J. (1967). Theoretical malaise and community mental health. In E. L. Cowen, E. A. Gardner, & M. Zax (Eds.), *Emergent approaches to mental health problems* (pp. 40–62). New York: Appleton-Century-Crofts.

Uba, L. (1982). Meeting the mental health needs of Asian Americans: Mainstream or segregated services. *Professional Psychology, 13,* 215–221.

U.S. Department of Health and Human Services. (1986). *Report of the secretary's task force on Black and minority health* (Vol. 5). Washington, DC: Author.

U.S. Department of Health and Human Services. (1999). *Mental health: A report of the surgeon general.* Rockville, MD: Author.

U.S. Department of Health and Human Services. (2001). *Mental health: Culture, race, and ethnicity–a supplement to Mental health: A report of the surgeon general.* Rockville, MD: Author.

Usher, C. H. (1989). Recognizing cultural bias in counseling theory and practice: The case of Rogers. *Journal of Multicultural Counseling and Development, 17,* 62–71.

van den Berghe, P. (1967). *Race and racism: A comparative perspective.* New York: John Wiley.

Vargas, L. A., & Koss-Chioino, J. D. (Eds.). (1992). *Working with culture: Psychotherapeutic interventions with ethnic minority children and adolescents.* San Francisco: Jossey-Bass.

Vázquez, L. A. (1997). A system's multicultural curriculum model: The psychological process. In D. B. Pope-Davis & H. L. K. Coleman (Eds.), *Multicultural counseling competencies: Assessment, education and training, and supervision* (pp. 159–183). Thousand Oaks, CA: Sage.

Vera, E. M., & Reese, L. E. (2000). Preventive interventions with school-age youth. In S. D. Brown & R. W. Lent (Eds.), *Handbook of counseling psychology* (3rd ed., pp. 411–434). New York: John Wiley.

Vera, E. M., & Speight, S. L. (2003). Multicultural competence, social justice, and counseling psychology: Expanding our roles. *The Counseling Psychologist, 31,* 253–272.

Vernez, G. (1991). Current global refugee situation and international public policy. *American Psychologist, 46,* 627–631.

Vontress, C. E. (1981). Racial and ethnic barriers in counseling. In P. B. Pedersen, J. G. Draguns, W. J. Lonner, & J. E. Trimble (Eds.), *Counseling across cultures* (2nd ed., pp. 87–107). Honolulu: University of Hawaii Press.

Wade, J. C. (1993). Institutional racism: An analysis of the mental health system. *American Journal of Orthopsychiatry, 63,* 536–544.

Wade, P., & Bernstein, B. L. (1991). Culture sensitivity training and counselor's race: Effects on Black female clients' perceptions and attrition. *Journal of Counseling Psychology, 38,* 9–15.

Wallace, A. F. C. (1970). *Culture and personality* (2nd ed.). New York: Random House.

Walsh, M., Smith, R., Morales, A., & Sechrest, L. (2000). *Ethnocultural research: A mental health researcher's guide to the study of race, ethnicity, and culture.* Cambridge, MA: Health Services Research Institute.

Warner, R. (1979). Racial and sexual bias in psychiatric diagnosis. *Journal of Nervous and Mental Disease, 167,* 303–310.

Warren, R. (1995). *The purpose-driven church: Growth without compromising your message and mission.* Grand Rapids, MI: Zondervan.

Warren, R. C., Jackson, A. M., Nugaris, J., & Farley, G. K. (1973). Differential attitudes of Black and White patients toward treatment in a child guidance clinic. *American Journal of Orthopsychiatry, 43*, 384–393.

Watkins, B., Cowan, M., & Davis. W. (1975). Differential diagnosis imbalance as a race-related phenomenon. *Journal of Clinical Psychology, 31*, 267–268.

Watson, D. L., & Tharp, R. G. (1997). *Self-directed behavior: Self-modification for personal adjustment* (7th ed.). Pacific Grove, CA: Brooks/Cole.

Watzlawick, P., Beavin, J. H., & Jackson, D. D. (1967). *Pragmatics of human communication: A study of interactional patterns, pathologies, and paradoxes.* New York: W. W. Norton.

Weiss, C. (1978). Improving the linkage between social research and public policy. In L. Lynn (Ed.), *Knowledge and policy: The uncertain connection* (pp. 23–81). Washington, DC: National Academy of Sciences.

Wellman, D. T. (1977). *Portraits of White racism.* New York: Cambridge University Press.

Wellman, D. T. (2000). From evil to illness: Medicalizing racism. *American Journal of Orthopsychiatry, 70*, 28–32.

Wells, G. L. (1982). Attribution and reconstructive memory. *Journal of Experimental Social Psychology, 18*, 447–463.

Westermeyer, J. (1987). Cultural factors in clinical assessment. *Journal of Consulting and Clinical Psychology, 55*, 471–478.

Whaley, A. L. (1998a). Issues of validity in empirical tests of stereotype threat theory. *American Psychologist, 53*, 679–680.

Whaley, A. L. (1998b). Racism in the provision of mental health services: A social-cognitive analysis. *American Journal of Orthopsychiatry, 68*, 47–57.

Whaley, A. L. (2001). Cultural mistrust and mental health services for African Americans: A review and meta-analysis. *The Counseling Psychologist, 29*, 513–531.

Wierzbicki, M., & Pekarik, G. (1993). A meta-analysis of psychotherapy dropout. *Professional Psychology: Research and Practice, 24*, 190–195.

Wilkins, R. (1992, November/December). White out. *Mother Jones,* pp. 44–48.

Williams, R. L. (1974). The death of White research in the Black community. *Journal of Non-White Concerns in Personnel and Guidance, 2*, 116–132.

Willie, C. V., Kramer, B. M., & Brown, B. S. (Eds.). (1973). *Racism and mental health: Essays.* Pittsburgh, PA: University of Pittsburgh Press.

Willie, C. V., Rieker, P. P., Kramer, B. M., & Brown, B. S. (Eds.). (1995). *Mental health, racism, and sexism.* Pittsburgh, PA: University of Pittsburgh Press.

Wills, T. A. (1978). Perceptions of clients by professional helpers. *Psychological Bulletin, 85*, 968–1000.

Windle, C. (1980). Correlates of community mental health center under-service to non-Whites. *Journal of Community Psychology, 8*, 140–146.

Wintrob, R. M., & Harvey, Y. K. (1981). The self-awareness factor in intercultural psychotherapy: Some personal reflections. In P. B. Pedersen, J. G. Draguns, W. J. Lonner, & J. E. Trimble (Eds.), *Counseling across cultures* (2nd ed., pp. 108–132). Honolulu: University of Hawaii Press.

Woodson, C. G. (1969). *Miseducation of the Negro.* Washington, DC: Associated.

Word, C. O., Zanna, M. P., & Cooper, J. (1974). The nonverbal mediation of self-fulfilling prophecies in interracial interaction. *Journal of Experimental Social Psychology, 10*, 109–120.

Worthington, C. (1992). An examination of factors influencing the diagnosis and treatment of Black patients in the mental health system. *Archives of Psychiatric Nursing, 6,* 195–204.

Wrenn, C. G. (1962). The culturally encapsulated counselor. *Harvard Educational Review, 32,* 444–449.

Wrenn, C. G. (1985). Afterword: The culturally encapsulated counselor revisited. In P. B. Pedersen (Ed.), *Handbook of cross-cultural counseling and therapy* (pp. 323–329). Westport, CT: Greenwood.

Wyatt, G. E. (1977). A comparison of the scaling of Afro-American life-change events. *Journal of Human Stress, 3*(1), 13–18.

Yamamoto, J., James, Q. C., Bloombaum, M., & Hattem, J. (1967). Racial factors in patient selection. *American Journal of Psychiatry, 124*(5), 84–90.

Yamamoto, J., James, Q. C., & Palley, N. (1968). Cultural problems in psychiatric therapy. *Archives of General Psychiatry, 19,* 45–49.

Yee, A. H., Fairchild, H. H., Weizmann, F., & Wyatt, G. E. (1993). Addressing psychology's problems with race. *American Psychologist, 48,* 1132–1140.

Young, A. S., Klap, R., Sherbourne, C. D., & Wells, K. B. (2001). The quality of care for depressive and anxiety disorders in the United States. *Archives of General Psychiatry, 58,* 55–61.

Young, M. E. (1992). *Counseling methods and techniques: An eclectic approach.* New York: Macmillan.

Zuckerman, M. (1990). Some dubious premises in research and theory on racial differences: Scientific, social, and ethical issues. *American Psychologist, 45,* 1297–1303.

Index

effectiveness studies and,
190–191
explicated presuppositions and,
187–188
mental health care reform and. *See*
Mental health care reform
multicultural competence and,
183–185, 212
multicultural training. *See*
Multicultural training
operationalized constructs and, 188
practice-based minority
research, 182–191
programmatic research and,
185–186
recommendations for, 189–191
research agenda for, 182–191
See also Mental health care reform;
Microsystem interventions
Malgady, R. G., 124
Manic depression, 77
Manson, S. M., 190
Marlatt, G. A., 152, 153
Master-slave pattern, 72
Matarazzo, J. D., 51
McCann, I. L., 5
McCauley, C., 98
McDavis, R. J., 44
Mechanic, D., 199
Medical model:
defined, 45
doctor-patient relationship
in the, 45, 149
failure to teach coping
skills of the, 48
focus on illness and the, 45
implications of the, 46, 99
inaccessibility to minority
clients of the, 48
limited social applicability
of the, 47–48
long-term treatment and the, 45, 48
modal personality and the, 49
psychoanalysis and the,
45, 47–48
role confusion of therapeutic
participants in the, 48
tendency to overpathologize
and the, 47

unintentional racism and the,
46–48. *See also* Unintentional
racism
verbal endeavors and the, 45
Meehl, P. E., 60
Mehta, H., 77
Melzack, R., 105
*Mental Health: A Report of the
Surgeon General,* 211
Mental health care reform:
accountability and, 195
availability/accessibility
of services and, 194–195
blueprint for, 193–194 (figure),
195–196
comprehensiveness
of services and, 195
data-driven policy making and,
192, 197
difficulty of, 191
equitable service
delivery and, 192, 218–220
evaluation of, 198–200
flexibility in, 193
funding and, 193–194
government and, 195–196
minority community
role in, 196–197
need for, 191
partnerships in, 193
philosophical foundation for,
192–193
policy makers and, 196
policy management for, 193–194
recommendations for, 196–200
research and, 197
resources for, 192–193
social policy, 193–194
See also Macrosystem
interventions; Microsystem
interventions
*Mental Health: Culture, Race, and
Ethnicity,* 10–11, 211
Mental health models:
as an aid to counselors, 42
biopsychosocial. *See*
Biopsychosocial model
conformity. *See* Conformity model
deficit. *See* Deficit model

About the Author

Charles R. Ridley (Ph.D., counseling psychology, University of Minnesota) is a Professor in the Counseling Psychology Program and an Associate Dean in the University Graduate School at Indiana University, Bloomington. Previously, he was Director of Training in that institution's doctoral program in counseling psychology. He has held academic appointments at the University of Maryland and the Graduate School of Psychology at Fuller Theological Seminary. In addition to those appointments, he was a consulting psychologist with Personnel Decisions, Inc. A Fellow of the American Psychological Association, he is also a licensed psychologist and consults with a variety of nonprofit organizations. He has published numerous journal articles, monographs, and book chapters as well as several books. His many scholarly interests include multicultural counseling, training, and assessment; organizational consultation; the use of religious resources in psychotherapy; and therapeutic change. In his work, he is committed to the scientist-practitioner model; he believes that a sound scientific and theoretical foundation is the only legitimate basis for psychological practice. He has served on the editorial boards of *The Counseling Psychologist* and the *Journal of Psychology and Theology,* and he has been an ad hoc reviewer for a number of professional journals.